Praise for *CO-CREATE*

"After reading *Relationship Economics* and *Return on Impact*, I heard David Nour speak at ASAE, hired him to advise my last association, coach me in the transition to a new association, and more recently work with me, our leadership team, and board on our strategic path forward. David Nour has done it again. *CO-CREATE* is the definitive guide if you want to *think and lead differently.*"

—STEFANO BERTUZZI, CEO—American Society of Microbiology

"Having our team work with David Nour over the past couple of years, we've seen his impact with critical change management initiatives such as elevate, our Customer Experience organization, evolution of our Modernization business strategy, as well as coaching several of our executives. *CO-CREATE* brings a lot of David's ideas together in how to fundamentally evolve an organization."

—RICH HUSSEY, CEO—ThyssenKrupp Elevator Americas

"I heard David Nour speak on Relationship Economics almost a decade ago and have been a strong fan of his work since! We've engaged him several times to work with our various internal and external teams and he consistently delivers. I'm sending a copy of *CO-CREATE* to every one of my strategic relationships."

—KATHY BEDELL, Senior Vice President,
Americas & Affiliate Program—BCD Travel

"David Nour has been a strategic, practical, pragmatic advisor to me. Having read *Relationship Economics* and been referred to him as a strategic relationship coach, I can definitely recommend *CO-CREATE* as the roadmap to the evolution of any forward-thinking enterprise and its leadership team."

—JEFF CARNEY, President, CEO—IGM Financial

"David Nour's ideas, elegantly captured and presented in *CO-CREATE*, were the genesis of much of my global talent agenda at Hilton Worldwide. I'm looking forward to working with David and his ideas again to replicate the same success."

—ROD MOSES, former VP of Global Talent—Bristol Myer Squibb

"I first heard David Nour speak at the IBM Global Commerce Summit in Monaco. Having followed his work with *Relationship Economics*, I was delighted to see him write about Cognitive Computing in *CO-CREATE*—a great example of the evolution many organizations and industries need to undertake."

—MANOJ SAXENA, Chairman—Cognitive Scale, Founding Managing Director—
The Entrepreneurs' Fund; former GM—IBM Watson

"We have engaged David Nour several times this past year to really help our internal teams, as well as our channel partners, internalize and apply his strategic relationship development ideas. *CO-CREATE* takes his foundational work to a new height!"

—KEVIN McNAMARA, Senior Vice President & General Manager—
LG Electronics A/C Business USA

"From speaking at our Annual Partners' Meeting, to helping us visualize our client journey maps and coaching several of our firm leaders, David Nour is astute in his observations, engaging in his thoughtful questions, and on-target with his advice. *CO-CREATE* will force you to think about what you're doing and why!"

—MARK D. WASSERMAN, Managing Partner—Eversheds Sutherland

"David Nour continues to innovate his global domain expertise in strategic relationships. First with *Relationship Economics*, then *Return on Impact*, and now with the much anticipated *CO-CREATE*. This is his finest work to date and I continue to believe that he's one of the best-kept secrets in America. His approach on leveraging relationships played an invaluable role in my previous role as an HP executive, as well as in starting and running my new companies; thanks David!!"

—RANDY SEIDL, CEO, Revenue Acceleration and Top Talent Recruiting;
a former SVP & General Manager, HP US Enterprise Group

"David Nour's tenacity, intellectual horsepower, and highly actionable insights elevate *CO-CREATE*. He makes it crystal clear that no organization can succeed by going it all alone."

—BRUCE KASANOFF, Co-Author, *Smart Customers, Stupid Companies*

"David Nour is a master at simplifying the complex and delivering solutions for his global clients in a practical and pragmatic manner. His ability to collaborate, nurture relationships, and coach executives to implement his strategies is uncanny. *CO-CREATE* is his blueprint!"

—LT. COL. ROB "WALDO" WALDMAN,
New York Times and *Wall Street Journal* bestselling author of *Never Fly Solo*

"We engaged David Nour to deliver his Relationship Economics message to a global audience of advertising and marketing leaders at the ICOM International Management Conference in Dubai. David's talk and workshop was the highlight of the meeting, and *CO-CREATE* builds on that valuable content and message. I'm excited to apply David's advice in the growth and evolution of my company."

—BOB MORRISON, CEO, The Morrison Agency; Global Chairman, ICOM

"Having known David for several years through our mutual involvement with the National Association of Corporate Directors (NACD), I've been impressed with the practical, pragmatic aspects of his work on Relationship Economics. *CO-CREATE* is definitely the next step and board members would benefit from David's keen insights on innovation through strategic relationships."

—ADAM J. EPSTEIN, Founder—Third Creek Advisors, LLC;
author of *The Perfect Corporate Board*

CO-CREATE

HOW YOUR BUSINESS WILL PROFIT FROM INNOVATIVE AND STRATEGIC COLLABORATION

DAVID NOUR

Illustrations by Lin Wilson

ST. MARTIN'S PRESS ⚑ NEW YORK

www.stmartins.com

Design by Meryl Sussman Levavi

Library of Congress Cataloging-in-Publication Data

Names: Nour, David, 1968– author.
Title: Co-create : how your business will profit from innovative and
    strategic collaboration / David Nour.
Description: First edition. | New York, N.Y. : St. Martin's Press, [2017] |
    Includes bibliographical references and index.
Identifiers: LCCN 2017001938| ISBN 9781250103024 (hardcover) |
    ISBN 9781250103031 (e-book)
Subjects: LCSH: Strategic alliances (Business) | Customer relations. |
    New products. | Diffusion of innovations.
Classification: LCC HD69.S8 N667 2017 | DDC 658/ .046—dc23
LC record available at https://lccn.loc.gov/2017001938

Our books may be purchased in bulk for promotional, educational, or business use.
Please contact your local bookseller or the Macmillan Corporate and Premium Sales Department at
1-800-221-7945, extension 5442, or by e-mail at MacmillanSpecialMarkets@macmillan.com.

First Edition: May 2017

1 3 5 7 9 10 8 6 4 2

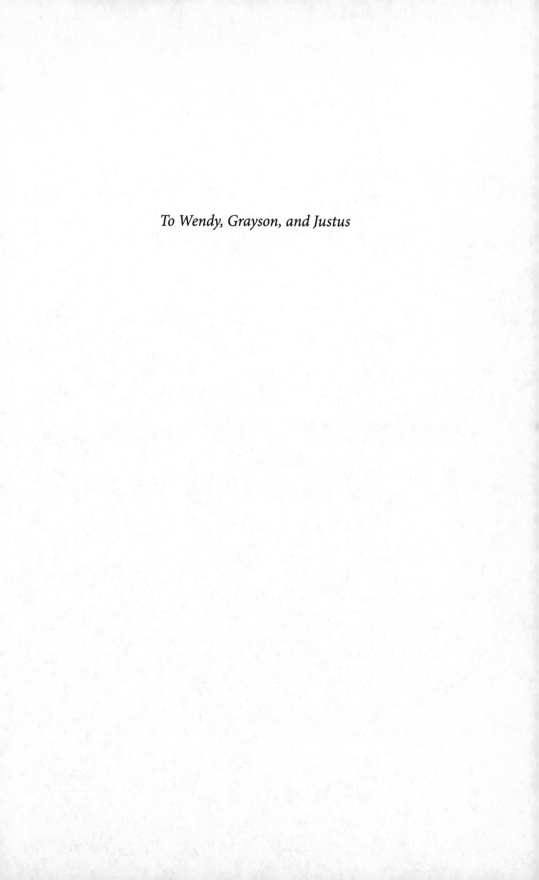

To Wendy, Grayson, and Justus

CONTENTS

FOREWORD

DON PEPPERS AND MARTHA ROGERS, PH.D.

The whole face of marketing today is changing rapidly, as our technologies and devices empower us all to stay connected, all the time, with everyone.

As customers in today's world—the world of Google and Facebook and Instagram, of smartphones and Wi-Fi and Uber and ApplePay—we no longer limit ourselves to learning about products and brands by encountering their ads in printed magazines or newspapers, or while sitting passively in front of one-way television commercials. Instead, whenever and wherever we *want* to learn about a product, we seek it out online, and pretty much instantaneously we get not just product specs and prices, but delivery dates and payment options, along with reputational information such as review opinions.

The Old Marketing of one-way advertisements pushed out by marketers to consumers has already been supplanted by the New Marketing of two-way interactions between consumers and marketers.

The Old Marketer would do research to find out what the most desired product attributes or qualities were for the planned product, and then the company would create that product and push it out for sale. Let's see how many customers we can get with this?

But the New Marketer operates entirely differently, interacting with each individual customer to learn what features or attributes are important to that customer and then, with the participation of the customer, the product is *co-created.*

In addition to getting a customer to Co-Create your product or service, however, the savviest New Marketers will also enlist the customer's help in evangelizing the product to others. Social media technologies make this kind of activity increasingly efficient, and in essence what it means is that the customer is not just co-creating the product or service itself but the entire marketing, promotional, and branding program.

In today's world, Co-Creation has become central to nearly all marketing.

As David Nour carefully and persuasively explains, to master the tasks in *Co-Create,* one must start with the individual customer, not the market. We have to think about the ant, not the anthill. And because customers are all different, this requires a great deal of insight into the nature of customer differences.

Now most companies comb through their customer data primarily to identify those high-value customers who buy the most products, or who have the most potential for buying more products. And knowing who your most valuable customers are is certainly beneficial to the company, because every company needs to know where the real money is. But if we stop with this, then we're looking at the issue through the wrong end of the telescope—the company's end.

Because for the most part customers couldn't care less about their value to our brand or company. What they're interested in is what value our brand holds for them. What problems can the brand solve for the customer? What can the brand do to improve the customer's life? So a far more useful insight for the marketer when it comes to Co-Creation is information about what different customers *need.* Needs-based differentiation is critical to the process, as Nour says, because the only way you can entice a customer into an act of Co-Creation is if the customer is motivated to participate in the process, in order to meet some need the customer has.

Co-Create might look like an easy-to-read business book with common-sense advice, tools, and metrics to engage in this new kind of marketing activity with your customers. And it is.

But I think it's also something else. I think reading this book might just provide an entirely different frame of reference for you when it comes to thinking about all business, and perhaps even about life in general.

Over and above the very useful lessons *Co-Create* holds for how to do better marketing, give this book a thorough read and you'll see that the stories, guidelines, tools, and cases within it are sewn together by an organizing theme that we might call "bottom-up" thinking.

Most of us think about marketing (and business management in general) in terms of top-down actions. The marketing manager decides on a program, he or she delegates authority downward, instructions are distributed throughout the organization, and then some semblance of the specified plan materializes from all the actions being coordinated.

But co-creation has to do with harnessing the effectiveness of people working as individuals according to their own motivations—customers, employees, partners, and others, collaborating with us and with each other, from the bottom up. Ants are a perfect example. No single ant knows how to make an anthill, but when ants get together and do the things they individually *want* to do, the anthill soon takes shape.

Old Marketing is top-down. We (the all-wise, all-seeing marketers) decide what products and services make sense and what kind of marketing will move customers to buy them. We gather facts and research to make smart decisions, but in the end the decisions are entirely ours to make, the messaging is entirely ours, and everything that results from this process will only be as good as we are, no better.

The New Marketing, on the other hand—the kind of marketing defined by *Co-Create*—is bottom-up in nature. We at the top don't try to dictate every feature and promotional benefit. Instead, we empower our customers to help us shape the product and its marketing. We enable them to help us meet their own needs, into which they will have far deeper insight than we could ever develop on our own, no matter how much we spend on research. Both the shape of our product and the cast of our marketing campaign are therefore impossible to predict, prior to receiving the inputs of customers.

Moreover, bottom-up thinking like this holds important lessons not just for marketing, but for the discipline of management in general. "Leadership by provocation," as Nour documents, can provide extremely effective outcomes. These outcomes are not planned and dictated in advance by the organization's leaders, but created ad hoc by empowered and motivated employees, acting on their own. Rather than detailed rules for a dress code or vacation time, such an organization might trust employees to "dress appropriately" or to "take whatever vacation time you need to come back recharged." And the benefits that come from such bottom-up policies will far exceed what any single leader could achieve, no matter how much insight went into the rules and policies he or she might have prescribed in advance.

Co-Create is a book that shows us how to harness the power of customers, employees, and other members of our value chain to achieve *better* results than we could manage on our own.

December 2016
DON PEPPERS AND MARTHA ROGERS, PH.D.
Co-Founders, CX Speakers, LLC www.cxspeakers.com
Co-authors of nine books including their latest,
*Extreme Trust: Turning Proactive Honesty and
Flawless Execution into Long-Term Profits* (Penguin),
revised paperback 2016

CO-CREATE

INTRODUCTION

I have long believed that a book is not just a book. Instead, it represents a journey of personal and professional growth. It is the culmination of good and bad decisions, which over time become invaluable experiences, which in turn help you make better decisions the next time.

A book is an opportunity to deeply examine an idea that may have been sparked by a single, random conversation. First, you find yourself talking about variations of the idea with friends and colleagues. Then you read about a related idea in an obscure journal. You bring the idea into your consulting, using it to frame a client's particular challenge or opportunity. You draw on the idea as you coach and mentor executives. You sprinkle parts of the idea into keynote speeches. And you workshop the idea with your friends, your spouse, and your kids—to the point that they beg you to talk about something, anything, else.

Some clients choose to listen, internalize, and apply your counsel; others defend their status quo. Either way, everyone you've drawn into the conversation provides valuable inspiration that you can use when you finally feel like it's time to get everything you have to say about your idea down on paper.

In this sense, a book is the essence of **Co-Creation**: a social approach to creating unique future value with multiple strategic relationships. Co-Creation can lead to attracting and retaining exceptional talent; it can lead to a great new product design or an unexpected path to market. By adopting Co-Creation as your business model, you'll learn to think and lead differently—and elevate yourself, your team, and your organization above the current market noise.

ATLANTA DOESN'T NEED ANOTHER CHURCH . . .

As we all know, inspiration often pops up in some unlikely places. I first felt the magic of Co-Creation at an Evangelical megachurch.

North Point Community Church founder and senior pastor Andy Stanley was facing essentially the same problems and questions as every mature company in a mature industry: How do you innovate when your core business is a two-thousand-year-old religion? How do you attract new members and retain your current ones when there are dozens and dozens of churches in your area competing for those same parishioners? (North Point is headquartered in Alpharetta, Georgia, smack in the middle of the Bible Belt.) To no one's surprise, Andy delivered the answer right in the middle of a Sunday morning service.

Now, when my teenaged children are up and dressed for church by eight o'clock on Sunday morning, when they come wake me and my wife, Wendy, to make sure we'll be ready to go, when they invite friends and sign up for church outings without prompting, you know there's something extraordinary going on. And it's not just my family. North Point currently averages more than thirty thousand people in attendance across its six physical campuses and thirty strategic partnerships across the globe. *Outreach Magazine* (the trade journal of the Christian ministerial profession) named North Point the largest church in the United States in 2014 and 2015.[1] Clearly, North Point has implemented what theorists W. Chan Kim and Renée Mauborgne would call a "Blue Ocean Strategy." Rather than competing in an overcrowded market, Andy and North Point identified a sizeable niche, developed a Customer Experience Journey with that target audience's specific needs in mind, and executed a growth strategy that has resulted in massive customer uptake.[2]

I submit that the reason for North Point's dramatic success is Andy's extraordinary talent for communication, leadership, and real innovation. North Point Community Church's mission is, quite simply, to lead people into a growing relationship with Jesus Christ. But isn't that the mission of most Christian religious institutions? Yes—however, Andy has found an incredibly innovative approach to doing it, even though he leads a mature company in perhaps the most mature industry in the world.

So there I was, sitting in church with my family that particular Sunday morning, and Andy was talking—just talking to the people assembled on their level; no sermons here. He told a story from his own traditional upbringing in which he was asked to lead a youth program at his dad's church. Andy soon figured out that "doing church" the same way his dad did wasn't working with young people—an absolutely essential market if any church is to thrive over time. He tried a number of tactics, none successfully, before finally concluding that *Atlanta didn't need another church. Rather, Atlanta needed a different church experience for the "unchurched."*

The term "unchurched" refers to individuals not belonging to or connected with a church. The majority of the unchurched claim Christianity as their faith but do not make church part of their regular activity.[3] In business speak, the unchurched represent a target market with awareness but little past buying history or current purchase intention.

So Andy set out to create an environment that is the opposite of everything you find in a traditional church. There is no steeple. There are no crosses anywhere. There is no communion wine, no wafers. The whole event feels like "prayertainment"—immersion in a whole new kind of religious experience from the moment you walk in: World-class music; Andy appearing on high-definition videos on big-screen TVs that make it seem like he is standing right on that stage, even though he's being simulcast to more than a million weekly viewers. The atmosphere is closer to a rock concert than a worship service.

And that's because it is built around an insight that the mission is better served by getting the faithful to invite others to "just come see," rather than by expecting every parishioner to be an effective evangelist. North Point delivers the experience the unchurched need—namely to feel engaged, relevant, with a sense of real belonging that may or may not be directly connected to Jesus.

And then—and this is the beautiful simplicity of Andy's strategy—he makes his parishioners partners in Co-Creating that value. He not only creates an experience that keeps people coming back for more, he makes them want to pull others in as well.

The operative word there is "pull." According to the groundbreaking work of researchers like Don Tapscott and Anthony D. Williams, evidence shows that "the old, hardwired 'plan and push' mentality" that defined "hierarchical, closed, secretive, and insular" organizations of the last century just doesn't work anymore. Increasingly, they argue, whether speaking to a conference room or a congregation, leaders who want to succeed in the twenty-first century must engage in a more dynamic recruitment strategy, with a sense of "openness, peering, sharing, and acting globally."[4] Like a number of my corporate and association clients, Andy realizes that neither he nor his limited staff is scalable. However, as the sheer success of North Point has proven, he clearly can energize an army of "customers as volunteers." People are compelled to take on unpaid roles—with verve—at all hours of the day and night, weekends, holidays. Some use their personal vacations from work to help; some even have left cushy corporate jobs to join his ministry full time.

I have developed a specific vocabulary to convey core concepts of my approach. The first term in your new "Nourcabulary" is **Market Gravity** (a term I first heard from a mentor, Alan Weiss).[5] Isaac Newton described gravity as a force of attraction that pulls objects in the universe closer together. Albert Einstein came along later and showed us that it's more likely that space and time actually bend themselves around objects with the greatest density. What remains true in either case, though, is that the more mass you have at your center, the greater the power you have to make *them* come to you, and that is key. It is Market Gravity that influences everyone—from new clients to new talent—to take unobligated interest in the success of something bigger than themselves. Gravity in the market is why app developers compete to test beta versions for hot tech companies—creating value for those companies without being asked. To be clear, Market Gravity isn't necessarily about the size of your firm, but the strength of your attraction. And that sense of "pull" brings us to another crucial Nourcabulary term: **Brand Influence**. It's no coincidence that this term "influence" has come to prominence in the Co-Create economy. From the Latin *influen-*

tia, it originally referred not to the aggressive "push" to assert dominance over others but to an *influx* or inward flow of positive new ideas. When technology company GoPro says "Be a hero" and 72.5 percent of the US action camera market answers, that's brand influence.[6]

Nourcabulary

Market Gravity, the prime measure of Co-Create outcomes, is defined as a company's ability to attract stakeholders' intrinsic interest.

Brand Influence is the ability of an individual or an organization to compel certain actions, behaviors, and opinions from others without any obvious authority to do so.

The very essence of Co-Creation of value is baked into the premise of Andy Stanley's evangelism. In his book *Can We Do That? Innovative Practices That Will Change the Way You Do Church*, he sums up his strategy in two words: "invest" and "invite." Andy's core insight is that bringing more people into the North Point fold will require Co-Creation of that pull, or Market Gravity, by getting believers to leverage their relationships and reputations. He writes:

> Instead of training our people in the art of personal evangelism, we instruct them to invest in the lives of unbelievers with the express purpose of inviting them to an event where they will be exposed to the gospel in a clear, creative, and compelling manner. . . . That's the part they can do that we—the church—can't. . . . They are not responsible for knowing the answers to every question their unbelieving friends may throw their way. But they are responsible for exposing them to an environment where they will be presented with the gospel.[7]

Co-Creation of value happens when believers help shape North Point Community Church into something to which they are comfortable inviting the unbelievers they know.

Let's talk about the impact of that strategy. How about raising $26 million to buy the land and build a church, without a single dollar of debt? How about creating an annual campaign that gets church members to volunteer approximately two hundred *thousand* hours of their time? Literally everything North Point Community Church does creates Market Gravity. Chat with people in the lobby after the service and nine out of ten will tell you they are there because someone invited them. More than 90 percent of the adults baptized at North Point Community Church were invited by a friend.[8]

That Sunday when I heard Andy tell this story of his remarkable innovation, I wasn't just being schooled in faith—I was the recipient of world-class strategy, marketing, and leadership wisdom. Andy fundamentally grasps Co-Creation of value. That morning he told the congregation,

> The key to us remaining a church that unchurched people love to attend
> is you—your willingness to invite your unchurched friends, and family,
> and neighbors. And here's why. Because inviters critique the right way
> and inviters complain about the right things. People who are inviting
> people want their guest to walk out and say, "Wow, that was helpful.
> Wow, I'm so glad I came."[9]

Think about when you're referred to a business that provides an exceptional experience; what do you think of the person who made the referral? How about the converse effect—if the business fails you miserably, what are you likely to think of the referring source? Would you take their next referral or recommendation seriously?

When twenty-five US Army officers banded together in 1922 to insure each other's automobiles, their motto was "Service to the Services." One of their original driving concepts was that helping the military community and their families—men and women from active duty through retirement—earned a loyalty that could be naturally extended across platforms and follow-on referrals. Today, after opening their service to the general public as USAA Bank, they provide auto and home insurance, as well as mortgage and other banking services, to tens of millions of customers. Along the way, *Fortune* magazine has included the company on its "100 Best Companies to Work For" list eleven times,[10] while Forrester Research ranks USAA Bank highest among all brands from all industry categories in "The Customer Experience Index."[11] To top it off, every customer is also a member, receiving a portion of unspent premiums in the form of a check or credit once each year.

Brand influencers are all around us, critical facets of the Co-Create economy. I'll explain in more detail as we continue. What I want you to begin thinking about is how to create and activate an army of flag-bearers for your unique value-add. What has to happen for them to become not just one-time recommenders but outright evangelists for you and the experience they've had with you?

I've spent most of the last two decades studying business relationships—what makes them succeed, how they break down, and how to make them yield strategic results. I call this the art and science of **Relationship Economics**. Going back to church, so to speak, I must point out the strategic relationship component of North Point's "invest and invite" strategy. Pastor Andy doesn't just say, "Invite anyone you know who is unchurched." That would be the equivalent of trying to cash in an investment without having given that asset time to grow. Instead, Andy exhorts his faithful to **invest** in the lives of others. It's similar to USAA recognizing that serving military men and women will return a dividend of loyalty. Or global talent leaders who think of their roles as investing in the organization's human capital assets rather than simply "doing HR!" Or the sales leaders who see their field force (in their strategic accounts certainly) as capable of providing opportunities to really listen to and learn from the market, as much as "sell everything on the truck!"

In my approach to strategic relationships, investing in others means using externally focused behaviors like empathy, candor, and accountability in order to be of unique value to others. The entire strategy is dependent upon purposeful, intentional, and strategic relationships.

Nourcabulary

Relationship Economics® is the art and science of investing in strategic relationships for personal and professional success. Its methods include exchanges of **relationship currency**, accumulation of **strategic relationships** across a balanced **relationship portfolio**, and accumulation of **relationship capital** as a strategic asset. These concepts are the subject of my book *Relationship Economics,* which is (to use the *Star Wars* vernacular) the prequel to *Co-Create*. If you haven't read it, please go to CoCreateBook.com and download my free PDF, in which I explain this methodology's six phases of strategic relationship development.

Andy and his church are dramatically succeeding at a time when other churches are in decline. He recognizes that it is far easier to lead people into a relationship with Jesus Christ by executing events designed to meet them where they are than it is to attempt to convince them that their worldview is incorrect. He's designed an experience that pulls what we would term "customers" through stages of progressively more meaningful relationships with his organization.

As does USAA, each and every day. The institution begins with an empathic connection of loyalty to country and troops and honoring that as a welcoming step to insuring your car. The experience of a breakdown or accident allows them to show just how well they can take care of you, another link in the chain of offering you help in other areas of your life, from credit cards and checking accounts to helping you buy a car or house and holding the mortgage or title. Periodic contact combined with truly useful services and stellar customer service lead naturally to an accumulation of trust such that millions of members end up turning to the company for both investing needs and life insurance as well.

Many of the clients I've been blessed to work with over two decades are mature companies like ThyssenKrupp Elevator or KPMG; they operate in mature industries such as manufacturing and professional services in the same way that most churches are mature because religions have been around for a while. So how do we, as leaders of companies and organizations large and small, respond to the urgent demand for innovation in today's highly competitive business climate? If you or your company are facing this immense challenge, I suggest you take inspiration from Andy's example. He's not a millennial in some Silicon Valley start-up, and, likely, neither are you! But the good news is that you don't have to be a start-up to act with agility and nimbleness. You don't have to be a tech powerhouse to achieve a breakthrough innovation. You just need to recognize and harness the power of Co-Creation and to get to know your customer-collaborators as well as Andy Stanley did. If a church can do it, you can too.

REQUIRED READING: *RELATIONSHIP ECONOMICS*

Co-Creation of value takes a certain level of respect, trust, intimacy, and, most important, an authentic commitment to one another's best interests. As such, familiarity with my strategic relationship concepts—discussed in my book *Relationship Economics*—is essential to understanding and applying what you are about to learn in *Co-Create*. In essence, *Relationship Economics* is the prequel to this book. To capture the ocean in a teacup, *Relationship Economics* teaches that we must purposefully build from relationship creation to relationship capitalization through behavior based in the Six Phases of Strategic Relationships. Those six phases are:

Mapping: Identifying relevant individuals who can add specific value to your life and how you can connect with them.

Relating: Actively expressing interest in others to create connections on which relationships can be built. Relating emerges most easily from a shared mission, vision, or enemy.

Nurturing: Prioritizing opportunities to offer help and acting on those with the highest value. Nurturing includes making relationship currency deposits and confirming you have delivered value.

Sustaining: Keeping the relationship strong by proactively staying in touch, creating touchpoints with others in order to broaden relationships, and making strategic plans for the relationship's future growth.

Requesting: Evaluating when to request help to achieve objectives, framing requests appropriately, and providing pertinent and appropriate information to make the request actionable.

Capitalizing: Accessing and gaining quantifiable business outcomes from the value in the relationship that encourage both you and others to grow in a mutually beneficial way.

We must understand the process of mapping, relating, nurturing, and sustaining before we can access the full value of strategic relationships by capitalizing on them.

Figure I.1: The Six Phases of Strategic Relationships

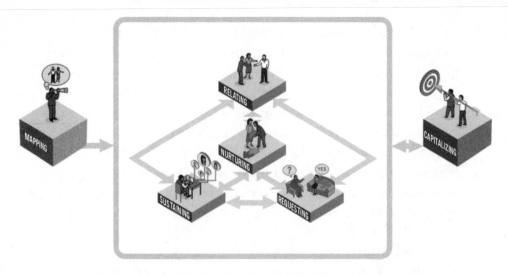

Let me explain why a grounding in Relationship Economics® is so important to the work that lies ahead for you. In my presentations I often tell people to stop asking other people to trust them, because they won't. They can't, until you demonstrate your goodwill through your behavior. Trust is earned through small gestures, early and often in your interactions, which become more significant as their belief in you grows.

Relating gives logical and natural context to the relationship. Instead of being two independent entities, you now have something in common. There is perceived value going both ways. In relationships we might express this as "You get me" or "We have chemistry." In a business context it means our firms are both better off because we are in this relationship. You add to my portfolio of products and services. You make me look better. You make me sound smarter. And our firm does the same for yours.

There's a "likeability factor" at work here, too. If I like you, I will invest time to get to know you. Through your consistent behavior, I see that I can trust you. Through what I read about you, or your demonstrated behavior over time, particularly in business-to-business (B2B) relationships that can be long, deep, and punctuated by regular contact toward a shared goal, I will encounter opportunities to develop respect for you and your work—and especially the value your work generates.

A critical distinction: relating is less about your input and more about the outcomes you have created. If I hear from your customers that they benefited in what they bought from you, if I hear from colleagues that they really enjoyed working for or with you—those are examples of outcomes that elevate you in my mind and in my heart.

The more of those positive comments I hear, and the more relevant they are to my current situation, the more your credibility and reputation are enhanced. You rise in my esteem. At this early stage in our relationship, you also gain a certain level of what I call "draft" or "preliminary" respect that leads to increased priority of access and response. You can see this happening in how responsive people are to your e-mails and your calls, in taking action on your behalf. As that respect grows, trust, intimacy, and commitment increase as well. The partners in this relationship start to open up to each other.

Only when you have allowed an organic process of mapping, relating, nurturing, and sustaining to flourish can you then access the true value of strategic relationships—the opportunities that open up for Co-Creation.

WHEN CO-CREATION WORKS

Co-Creation works—most of the time, in most circumstances. So let's talk about what creates the conditions for successful Co-Creation of value.

Co-Creation works when both sides reduce their self-interest. I'm not saying anyone completely forgets self-interest; I am saying all parties believe in a dramatically stronger path forward, together.

In some ways Co-Creation has its roots in dynastic eras, when enemies would marry their sons and daughters to one another to bond the families for a common goal or against a common enemy. It was a successful strategy; it created great wealth and power. Today, companies engage in "co-opetition"—a judicious blend of cooperation with competition, and of suppliers, customers, and firms producing complementary or related products. We have a reason to come together for a specific part of our business, to achieve a common mission, such as streamlined supply channels, or a common enemy, such as overregulation.

Netflix is an interesting example of a Co-Create economy eco-system because it creates value by bringing together old-economy and new-economy players. Producers of movie and television content still operate fundamentally as they always have, but the distribution and viewing of that content takes place in a radically altered—and con-stantly evolving—landscape. Digital devices for viewing that content now include computers, mobile devices, and televisions with set-top media players, all of which may be receiving signals through cable or, increasingly, powerful Wi-Fi connections. As a distributor, Netflix has evolved with these changes, first by partnering with content creators on both the corporate level (movie studios) and, more recently, directly with respected actors and directors like Kevin Spacey and Ricky Gervais. Netflix's launch in 1997 as a DVD-by-mail service disrupted the traditional movie rental business by innovating customer conve-nience with mail-in pouches that turned every US Post Office box into a video store. But behind the scenes, Co-Creation of value was afoot: Netflix developed industry-leading predictive software to guide cus-tomer choice, thus making its members partners in improving its ser-vice. During this rent-by-mail phase, Netflix's marketing department iteratively improved its movie selection website for seamless customer experience, in the process gaining valuable experience it would later apply to designing its streaming platform.

Netflix read faint market signs to gain a first-mover advantage through two major upheavals. The first was the transition from VCR to DVD, where Netflix innovated evolutionary pricing, content availabil-ity, and consumption limits. Then Netflix began its transition to broad-band streaming away from DVD. How Netflix transitioned its customers (including supporting late adopters who still rely on the postal service) is by itself a case study in value delivery.

What is, on the surface, a business-to-consumer (B2C) company employs a number of B2B strategies—and it is partly in those strategies that we find the principle of Co-Creation at work. Netflix has funded the media player Roku, a vertical-integration streaming player that brings over 350,000 movies and TV episodes, live sports, news, and music across 3,500+ free and paid entertainment brands. (This is a classic case of disrupting yourself before a competitor can since users can rent, buy, subscribe to, or watch for free.) Roku needed that real estate in its battle with Apple TV and others. Netflix has further positioned itself as strategic partner in tech by adding Netflix apps to every TV, game console, and set-top box sold anywhere.

Partnering with movie studios for original content development, like *House of Cards* and *Orange Is the New Black,* further builds brand loyalty. Here, the company uses two kinds of common Co-Creation thinking. First, it realizes it is not Hollywood (yet), but it goes to Hollywood for its expertise, learning through collaboration before producing original content. That period of successful co-branding evolves into a new era in which, while it still licenses much content, it grows its own brand with daring original series by inviting Co-Creators into the tent. They didn't even ask executive producer and lead actor Kevin Spacey for a pilot, and they ordered two full seasons—both unheard of in episodic television, giving the show some breathing room. That investment paid off with nine major-category Emmy nominations, the first for an online-only web television series.

Another example of successful Co-Creation comes from LEGO, the maker of interlocking toy bricks and a universe of accompanying parts for construction play. In 2005, the family-owned toy company nearly went bankrupt. Today, the $2 billion business is solidly profitable and has gained a worldwide reputation for constant innovation and reinvention. Much of that is based on various kinds of Co-Creation inside and outside the company.

Inside the company, a division called Future Lab declares its belief that nothing is out of bounds, which has led to productive Co-Creation in several ways. First, the company enables every LEGO player to become a potential source of new ideas (at the highest level of LEGO art are what they call "wizards"). Second, the company isn't hesitant to partner with outside organizations and creative communities to innovate cutting-edge product categories. Finally, LEGO engineers are able to observe how actual children use the toy in an open online environment in which users can manipulate "bricks" (actually pixels) to build anything they imagine.[12]

While the company had long suspected that adults were also playing with the plastic blocks, it was a Chicago architect named Adam

Reed Tucker who, in 2007, suggested that the company begin a line dedicated to great architectural masterpieces around the world, beginning with the Sears Tower. Today LEGO Architecture continues to add products every year as a successful standalone line. There is also LEGO Ideas, where customers both vote on proposed products and suggest products of their own, with a tipping point of ten thousand votes triggering a formal study by the company. Stemming from the insight that there were pros who knew more about innovating across the digital/physical divide, a space they needed to explore, LEGO partnered with MIT's Media Lab to create Mindstorms Robotic Invention Systems.[13]

CO-CREATE: A TRANSFORMATIONAL JOURNEY

Co-Creation is fundamentally a transformational journey. It's not a transaction. It's not an event. It's also not a partnership, an alliance, or a merger in the traditional sense. Not every individual reading this book or every organization thinking about these ideas will be able to make that transformation or make it smoothly. And for some organizations, it might not be a good fit at levels farther down the corporate ladder.

I've never met an individual, team, or organization that doesn't need to evolve somehow. As **individuals**, we constantly have to learn and grow if we are to remain relevant to our relationships. Our **teams** must grow and evolve. A skill set within a team that was really useful two or three years ago may not be the skill set needed going forward. Ideally, we train and develop individuals not just in the skills they need to have today but also in how to anticipate what the organization will need in the future. But you also have to evolve the dynamics of the team, through actions like job rotation, without diminishing the team's portfolio of relationships.

And the **organization** must grow and evolve. If you are still making and selling or distributing the same products you sold thirty years ago, are you really surprised that you are losing market share? Organizations must audit their products and services portfolio on a consistent basis. If you are not leveraging insights from quantifiable win/loss analysis, how will you know what is or what isn't resonating with today's market, much less tomorrow's? Supporting the same products you did ten or twenty years ago is not going to enable you to move ahead.

As should now be clear, I believe the organizations that achieve best-of-breed performance in the future will take this transformational journey. Now, let's spend a moment on *how* this transformation happens. As I look at my global client base, I see five key components differentiating the organizations that are successful in transforming themselves from the ones that struggle in the present or see a cliff dead ahead:

1. **Visionary leadership.** CEOs focus on managing the present, while they lead the future by investing in opportunities to evolve. CEOs have to produce results, but they also have to invent their organizations' futures.

2. **SEAL Team Six.** In my view, transformation of an organization does not require a battalion, particularly for mature companies in mature industries. You cannot—and don't want to—turn an oil tanker on a dime. You need a SEAL Team Six to get in, get the job done, and get out. A SEAL Team Six starts small, proves the model, creates the success, and then finds ways to scale that success, taking it wide and deep across and throughout the organization. Then you can start to build momentum that leads to the next stage of this transformation.

3. **Think transformation, not incrementalism.** "Doing things better" is incrementalism. Real transformation is about doing things *differently.* It's about aligning culture, innovation strategy, and exceptional global talent—within and external to the organization. When groups work across functional boundaries to share insights and gain new perspectives, they generate more innovative solutions, faster and with greater agility, and thus increase the chance of successfully implementing the new path forward. Here is a simple litmus test: How will your organization look, feel, or behave *differently* in eighteen to thirty-six months?

4. **Your relationship ecosystem.** Transformation leverages a strategic relationship ecosystem. We are always so focused on what we should do and how we should do it. Co-Creation is where you really leverage, asking instead, Who do we need? Who do we know? How do

we leverage a broader ecosystem in our portfolio of relationships to accelerate this journey? Inside and outside of our organization? Inside and outside of our industry? Inside and outside of a particular geography?

5. **Metrics and compensation.** Only a dramatic, wholesale change in behavior will drive the impact that you are after, the results that investors and boards of directors are after. It is generally accepted that metrics and compensation are the levers that deliver desired behaviors. Yet how often do we see an organization incentivizing or compensating one set of behaviors but demanding a completely different set? Metrics and compensation are too often relics of past priorities, disconnected from the results required for success today, much less tomorrow. These levers can drive a company toward Co-Creation by rewarding outcomes instead of input, thereby encouraging people to focus on the value their work creates for others. Measuring and compensating Co-Creation behaviors inside an organization may be the most disruptive transformation of all.

In order to take this transformational journey, individuals, teams, and organizations must first understand and develop these five key traits, and then internalize them.

TOOLS: THE ELEVATOR RIDE

Throughout the upcoming chapters, my goal is to present a theory, then through case studies and examples illuminate that theory and demonstrate its applications. Each chapter closes with summaries and references to unique tools (available as a free downloadable PDF on CoCreateBook.com) to help you with the implementation of what you have learned.

I begin with theory because it is critical to understand the intellectual underpinnings of any strategy. One of the painful lessons I learned during the dot-com bubble is that wishful thinking never pays the bills. I saw companies engage in asinine behavior that ran counter not only to best practices but also to basic economics: you cannot buy a product for two dollars, sell it for one dollar, and try to make it up in volume!

I see it again in incubators and innovation hubs today: faith in certain tools and behaviors that isn't based on any quantifiable construct—such as counting simple page views without measuring engagement or giving away free content in the hope that it will be offset by some future, undetermined revenue stream. I believe it is critical to start with a solid foundation. Otherwise you're building on quicksand.

But the theoretical concepts alone won't suffice in your transformational journey. The theoretical isn't going to help you as a manager of a team desperate for fresh ideas. The theoretical isn't even going to help you think differently in your industry of sameness. That is where real case studies and examples come in. Look for interviews with leaders who have created definitive results. At the close of each chapter, I summarize the key ideas and give you action items, questions to think about, and a tool or two that will ultimately lead to the Co-Create Canvas presented in chapter 8.

My goal is to give you a path to implement the Co-Create transformation. In many ways I've begun the work for you in introducing these ideas. But just like I tell my kids from the sideline of the ball field, I can't do the heavy lifting for you. I need you to read (or listen to the audiobook) proactively and really ask, "What is David trying to say?" And more important, "What does it mean to ME?" In the background, throughout this book, my fundamental questions remain the same: How will your organization think, feel, or behave differently in eighteen to thirty-six months? How will Co-Creation of value keep you relevant to your biggest asset—your portfolio of strategic relationships?

Turn the page to begin your transformative journey and Co-Create your new path. Because I can guarantee you this: your industry doesn't need another product or service. What it needs is a company anticipating and evolving to innovate solutions for the *next generation* of its customers' needs!

ONE

CO-CREATE IN: INTROSPECTION LEADS TO RIGHT ACTION

 In this chapter you will learn about:

- General preparatory steps to Co-Creation from individual to team and company;
- Disruption: how to accept and embrace it;
- The four interdependent principles on which organizational growth in the Co-Create economy depends;
- Ways in which winners in the Co-Create economy generate Market Gravity;
- Strategies used by large organizations to align with nimbler Co-Create economy firms;
- Leadership strategies to generate the organizational agility the Co-Create economy requires; and
- The advantages contextual intelligence confers on leaders and organizations.

Modern business is pure chaos. Those who succeed are the people who continually adapt to the disruption all around them without losing sight of the fundamental mission: creating exponential value through consistently delivered exceptional experiences for their key stakeholders, thus capitalizing on strategic relationships.

That's saying a lot, so let's break it down.

- **Creating exponential value:** In the current push economy, everyone is aiming to outdo one another—by being a little bit better.
  But the value of merely being better than your competitors is
  incremental—there's no guarantee that you'll have real staying
  power. The Co-Create economy is not about being a little bit better
  than your competitor, but dramatically stronger.
- **Consistently delivered exceptional experiences:** The Co-Create
  economy is about incredible consistency, everywhere from the
  executive suite to the point of sale. Co-Creation goes miles
  beyond "good enough," for various internal and external stakeholders.
- **Capitalizing on strategic relationships**: When you apply the first
  two elements of this mission, it elevates all of your business relationships, which raises you not just above your competitive peers but
  also above the broader market noise!

My purpose in this first chapter is to call you to introspection: Personally and organizationally, what is your readiness for the transformational journey that is Co-Creation?

Nourcabulary

Push Economy is my definition of what we're living in now. All around us
are overt and covert push messages—from product placements in movies,
to pervasive ads in advance of every commercial video we watch on news
sites, to intrusive ones on our mobile apps when we're in need of driving
directions. Unfortunately, it's not just marketing and advertising. Push
messages from HR, irrelevant communication attempts by managers and
leaders that completely miss what employees are really concerned with,
most political messages that talk more about how rotten the other guy is
than about any fresh ideas by the candidate—all are constantly competing
for our time and attention. All this noise is in fact making us desensitized
to the brands and messages that promote versus those that attempt to engage and influence. Therefore, many of us can't remember the ads we see
throughout the day, and when we channel surf, DVR our favorite TV shows,
or subscribe to satellite radio and streaming services we skip the ads. This
push mindset, both within organizations and external to them, often creates nothing more than noise that many people simply choose to ignore.

I equate it to the car alarms that go off in the parking lot. When was the last time you saw someone respond to one? It's time for a fundamental shift in our mindset. Read on to learn more . . .

Organizational growth in this new paradigm depends upon three interdependent principles:

- outcome-focused brand experiences;
- collaborative Co-Creation; and
- purposeful, provocative leadership.

Though we will explore each in depth in this chapter, let's start by considering where you are today. What has to happen for you to start thinking and leading *differently* to help your organization transform itself to thrive in the Co-Create economy?

Let the Introspection Begin

To transform a business, it is essential to balance learning with performance, execution, and results. First, let's examine what kinds of change your organization must execute to become more proactive—if not predictive—in uncovering market opportunities.

In the vast majority of organizations today—particularly in mature industries where change comes slowly—there is such enormous pressure, regardless of your firm's ownership structure, regardless of your business or revenue model, to focus first and foremost on the numbers, with everything else a distant second. How does a leader under that kind of pressure adapt the organization to enormous disruptions from multiple directions? By transforming it at its most fundamental level— the interactions between individuals.

Whether it is spec'ing out a new product, evaluating a job candidate, analyzing intelligence gained from a trade show, or simply getting through a meeting agenda effectively and efficiently, individual interactions are the medium through which work gets done. Teams interact with other teams in functional areas that interact with other functional areas. And thus, the organization lives, breathes, survives, or thrives.

Every one of those interactions is an opportunity to learn and grow, and yet the vast majority of organizations do not allow enough time and space for that learning to occur. Most interactions remain confined to their immediate context, with no potential for larger effect. A very simple example would be when an exec from two levels up "pops in" on a weekly ground-floor progress meeting. The exec's presence is the rare exception. Awkwardness ensues, maybe a little paranoia because, let's be honest, if the boss is there, something must be wrong. Unfortunately, because most organizations are inherently hierarchical, any sense of lurking adversity—real or imagined—tends to spark a "kill or be killed" mentality among colleagues. In various client meetings, I've actually heard seemingly nice people discussing delay tactics, such as "Ignore her long enough and she'll go away," "It's just the flavor of the month," or "Here come the out-of-the-blue mandates by the senior exec who just read a book or came back from a TED speech." Obviously, random gestures like this aren't the way to build the trust necessary for true Co-Creation. But what does work?

Transforming an Organization at the Team/Function Level

Consider if your teams took the first Friday of every month and went off-site. What if we used those First Fridays to give people one-on-one time outside the office together, or for group participation in a shared learning experience, or for a chance to vet a potential new hire, or to nurture relationships with key partners or customers?

By prioritizing collaborative interactions at the individual, team, and function or division levels, you start to introduce this simple notion of Co-Creation inside the organization. You infuse strategic relationships into the culture from the cellular level on up, all the way to the complex level of living, breathing companies interacting in a global marketplace.

When Alan Mulally took over as CEO of Ford Motor Company, he brought with him an engineering background from decades at Boeing, where he had overseen such super-complex projects as the launch of the

777. In 2006, Ford was widely regarded as flailing; it was losing market share and was without a significant new product line in the showrooms. Instead of panicking and throwing money at new products, Mulally took a deep breath—and instituted unpopular cost-cutting and debt-consolidation plans that some thought signaled desperation. His thinking was guided largely by weekly business plan meetings, wherein several handfuls of top executives, starting with Mulally, each presented programs and plans, issues, and forecasts from their particular area, categorizing each as "red light," "yellow light," or "green light," meaning, respectively, "of concern," "to follow," "good to go." Then came 2008 and the Great Recession. Because of Mulally's foresight in restructuring Ford's debt and going lean, and because they were so closely following what was happening inside the company and out, they were the single automaker of the Big Three to avoid bankruptcy.

Given that the focus of this first chapter is on assessing your organization's readiness for the Co-Create approach, stop a moment for a gut check. Did the idea of a culture-wide expectation of team off-sites strike you as unrealistic, impractical, "not the way we do things here?" Then buckle your seat belt—you might be in for a bumpy ride. And note that a few of those top Ford executives, who couldn't or wouldn't adapt to Mulally's methods, were in fact shown the door.

ADAPT TO DISRUPTION

If you don't disrupt your business, someone else will.

Disruption, by definition, is going to happen to every industry sector and, by extension, every business. Every business is currently or will soon be under attack. And disruption isn't always of the overt, "Oh my God, Uber just ate my lunch" kind. It may also come in the creeping loss of customers migrating to other choices of consumption, until you're a Polaroid, a Blockbuster, or a CompUSA. Companies that thrive in the Co-Create economy are already responding to, learning from, and growing through that disruption, no matter how large they are or how mature their industry is. Quite simply, they are adapting to this new landscape where disruption is the norm.

Consider Randall Stephenson, the chief and chairman of AT&T.

Stephenson is fighting to transition his company as fast as he can in the face of disruption to many areas of his core business. (How many of us have landlines in our homes anymore?) He sees his company's future not as one tied to fiber-optic cable and linemen in trucks, but workers manipulating software in the cloud to deliver real-time sports footage to your smartphone app or using traffic-cam data to continuously reprogram stoplights for better traffic flow. With the acquisition of DirecTV in 2015, along with a handful of wireless companies in Mexico and 5G collaborations with Ericsson and Intel, his vision is of a company that not only delivers services for phones and satellite TV but also manages cloud-based data for other businesses.[1]

To do this, Stephenson needs his 280,000 employees, many of them in midcareer, to retool. He is challenging them to become better coders and to learn how to *predict* market needs rather than follow them. As such, he is asking them to spend five to ten hours a week in online retraining—sometimes at their own expense. Every week.[2]

Walk around the annual Consumer Electronics Show (CES), and you'll see the evidence of such dynamic disruption at each turn. Anything "dumb" (not connected, responsive, or intelligent in every interaction) is being replaced by a "smart" device that incorporates or accesses learning machines and near real-time feedback, using contextual intelligence to create customer experiences with greater impact. (We will explore contextual intelligence in detail in chapter 7.) Even a standard practice like basing marketing on demographic profiles is being replaced by a "smart marketing ecosystem" that connects the dots, recognizes that, say, "this individual is getting influenced by the Tesla brand," and responds with intelligence to the customer's desire for the next insight, emotional connection, or experience that will move them along their need continuum to the perfect new car purchase.[3]

If you don't disrupt your value chain, someone else will. To see this in action, just look at the disruption now taking place in global transportation. Until recently, one of the most profitable investments in any metropolitan global city was to buy a taxi medallion, because the average return on it was 10,000 percent. Then came Uber, whose founders' breakthrough insight was that most cars on the road in urban cities

Figure 1.1: Adapt to Disruption

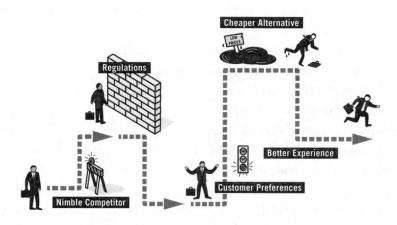

If you don't disrupt your business, someone else will.

have only one passenger in them. The idea of aggregating the available space in private vehicles to directly impact global traffic congestion led to providing a service that creates operational efficiencies and market effectiveness—regardless of geographic or language barriers. Bang! It disrupted traditional taxi and limo services overnight. And now it's having a ripple effect into rental cars, couriers, and food-delivery services. The car was never more than a means to an end; Uber provides the same outcome with a dramatically accelerated *resource-to-results* outcome. For me, Uber's value proposition in New York City—as well as in Dubai and Kuala Lumpur—includes eliminating such complexities as language barriers, potential for fraud, and safety concerns with the transparency that the app provides, while adding the exponential convenience of getting me and my stuff from point A to point B effortlessly.

If you own a company involved in almost any aspect of transportation right now, you'd be astute to study how to change your business model in response to this paradigm shift in market dynamics. But the assets for hire aren't just taxis; you have to think about the ripple effect.

Uber is allowing more people to live without owning cars. If people aren't buying cars, they're not going to buy car insurance, use as much gas, pay as much in tolls, incur traffic tickets (which are a revenue stream to local municipalities), etc. And so the ripple expands outward, industry by industry, based on a single company or business model.

Another disruption stems from the increasingly pervasive digital mindset. Every customer is now a digital customer. By this I mean that not only do we act on digital input but we are also acted on by that same network through an endless loop of connectedness. So the Co-Create evolution of your business model must definitively reflect digital customers and their real-time expectations. Digital technology now inhabits every dimension of our lives. Your business model and value proposition are expected to deliver seamless end-to-end experiences. "What do you mean I can't order that part from my smartphone?" or "Why can't you download that data from our private cloud before I arrive on-site?" or "Why didn't I get an alert and a reroute about that supplier incident?" You too will face a barrage of indignant reactions like these if you stick to antiquated ways of interacting with key stakeholders.

We're reaching the point where push truly gives way to pull—where search engine optimization transforms into "needs engine prioritization." Optimized search is still geared to assist the sellers of information, products, and services. It's high time that search focused much more on what the buyer needs to make their next decision—not just in terms of buying products and services but also in buying *into* an individual or organization's credibility, reputation, and trustworthiness.

Some of these changes are being driven by your changing consumers and how they prefer to receive information, goods, and services. Before 2020, millennials will surpass boomers in spending power. And unsurprisingly, researchers have found distinct differences in buying behavior between the two generations. Older people trust friends' opinions and recommendations—66 percent—while half of millennials prefer online reviews to advice from family and peers. What's coming—from the manufacturers showcasing their latest wares at CES and from the companies inspired by those dazzling SmartThings—will arrive in whole ecosystems designed to take advantage of real-time access, human responsiveness, and actionable intelligence from a multitude of data sources.

British technology pioneer Kevin Ashton coined the phrase the "Internet of Things" (IoT) to refer to that web of objects—from smart watches to sensors in buildings and traffic cams and refrigerators—whose interconnectedness allows them to passively collect data and then act to optimize processes, and which can be conveniently controlled via a mobile device. In his lab at the Massachusetts Institute of Technology (MIT), Ashton's team created technologies that, for example, make your house a SmartHome whose every appliance, garage door, thermostat, and security system is being monitored and manipulated remotely. Without human intervention, the IoT will increasingly run in the background, making decisions like when to turn on the heat or air-conditioning for optimal home energy use, and informing you by text message or e-mail. While this may seem banal, the day is coming when you'll get to the gym in a driverless car that takes itself in for service around your schedule, and when your workout clothes will warn you about overstressing that injured shoulder, relaying data continuously to the cloud to be downloaded by your physical therapist before your next appointment to adjust your workout.[4]

The disruption ahead means big changes for your organization's go-to-market strategy. In what ecosystem will you find your unique niche? It's time to develop the skills of rapid, agile innovation (chapter 2) you are going to need to compete and evolve. Thinking about this now will allow you to become that agile innovator, prepared to adapt to disruption. Ignoring these changes creates the conditions to be disrupted by someone else—on their terms, at the time of their choosing. What is your company's baseline behavior on this dimension?

When it comes to disruption driving innovation, you will discover that the Co-Create difference is not just anticipating and reacting to these earth-shattering changes. Rather, it is reimagining your organization and how it does business in such a way as to build the opportunity for Co-Creation into every relationship and interaction. Then, as illogical as it may seem, there is no longer a customer or a buyer and seller but partners working together to create exponential value. If this seems a little opaque, don't worry. Just keep reading, and it will get clearer.

Benchmark, Profile, then DISRUPT Yourself!

I realize I am asking leaders to perform an unnatural act, which is to think in an intentionally disruptive manner, despite the maturity of their firm or industry. This is all about changing leaders' perspective from "we've always done it that way" to a radically fresh lens.

Here's a sample taken from my work with a Fortune 500 company whose research revealed that the best and brightest recruiting prospects among millennials perceived their organization as decidedly back-of-the-pack. The company was using the timeworn sequence of campus info session, job fair, and selective interview followed by trial employment—with less than stellar results. Their focus was all push and no pull, all "Do you fit with us, how can you help us?" and no "Here's what we can do for you, here's how we can help you reach your goals." I urged them to take a more Co-Creative approach to the campus recruitment train via the following program:

1. **Information session**: The focus is now on how the young people might be better off because of the relationship. Gone is the one-hour, one-way session. Half-day conversations now bring in relevant local expertise. We meet prospects as freshmen, gradually building a community in which they can feel connected to a career path for the duration of their college career.
2. **Career fair:** If we can't change the ritual, we can at least disrupt it. Instead of tables, we'll group some couches and comfortable chairs to encourage conversation. That evening, we'll invite the students to a casual dress event where they can relax, and so can we. We'll deepen relationships with these young people beyond their résumés—how 'bout them Falcons!—as we get to know each other.
3. **Interviews:** Sure, the HR people will interview for most of the day, but at the end we will offer a one-hour workshop on interviewing best practices with specific feedback, giving them something of value—and deepening our relationship in the exchange.

4. **Internships:** More internship opportunities, started earlier, to encourage young people to come back, summer after summer. We'll explore work/study cooperative programs in which students can balance their academic education with practical field experience.

5. **Management-development program:** We're finding ways to extend this program, so that we have the opportunity to retain more of the bright young people we've invested in.

So the process that starts with sentiment analysis, to see how we are perceived by prospective employees, leads to a step-by-step deepening of the relationship.

Nourcabulary

Sentiment analysis identifies and extracts subjective information from source materials using techniques like natural language processing (NLP), text analysis, and computational linguistics, usually to determine the attitude of a speaker or a writer with respect to a topic. Sentiment analysis can be widely applied to reviews and social media to guide innovation, sales and marketing, and customer service.

We can accent this by building an online community through which they can talk to us—and one another—about their experiences along the way. The whole effort is part of rebranding our campus recruiting by creating awareness of our career opportunities with multiple stakeholders—not just students but also career-planning services, faculty, and corporate partners.

It should now be clear why I believe it is imperative that organizations take on and internalize the role of disruptor in order to avoid becoming the disrupted. The catalyst is the spirit of Co-Creation.

OUTCOME-FOCUSED BRAND EXPERIENCES

Groupon, Fab.com, eToys.com, Pets.com—these are just a few e-commerce outfits launched with great fanfare, and big bucks from Venture Capital—that have foundered on the rocks of overpromising and underdelivering (sometimes literally). Instagram, Warby Parker, eSalon, Houzz, Carta—these are sites that have succeeded, some in quite mature spaces, because of their creators' razor-sharp attention to **outcome-focused brand experiences** and how heeding consumer input can help perfect a brand's products and services. In the introduction, I defined Market Gravity as a company's ability to attract stakeholders' intrinsic interest and the prime measure of Co-Create outcomes. In this chapter I will lay out the attributes of these experiences and the techniques by which organizations create them.

What are you doing that is more than just a clever management gimmick or manipulative marketing ploy? What about your organization is truly unique, engaging, and impactful enough to set you apart? You must do something that grabs people's attention in an authentic, meaningful way, so that your customers cannot wait to tell their friends about the experience. Suppliers recommend it to other suppliers. Investors bring in other investor friends. They forward your video to not just one friend but ten. They discuss your unique passion for being different on their social channels, thus dramatically extending your market reach.

Outcome-focused brand experiences activate an army of ambassadors as the ripples spread. Potential buyers start hearing about the same event, experience, or product from multiple sources. Candidates currently not on your talent-acquisition radar begin to make inquiries about joining your team. They feel pulled to search that term or click on that link or attend that event. As a consumer, how did you hear about Fitbit? How did you hear about GoPro? Chances are good it was through this kind of Market Gravity.

L.L.Bean was founded in 1912 on the back of a single product, a then-revolutionary "duck boot" that married a waterproof rubberized bottom to a lace-up leather top. One hundred years later, that same boot was named "the" boot to have by a handful of media, including pubs as various as *InStyle*, *Us Weekly*, and *The Wall Street Journal*. Spontaneous social media boosts on Instagram and Pinterest grew partly out of its popularity—and visibility—on college campuses, particularly in northern climates. Every year since, come winter, the company has had to announce back orders—sometimes as many as fifty thousand a season—such has the demand grown.

Figure 1.2: Outcome-Focused Brand Experiences

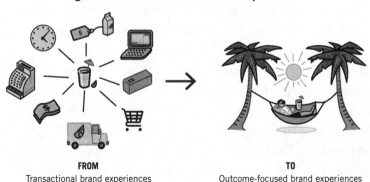

FROM	**TO**
Transactional brand experiences	Outcome-focused brand experiences

With 450,000 pairs sold in 2014 and that number only growing, one can ask, "What is going on?" Remember how I suggested that Market Gravity is like word of mouth on steroids? Here, a combination of initial fashion and media interest fueled by the firehose of social media turned a "heritage" product into a runaway seller—now perceived as a must-have accessory by key trendsetting and spending-market segments.

Made by hand in Maine out of US-sourced materials on shoemaking machines many decades old, the boot is not something easily outsourced, nor is its production easily ramped up. The company would not want to do that anyway. For the other leg of the Bean boot phenom is the way it invites the customer into a whole family of well-made, classic American products, while at the same time allowing them to enjoy Bean's legendary customer service and unimpeachable quality.

Now, let's take a closer look at what makes for an outcome-focused brand experience. For starters, most companies concentrate on a specific market niche.

Market Gravity is a force created between an organization and its target stakeholders. As such, intentional focus on fewer, more targeted relationships is dramatically more critical and effective than trying to appease the masses. That's why Ducati doesn't make a scooter—they're known for high-performance motorcycles. Can you imagine a Ferrari or a Lamborghini built for the consumers of the Nissan Leaf? Yet, you see organizations of all types, sizes, and industry foci chasing every conceivable type of employee, trying to work with completely inappropriate suppliers (or worse yet, ignoring the ones who aren't proposing $10 million for a strategy engagement up front or a six-figure retainer), or appealing to the wrong customer!

How do organizations design these outcome-focused brand experiences? By understanding, deeply, the results that their customers or other stakeholders are after. A lot of companies, individuals, teams, and brands confuse *inputs* with *outcomes*. To keep the focus on outcomes, you have to ask, and keep asking until you run out of questions to ask, how is the recipient of your value—be it your employee, a partner or investor in your company, your customer—better off because they are in a relationship with you?

Journalist Malcolm Gladwell does this deep inquiry in areas in which he's trying to develop an expertise—driven mostly, as he told the *Sacramento Bee*, by his knowledge of how poorly we make decisions, in business as well as in daily life. "The kinds of cognitive errors that lead to disastrous decisions are common to all of us. By definition, human beings are flawed decision-makers."[5] His oft-cited illustration is New Coke, a fine example of a new product nobody wanted, the result of shallow market research that failed to ask the right questions to identify customers' needs. Gladwell reminds us to make decisions based on what recipients of our value tell us—not on our presuppositions.

If you can get and keep your finger on the pulse of customers' experience with your organization, then you can begin to anticipate what they will need from you next in the relationship. And that is how you instill and nurture lifelong loyalty, in both your personal and organizational brands. Instagram and Warby Parker have both done this and built tremendous growth and brand repute using this strategy.

When Instagram was founded in 2010, it was mostly known as a platform where fashion industry professionals, particularly designers, could post images of the latest and hottest looks. As of late 2016, they had 500 million monthly users posting images of almost anything. That growth came by recognizing a need that Facebook in particular was not filling: the ability for users to very quickly and easily post photo content and then sort, curate, follow, like, share, and comment. Entire communities of like-minded individuals coalesced overnight into groups eager to let (for example) the Nordstrom's and Macy's of the retail world know what they loved—and were more likely to buy. Anticipating their loyal followers' next deep desire, Instagram added a short video function in mid-2016 with promises of longer video upload options to come.

That same year the founders of eyeglass retailer Warby Parker saw an opportunity for a "David and Goliath" play in the eyewear industry, which was dominated by Luxottica, the world's largest eyewear company. Warby Parker shook the industry with exceptional customer experience elements, such as fostering human interactions at their store entrances; designing customer experience with the customer in mind (vs. letting marketing or merchandizing considerations override what's best for the customer); hiring and investing in exceptional talent to engage customers right the first time; and using technology to streamline the customer experience, rather than letting it overwhelm it. Enormous attention to detail around the customer experience online and off is baked into the DNA of Warby Parker, which designs and manufactures its own products to avoid the captive pricing of Luxottica. Customer service is so great that real interactions often become advertising storylines.[6]

Customers—including business-to-business clients—might be overjoyed with what you offer them today, but they will leave you tomorrow if a disruptive competitor can offer them superior outcomes. The speed with which this can happen to companies and industries is often breathtaking. Remember Nokia and BlackBerry? At their height, they were the most sought-after brands with leading-edge products. Whether B2C or B2B, today's successful Instagrams and Warby Parkers cannot rest on past performance. What will you do to disrupt yourself tomorrow?

This brings us to another aspect of how Co-Create companies find unique, differentiating value: they collaborate with other companies to strategically extend their market reach. While Google is consumer focused, they derive a great deal of their success from their business play. They didn't stop at search; Google Docs, Google+, and Google Apps create a better online experience for their users, many of whom are already using Google in business contexts. With its acquisition of the immensely popular social traffic app Waze, it's easy to see how Google can now deliver your fresh groceries more quickly and efficiently than the grocery store itself, or how its autonomous driving vehicles will be a threat to Uber, Tesla, and Apple as well as the traditional car manufacturers.

Great companies like Google have mastered creating great brand experiences. To be truly differentiating, to create Market Gravity, those experiences have to be focused on the customer's desired *outcomes*, not on what it takes to get to that outcome (the *inputs*). This is the essence of listening—a bedrock principle of all good Co-Creation.

Co-Creation Demands Constantly Listening

The Co-Create economy demands constant reassessment of what is currently working in terms of meeting customers' needs in order to discover, meet, and exceed their ever-rising expectations. The Net Promoter Score (NPS)® system introduced by Fred Reichheld and Satmetrix in 2003 has become a widely used tool for gauging customer satisfaction, championed by many as one of the leading drivers of brand success.[7] However, I see limitations in the NPS® system as it is currently used, for three reasons:

1. It is overly simplistic. It only captures a single point in time, and even in that one moment, it obscures subtler facets of the customer experience.[8]
2. It doesn't take into account the outcome that a customer used a product or service to achieve.
3. It is a lagging indicator, which means you learn too little, too late.

More useful, in my opinion, are methods of listening to customers that allow you to analyze *why* they feel a certain way. I am more likely to recommend sentiment analysis to my clients.

Listening to customers—which is what both NPS® and sentiment analysis is about—is treated in more depth in chapter 2.

A more useful focus than generalized NPS® scores, introspection, is the primary task of this chapter—a frank evaluation of how well your company performs at what I refer to as "passing the baton." Much of the time, those track-and-field relay races are won or lost in how the baton is passed. Both internal to the organization and among partners in the value chain, how we pass the baton determines if we give recipients of our value a seamless experience in which they achieve their desired outcome—or if we fall short.

An example of genuine Co-Creation of value, achieved by paying attention to customers' experience of passing the baton, can be found in the Hilton hospitality brand. Hilton, recognizing that millions love Uber's app and demonstrate that love not just by using it but by including it in their social media interactions, has announced a partnership with the transportation disruptor. Connect your Hilton Honors account to your Uber account and they'll automatically know where you are, pick you up, and take you where you want to go. Hilton understands there is an opportunity for creating a more holistic experience for its guests by incorporating Uber. Guest satisfaction is no longer limited to the experience inside the hotel property; it is deeply linked to the outcome that brought the guest to that hotel location.

The same idea applies in any company. I could have a great sales force, but if my marketing team isn't equally competent, or if I have great sales and marketing but IT is behind the curve in keeping our team at the leading edge of where they can provide value, we won't move forward. Any part of my organization can dilute the experience of an employee, partner, customer, or investor.

Another way to create unique and positive outcome-focused brand experiences in the B2B space is by partnering with others who specialize in what you don't, where one plus one equals three, or even four or five, because you leverage your competencies. Boston-based HubSpot (NYSE: HUBS), founded in 2006, is a fast-growing inbound software marketing platform created because, as its founders put it, "people have transformed how they live, work, shop, and buy, but businesses have not adapted."[9] The company's mission is to integrate your business with applications that are not only helpful and easy to use but also reactive and proactive. "Any marketing software can help you automate e-mails or build campaigns," Hubspot's VP of marketing Meghan Keaney Anderson told me, "but HubSpot was built around the idea of treating prospective customers differently: relying more on content than ads to attract visitors to your website and using context and personalization to convert those visitors into leads and customers."[10] The customer may never even know HubSpot is a partner in their experience, making you look good with every page view, helpful blog post, and curated content experience.

What this looks like on the screen is responsive design, easily experienced across all devices. At every turn, the user is met with integrated analytic tools that maximize the inbound marketing experience. Crafting a blog post? The app recommends keywords, calls to action (CTAs), and internal links, and even curates blocks of content to be personalized for relationship-driven marketing. Your corporate website is no longer static, updated manually with bits of information. Instead, it is dynamic, with different content and customized CTAs appearing depending on who is visiting and from where.

And if you think this tech-driven company must work best with, well, other tech-driven companies, think again. "Some of the best inbound stories come from traditional companies," Anderson said. "I'm reminded of a plastic sheeting company that became a HubSpot customer and began creating content around, what else? Plastic sheeting. After a year of blogging consistently, they saw a 100 percent increase in sales, largely attributed to that content. Why? Their competitors weren't blogging about plastic sheeting. They weren't doing much at all. So when it came to getting found online through Google or other search means, their content quickly rose to the top, and that niche audience found them first. There is no industry too 'dull' or obscure to leverage inbound marketing." Indeed, Hubspot counts Shopify as one of its first customers, but it is also used by companies in tech, manufacturing, nonprofit, consulting, recruiting, health care, and marketing.

HubSpot thinks of everything, generating shorter forms for a visitor on a smartphone, and also using continuously harvested feedback on how people find you so that you can add adapted, "smart content" to strengthen visitor engagement. Their social media analytics tell you whom to respond to and who is responding, keeping track of relationships to guide you to strengthen them. Customer Relation Management (CRM) and Sales suites complete the package. The result? HubSpot had over $180 million in revenues in 2015, up 57 percent compared to 2014.

As should now be clear, organizational growth depends on outcome-focused brand experiences because they create Market Gravity. Not only do they attract net-new customers, they also keep existing customers coming back for more, because their brand experiences meet their ever-rising expectations over time. Compelling outcome-focused brand experiences create loyalty in customers and other stakeholders, inoculating them against temptation to defect to a potentially disruptive competitor.

Take a moment now for introspection: How is your organization's current performance in terms of the experiences that you create for employees, customers, investors, and suppliers? Remember, focus on the outcomes they seek, not on the inputs to that outcome that your job descriptions, preferred vendor programs, product or service offerings provide. Keep that finger on the pulse of your customers' rising expectations with a plan to consistently exceed them. The ability to create outcome-focused brand experiences is a key component of your organization's readiness for the Co-Create approach.

COLLABORATIVE CO-CREATION

When companies think creatively about how to develop compelling experiences for their customers, the brainstorm often leads beyond their own internal capabilities. They begin to see how to create greater value for their target relationships by partnering with other firms to Co-Create exceptional value.

The real opportunity for organizational growth in the Co-Create economy is in collaboration. Specifically, Co-Creation's greatest potential is achieved when large organizations work intimately with nimbler Co-Create economy firms. Various methods can be used, ranging from high-profile "accelerator" competitions to strategic investing using such tools as peer-to-peer lending and crowdfunding.

Nourcabulary

Collaborative Co-Creation: Collaboration for its own sake is a waste of time! Who really needs to read another hundred e-mails about preparing for a dozen conference calls or web meetings for a face-to-face that's coming up? Conversely, collaborative Co-Creation, which makes the end result dramatically stronger or more effective, is priceless. Might you eventually be able to create that result by yourself? Sure. But why not get there faster, and at a fraction of the cost, through collaborative Co-Creation? The relationship is the secret sauce.

What are these firms creating when they come together? There is plenty of room on this "workbench" for all kinds of value generation, from Co-Creation of content to co-opetition to achieve vertical integration of manufacturing, distribution, and retailing. Partners are proliferating in all different kinds of channels, demanding understanding and a proactive response from leaders. With this proliferation, the ecosystem of relationships grows exponentially and is mutually beneficial.

A great example of a large organization choosing to collaborate with smaller, nimbler firms is Coca-Cola Founders (coca-colafounders.com). The Coca-Cola company has been around since 1886, and it's as good an example of a mature company in a mature industry as you could ask for. How in the world can a soda company with a product they dare not change dive into a Co-Creation approach? And yet, knowing that it cannot afford to ignore innovation when little start-ups are disrupting big businesses left and right, Coca-Cola has launched a new model for incubating start-ups that leverages the mutual interest that characterizes the Co-Create economy. In ten cities around the world, they have handpicked experienced entrepreneurs and given them not just a start-up platform but potentially their first big customer as well.[11]

It's called the Founder's Platform, and here's how it works: Experienced entrepreneurs are identified and invited to join. They are given unprecedented access to senior-level advisors within one of Coke's

Figure 1.3: Collaborative Co-Creation

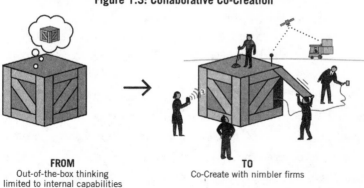

FROM
Out-of-the-box thinking
limited to internal capabilities

TO
Co-Create with nimbler firms

business units, where they take a deep dive into Coke's challenges and opportunities. The entrepreneurs benefit from Coca-Cola's relationships, resources, and reach, as well as seed funding, in exchange for 20 percent equity. All this before any ideas are on the table! "Our goal is to help our founders grow big new, high-growth businesses while helping us grow Coca-Cola at the same time," said Coca-Cola's VP of innovation and entrepreneurship David Butler.[12]

In fact, Co-Creation has been in Coca-Cola's DNA from the establishment of its first bottling agreements. From the start, Coca-Cola pioneered an outsource partner approach to its supply chain rather than vertically integrating. Nothing has changed in that formula either, as the company has grown into a global brand.

Look at some of the start-ups generated since the launch of the Coca-Cola Founders Platform in late 2013: Home Eat Home on-demand meals; Weex, a mobile network operator for millennials; Hivery, a provider of vending analytics. With some of these companies, it's relatively easy to see how Coca-Cola stands to benefit. With others it's less clear, but I'm willing to bet that they see an angle—or the future potential for one, at least.

The pairing of agile start-up entrepreneurs with the relationships, resources, and reach of Coca-Cola fully illustrates the potential of Co-Creation as a philosophy. As we will see in detail in chapter 7, IBM used the same approach under an umbrella program called the Watson Ecosystem, in which they invited app developers to apply to use its cutting-edge artificial intelligence (AI) technology behemoth Watson for initial business development and then selectively invested in some of those companies from a dedicated $100 billion fund. Recent partners are nimble, relatively new youngsters like Engage, Macaw Speech, Opentopic, StatSocial, Vennli, and Domus Semo Sancus, creating real innovation in call-center support, speech telephony, content marketing, social media analysis, survey analysis, and risk management.[13] But bigger fish have come to swim as well, including Under Armour, SoftBank, Whirlpool, and Medtronic, all of whom need Watson's massive data-crunching ability for applications from fitness monitoring to personalizing home appliances to diabetes management.[14]

Can you see your organization in the story of the Coca-Cola Founders Platform or the Watson Ecosystem? Whether you're one of the giants like IBM or Coca-Cola or just a start-up, it's time for some introspection about the Co-Create economy advantages achieved when large organizations partner with nimbler firms. Like creating outcome-focused brand experiences, collaborative Co-Creation is a key component of your organization's readiness for the Co-Create approach.

PURPOSEFUL PROVOCATIVE LEADERSHIP

Nourcabulary

Purposeful, provocative leadership: A mindset that balances organizational learning with performing, welcomes prudent risk-taking in making multiple evolutionary bets, doesn't fear failure, and encourages a relationship-centric culture that's unafraid of retribution.

The challenge of effective leadership is all around us. Kevin Plank of Under Armour offers an example worthy of study.

Kevin Plank of Under Armour: Poster Boy of Purposeful, Provocative Leadership

I became aware of what defines a provocative, purposeful leader in this dimension when I attended iCONIC:DC, presented by *Inc.* magazine and CNBC, where I heard Kevin Plank, the CEO of Under Armour, speak.[15] I have been drilling into his leadership and performance since.

Plank's prudent risk-taking consists of betting almost a billion dollars on technology, all through acquisitions, specifically to outperform Nike. Particular features of his leadership include an ability to balance learning with performing and facing failure without fear. While Under Armour is performing well as an organization, Plank speaks unapologetically about products they've launched that were flops. They are learning from their mistakes. Who in their right minds would spend a billion dollars on technology if they feared failure?[16]

Plank talks about a battle among the company's leadership over whether or not to invest in devices. You would think Under Armour might take a keen interest in developing personal fitness tracking devices to compete with Fitbit. But they quickly figured out that there are other firms much better at building the physical devices. Plank encouraged Under Armour to focus on building customer communities instead. (Notice how this supports a relationship-centric culture inside and outside the company. Do you recognize Relationship Economics®?)

Tolerance for a prudent level of risk is important: we all know that old saying, "nothing ventured, nothing gained." But how do you delineate what is a good risk and what is a "bet-the-company" risk?

Under Armour bought three leading makers of activity- and diet-tracking mobile apps. Any conservative CEO would say they were crazy to spend $710 million on the three, especially since two were unprofitable at the time of the acquisition. How do you expect to ever get a return on that investment?

But look closer. The strategic advantage in these tracking apps is the data stream they produce from the 150 million–strong digital health and fitness community members those apps represent, creating at a single blow a massive data collection and analysis engine unique to Under Armour. The company can now learn and analyze what their customers eat, where they exercise, how long they run, and what their favorite routes are. They are harvesting masses of information that can drive everything from product development to merchandising to marketing. (And, likely, they can also repackage that information and sell it, too.) Plank's willingness to risk steep investment costs in exchange for a prolific stream of customer-centric insight exemplifies the courage required of a purposeful leader—and definitely illustrates what you might call the absence of fear of failure.

Mobile apps share very little with Under Armour's core business; they have nothing to do with making fitness shirts, shoes, and gear. When a CEO does something as bold as that, it is provocative leadership. The bet on a vision that will transform the organization sends a clear message: We're about more than simple iteration, doing the same things better, cycle after cycle. We're more than innovation, doing things differently. Even if—especially if—it makes our old way of doing things obsolete.

Such acquisitions naturally lead to a new cycle of balancing learning with performing, as the company cultures come together and managers at every level must learn how to achieve the outcomes they are responsible for in a new milieu. I have long believed that appropriate metrics and performance-based compensation drive desired behaviors. With those in place, if I am an employee, I am now worried about what's going to happen to our company's performance and how that may impact my bonus. I might also be thinking about changes that divert my resources—my budget, my people—to the CEO's side project from the core business for which I'm personally responsible.

The success of acquisitions relies on leaders' purposeful encouragement of a relationship-centric culture that's unafraid of failing and, thus, unafraid of retribution. At the iCONIC event I attended, Plank talked about spending a massive amount of time in one-on-one conversations persuading key people that the negative consequences they feared were not going to be realized. He was savvy enough to understand that to succeed, he needed internal relationships aligned with his strategic, company-evolving initiative. While this may seem obvious, I point it out because I find strategic relationships so frequently overlooked by senior leaders. Unfortunately, a fundamental appreciation of the value of relationships, not to mention the skills, knowledge, and behavior that develop those assets, is still not taught in business schools or executive education.

Kevin Plank is the quintessential purposeful, provocative leader.

Can you imagine how that *huge* investment must have seemed to top executives used to overseeing Under Armour's core business of shirts and shoes? By the way, with almost fourteen thousand employees and $4 billion in revenue, this is no start-up. This is a mature company in a mature industry. Even so, it has figured out how to replicate its entrepreneurial DNA going forward.

Now, apply the lens of common mission, common vision, or common enemy. Under Armour dislikes Nike, its fiercest competitor. Nike and Adidas are seen as public enemies at Under Armour, and rightfully so. Nike delivered $30 billion in revenues, but they have only one-fifth as many users on their technology platform, Nike+, as Under Armour has with their acquisitions.

Plank sees the mobile app acquisitions as a multipronged approach. He understands that purposeful leaders must manage the present while inventing their future. Taking care of the present means keeping Under Armour's athletic-wear business healthy. They still have to produce T-shirts and shoes. But to invent and invest in a future in which Under Armour eclipses its competitors, to start to adopt (to quote a 2015 *Inc. Magazine* article), "the kind of world-changing ambitions more common to a Google or Facebook,"[17] Plank must steer the present company toward making Under Armour Connected Fitness a platform that has an impact on fitness globally. Partnering with Taiwanese smartphone maker HTC, Under Armour is going to start making biometric fitness devices and a smart scale, which will put them in competition with Fitbit and Apple.

Yes, Plank admits, his strategy is risky. But their stock is up over 2,000 percent in the ten years since their IPO. His purposeful leadership is paying off.

Plank is a visionary, but he is also a realist who recognizes that the Connected Fitness initiative is extremely ambitious—and not a sure thing. But, to quote a line from a former US special operations commander that graces a whiteboard in Plank's office: "Nobody ever won a horse race by yelling 'whoa.'"

Of course, such high-caliber leaders aren't just born that way. They are made through mentoring, through coaching, through failing and succeeding and learning from both inside and outside the corporate world. And they are made through the very overt, intentional processes we've been examining here.

What is your organization's readiness for purposeful, provocative leadership? This, too, is a key component of your organization's readiness for the Co-Create approach.

CONTEXTUAL INTELLIGENCE

We have discussed three interdependent principles essential to organizational growth in the Co-Create economy so far. A related concept is **contextual intelligence,** which helps leaders interpret market signals, partner input, and customer feedback in their proper respective contexts, and quickly take appropriate action. In fact, contextual intelligence is becoming more important at every level within the organization. Nowhere is it more important than at the edge of where business happens—where customers and other stakeholders experience value.

Nourcabulary

Contextual intelligence: When you combine situational awareness with the ability to apply intuition to sense and respond to trends, you understand events in a way that enables more informed decisions and more effective action in varied, changing, and uncertain conditions.

Contextual intelligence concerns the practical application of knowledge and information to real-world situations. (The concept is an evolution of one part of Robert Sternberg's "Triarchic Theory of Intelligence,"[18] which incorporates a more cognitive approach centered on defining intelligence in the context of reacting and adapting to the environment instead of on some concrete set of measurable skills.) A key concept as applied to leadership is that contextual intelligence views one aspect of true intelligence as dynamic, both in the short and long terms. This true intelligence evolves across a given situation or problem (Where is my team right now and what resources do we have access to?) and is then extrapolated in subsequent events (What should we do next given our condition and resources?). It stems from situational awareness, meaning the ability to understand the context surrounding events as they unfold. The "intelligence" comes into play via both human and system factors—the "nature and nurture" that individuals bring to a situation, complemented by the capacity of the organization to make real-time information available to individuals when and where they need it.

Contextual intelligence is easier to see than to define. Here's contextual intelligence in action:

Your HR pro has taken the first steps to recruiting a major prospective employee who was partly responsible for developing a key technology that will play an important role in your company's near-term growth. You take two influential team members along for an initial meet-and-greet lunch at a swanky, but discreet, restaurant. During the meal, you notice the prospective employee running his finger around his collar as if it were too tight, as well as taking frequent small sips of water. He barely touches his food. During a long, sometimes technical conversation, he mostly listens and nods, citing his current employer positively and brightening considerably when the talk turns to his family, his love of outdoor sports, and the local ball club's ongoing terrible season.

When the meal comes to an end and it is time to set the next meeting, you ask your co-workers to hang back. You walk him out to his car and suggest that it's a lot to think about. You've got tickets to the next game a week away. Why not meet there, bring the family, relax for a few hours. At the game, you talk about your recent family trip to Disney World, your company's school volunteers program. Yes, people work hard at your company and the expectations are high, but you also work closely, supporting each other to reach those goals. You listen more than you talk, you offer your own personal goals, sketch a bright future. You part with a handshake—and a hire. Though you would have liked to have wrapped it up at the lunch, given time pressure, you resisted. You asked not, "What can you do for our company?" but instead offered, "Here's what we can do for you—and those you care about."

You just displayed your contextual intelligence.

I predict you will hear a lot more about contextual intelligence in the near future. We are fast moving from the app era to the era of the intelligent agent. Over the next half decade, we'll witness the birth of hundreds, if not thousands, of autonomous intelligent devices that function as our personal agents. Remember the Internet of Things? By definition, these agents complete entire jobs by themselves, which means they must learn to understand us and our human objectives. In this world, there is no room for last century's "command-and-control" approach. We must shift to an "equip-and-empower" approach that uses contextual intelligence. The customer will be an equal participant in this new dynamic, and all customer touchpoints must be equally "smart" and contextually aware to deliver the seamless experience customers expect.

Too often, both among my clients and in the marketplace, I see a complete disconnect between what an organization wants its public to hear and what people actually experience. The CEO of Delta Airlines appears in the media talking about the company's turnaround performance and its customer service, the "Delta Difference." Then I witness a Delta flight attendant berating a passenger. Or they send me a survey, "How was your gate agent experience on your last flight?" The gate agent was fine, but the flight attendant was inattentive, or the food was awful, or the seat was broken. When you are asking about something that is irrelevant, you are not being contextually intelligent. Too many leaders are still running an organization through command and control instead of really empowering the front line, where the customers experience the brand.

"Contextual intelligence" is a key component of leadership courses at our nation's military schools—the National War College, Naval Academy, and the Air Force Academy, for example. The days of the Pentagon sending in the mass manpower are long gone. A battalion didn't go in to get Osama Bin Laden. No, it was SEAL Team Six, and they only moved based on intelligence and years of groundwork, using advanced warfare equipment and an intelligence unit made up of our finest soldiers. That is contextual intelligence in action!

Now, does your company have the right DNA to apply intuition, observation, and groundwork, including real-time access to data, to respond to what's happening at a moment of truth with a stakeholder? Today's challenges require a much more intuitive, knowledgeable "soldier," with real-time access to supporting information, at the edge of where he or she needs it most.

Take the same military concept and apply it to employees. Is contextual intelligence relevant to everybody in every role? Probably not. But customer-facing roles have to become more analytic, use better tools, and be empowered to make real-time decisions. They should also receive training on how to sense and respond to what is happening around them. Not "Just let me check with the office," but "Given my experience, my tools, my resources, here's what I can do to help."

Recently, I was speaking at a Ritz-Carlton property in Lake Oconee, Georgia, to about four hundred executives. On this particular day I was wearing black slacks. At breakfast, I asked one of the waitstaff for a black napkin because I wanted to avoid the lint a white napkin can leave behind. Sure enough, she quickly brought me a black one. After breakfast I gave my speech, and later that morning the group came back to the dining hall for lunch. I was just one of four hundred people, but that staff member was standing with a black napkin on a platter at the entrance, looking for me. I could not have been more pleased, with her and with Ritz-Carlton for this thoughtful gesture. Was it in her nature, her DNA, to anticipate a customer's needs like that? Or was it Ritz-Carlton's legendary training and development culture that nurtured it?

You'll notice in that story, I'm not talking about the catering manager or the director of facilities. I'm not talking about the hotel IT guy. I'm not even talking about Ritz-Carlton corporate. I'm talking about a single frontline employee who doesn't get paid a large salary, but with her effort, her intuition, her training, she creates that brand experience, that affinity. I can't tell you how many times I've told that story. It's such a good example of the gravity contextual intelligence can create.

Contextual intelligence applies across the board, from positioning a brand, to the execution of its value delivery, to closing the loop with analysis of insightful data. It's a steady process of course correction, typically in response to a market trend or a competitive peer. Contextual intelligence helps leaders interpret market signals, partner input, and customer feedback in their respective contexts and then take appropriate action.

Big data offers unprecedented opportunities for discovery and insight. But without context, data is meaningless or misleading. Competitive differentiation in the era of big data requires contextual intelligence that marries empirical rigor with intuition. To harness this, leaders must shift from a "command-and-control" approach to an "equip-and-empower" one, and to deploy their company's resources in support of human factors at those black napkin moments and experiences where business happens—where your brand creates your customers' experience.

Like the topics discussed earlier in this chapter, contextual intelligence is a key component of your organization's readiness for the Co-Create approach; it is the fourth of the interdependent principles on which organizational growth in the Co-Create economy depends.

TOOL 1: CO-CREATE PRIORITIES DIAGNOSTIC

Don't forget to download the Co-Create Toolkit PDF from CoCreate-Book.com and apply some of the key ideas you've just read in this chapter. In my experience, application of these ideas tends both to help you internalize them, and to make them more relevant to your realm of responsibilities.

The first tool prompts you to evaluate up to twenty ideas, narrow those down to ten, then identify a single initiative to receive top priority as you begin actively implementing a Co-Create approach within your company.

Chapter One Takeaways

- If disruption hasn't already begun to affect your business, it soon will. Companies that thrive in the Co-Create economy adapt to this new landscape.
- Organizational growth in the Co-Create economy depends upon four interdependent principles—outcome-focused brand experiences, collaborative Co-Creation, purposeful, provocative leadership, and contextual intelligence.
- Winners in the Co-Create economy generate Market Gravity by delivering on the outcome-based experiences desired by customers and other stakeholders.
- Large organizations can collaborate with nimbler Co-Create economy firms through various methods, including competitions, strategic investing, peer-to-peer lending, and crowdfunding.

- Organizational agility requires leaders who balance learning with performing, welcome prudent risk-taking, and do not fear failure or tolerate infighting.
- Contextual intelligence allows leaders to interpret market signals, partner input, and customer feedback, and to take appropriate action.

TWO

CO-CREATE TOGETHER: ADAPTIVE INNOVATION

 In this chapter you will learn:

- What adaptive innovation requires of a company's various organizational functions;
- How "listening louder" brings relevant information to light;
- The impact of faint market signals;
- How to verify, validate, or void critical assumptions;
- Why pilots and prototypes are essential;
- How needs-based segmentation of customers fuels adaptive innovation.

You can either embrace the disruption that comes with adaptive innovation, or you can become irrelevant. Put another way, your company can either enter the Co-Create economy willingly, or it can be sidelined by the companies that do.

Sales of Apple's iPod were still on the rise when the company introduced its first iPhone. But why would Apple introduce a product that would steal so much of the market from its own bestseller? Because, as Steve Jobs famously said to his biographer Walter Isaacson, "If you don't cannibalize yourself, someone else will."[1] Apple wanted to be the company that continually brought the public new and delightful customer experiences, not the one that coasts on its last innovation straight into irrelevance. For an example of the opposite approach, look no further than the cable companies that tried to hold on to their outdated business model while streaming media players gained market share. When the Federal Communications Commission ruled in February 2016 that consumers could access video programming without having to rent a set-top box from their cable provider,[2] it was the final nail in the coffin for pay cable, an industry already known for customer service so terrible that it's long since been retired as a running joke. Apple, meanwhile, with its streaming media device Apple TV, once again came out the hero: they embraced adaptive innovation when the cable communications industry did not.[3]

In this chapter, I hope to help you discover new opportunities through close collaboration among your company's various functions. We'll focus primarily on the innovation and marketing functions, but no division, business unit, or team is unaffected by the demands of the Co-Create economy.

We'll learn how adaptive innovation can help you achieve four key objectives:

1. Separating signal from noise by listening closely to your environment;
2. Identifying faint market signals;
3. Rapidly validating critical assumptions; and
4. Rolling out pilots and prototypes rather than full-blown launches.

This chapter concludes with a discussion of needs-based segmentation of all organizational stakeholders, an assessment tool that will help you identify opportunities to Co-Create adaptive innovation. Let's get started.

WHAT IS ADAPTIVE INNOVATION?

Creating new products and services in today's economy requires a process of **adaptive innovation**—in other words, the ability to adjust to the fast-changing needs of target markets. For that reason, it begins at the edge of the business, with the individuals closest to the customer—or to anyone else receiving value from the company. Yes, customers are important recipients of value, but by no means are they the only audience worthy of attention. Employees, value-chain partners, investors, the media—all will experience value flowing from the organization and will need to be invited to collaborate in creating that value.

To adapt to a dynamic market's demands, organizations need relationship centricity embedded in their very DNA. Strategic relationships, both internal and external to a company, are the assets that drive adaptive innovation.

Examples of Adaptive Innovation

Apple is the most famously secretive company in technology, but among the numerous initiatives in 2014 that bucked its reputation was the release of a public preview version of its Mac OS X Yosemite. Available months before the final version shipped in October, the software was freely available to anyone curious enough to give the new operating system a try. This was the first time since the original version of OS X back in 2000 that nondevelopers had the opportunity to use a version of the software that was still a work in progress.[4] Why? Because many of the company's most meaningful accomplishments are focused on subtle software refinements that make its existing hardware products more useful.[5]

To understand the genesis of adaptive innovation, just consider one of its purest exemplars, Apple's iTunes store, which opened in 2001, grew to be the world's largest online music retailer by 2008, and surpassed 25 billion songs sold worldwide by 2013.[6] And to think that it all began with the company's constant examination and reexamination of its customers' needs, even those the customer wasn't aware of yet, like "personal" music you carried with you not just like your phone, but *on* your phone. And, of course, the media could be playable on all your devices, and shuffled and organized in whatever fashion necessary for every occasion—all at what seemed a laughable price for an ever-expanding list of customer-driven offerings, from TV shows to music videos to sports and special events.

And adaptive innovation doesn't just exist in the B2C space either,

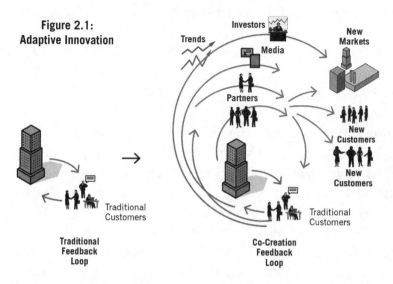

Figure 2.1:
Adaptive Innovation

Trends

Investors

Media

Partners

New Markets

New Customers

New Customers

Traditional Customers

Traditional Customers

Traditional Feedback Loop

Co-Creation Feedback Loop

with a clearly defined product like an app or song. One of the reasons Alphabet, formerly Google, had changed its name and the company's organizational structure was purely functional: they had become much more than a search engine and had learned an awful lot about how to leverage vast amounts of data—both historical and real-time—to build new businesses. Everyone has heard of Alphabet's self-driving car project, but many probably haven't heard of Sidewalk, which in early 2016 announced a partnership with the US Department of Transportation and seven large American cities, among them Austin, Texas, and San Francisco. Sidewalk's chief executive Daniel L. Doctoroff told *The New York Times* that, under the plan, Sidewalk will use anonymized cell-phone data scraped from billions of trips, traffic sensors, and other passive data sources in cities to construct a new software platform called Flow. Flow will synthesize and process the information to share in real time with public and private organizations, aiming to predict and address traffic congestion, with analysts and instant messaging capable of directing corporate fleets, private citizens, and public transit.[7] It began with the US government's Smart City Challenge program, an innovation incubator that solicited proposals for all kinds of ideas to improve life in urban environments, with seven cities selected for a first round of the $40 million of funding. Government, corporate, and municipal stakeholders will work together so that Flow advances through more rounds in constant evolution with stakeholders' needs and wants.[8]

Ask a simple question like "What is the product?" in this scenario, and you begin to understand how adaptive innovation brings value to all stakeholders. That value *is* the product, and it is not some static endpoint, but rather a deep relationship that has ongoing, evolving rewards. Cities avoid the waste, pollution, and danger associated with traffic congestion; drivers and transit riders get to work faster and more safely; while Sidewalk gets a presence—and its hardware—in major cities, collecting priceless data it can use and resell to other companies. For instance, Dunkin' Donuts might like to know that you've been stuck in traffic for thirty-five minutes at 8:15 on a Monday morning and are approaching one of their outlets. Commuting in your driverless car in a few years, with a dashboard screen, cell phone, or tablet on your lap, you won't be surprised to receive a sponsored message reminding you that your tires are reaching their limit in miles, along with a Firestone ad from a nearby store and a "Take Me There" button that interfaces with your car—dramatically more personalized and customized than geocentric ads on the Waze app now.

Key Adaptive Innovation Principles

In chapter 1, you learned that the Co-Create economy demands purposeful, provocative leaders who encourage failure as part of growth. Those leaders create the culture that makes adaptive innovation conversations possible. In many ways, this behavior is going to feel unnatural. It is the antithesis of what we've learned in business schools, what we've been taught since the first day on the job, things like failure is "bad" and a business plan is a "necessary" step in launching every new venture. In today's dynamic Co-Create economy, the mindset around failure has to change from failure with negative connotations to appropriate risk-taking with the motto "fail small, fail early, fail fast."

Innovation in a silo, a cocoon, or some corner lab has fundamental flaws. It encourages us to build something *we* think is cool, with no guarantee that the customer will agree. On the other end of the spectrum is research and development, which takes its cues from customers in order to drive innovation. But in some ways that also lacks vision. To paraphrase Steve Jobs, it is not the consumers' job to know what they want,[9] it is our job to tell them what they want. Adaptive innovation finds a happy medium between those two points of view.

To understand adaptive innovation, think about the notion inspired by Matt Ballantine of "iteration, innovation, and disruption." To explain the first term, *iteration*, Ballantine points to the television remote control as an example of something that keeps getting redesigned to ultimately do the same thing, just a little bit better.[10] Imagine holding your own all-in-one remote control in your hand. Admittedly, we've come a long way from the days when we all had four or five clunky behemoths parked on the coffee table, each with its own five-hundred-page code book and three different-sized batteries. But no matter how many ways the buttons are rearranged, a remote control is still a remote control, a device that seemingly screams to be disrupted.

Have we already seen any innovation in this category? *Innovation* is about process, doing things not necessarily *better,* but differently. Imagine changing the channel on your television set not with yet another handheld remote control, but with the sound of your voice. Samsung and LG already sell so-called "Smart TVs" capable of responding to voice commands, which are nothing if not innovative but don't rise to the level of disruption. Even while offering a hands-free option, these designs still revolve around the set-top box, using the same framework of menus and channel selections but just changing the inputs.

The third term, *disruption,* means using new processes to make old things obsolete. What would it take to eliminate the need for your remote control? Unlike many Smart TVs currently on the market, which require the user to memorize commands and interact with menus, the *disruptive innovation* coming to a Consumer Electronics Show (CES) near you would allow the user to simply converse with the technology as if it were a member of one's own family. The innovation that led to the development of Apple's Siri, Google's Home, Amazon's Echo, and Microsoft's Cortana was the result of a landmark collaboration between the US government's National Security Administration and the Defense Advanced Research Projects Agency (DARPA), with contributions from the Universities of Pittsburgh, Washington, and Cambridge alongside

Figure 2.2: Disruption

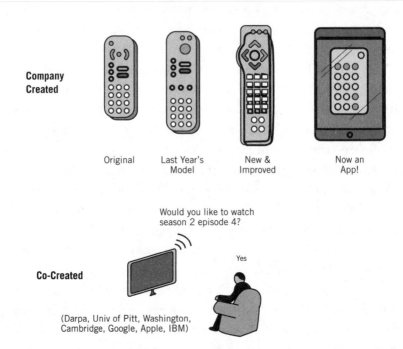

Company
Created

Original | Last Year's Model | New & Improved | Now an App!

Would you like to watch season 2 episode 4?

Yes

Co-Created

(Darpa, Univ of Pitt, Washington, Cambridge, Google, Apple, IBM)

private partnerships with companies like Google, Apple, and IBM. And that consumer-ready tech wasn't even the goal of that project. It also yielded powerful national security systems that analyze massive amounts of language data and produce new and exciting results every day. Are you tired of the same old program? What might you find if you opened your channels to more adaptive innovation?

It would be very easy to simply focus on disruptive innovation; Clayton Christiansen radically changed the way we talked about change in the business world when he introduced the concept of disruptive technologies back in 1995.[11] But even Christiansen warns that disruption theory has long since become "a victim of its own success," noting in a recent *Harvard Business Review* article that

different types of innovation require different strategic approaches. To put it another way, the lessons we've learned about succeeding as a disruptive innovator (or defending against a disruptive challenger) will not apply to every company in a shifting market. If we get sloppy with our labels or fail to integrate insights from subsequent research and experience into the original theory, then managers may end up using the wrong tools for their context, reducing their chances of success.[12]

Simply identifying innovation isn't enough. Because market conditions constantly change, innovation must also be continual. Using adaptive innovation, companies create a "virtuous spiral" of new offerings that lead to increased adoption, Co-Creation, and evangelism.

Adaptive innovation requires ongoing conversations with those you strategically partner with. These people function as your signal scouts— those who are at the edge of your sphere who can detect faint signs before they come over your horizon. If you have these relationships, both across the distribution partners who make up your value chain and also across multiple industries, you inoculate your innovators against groupthink. You minimize time lost on ideas that are unlikely to gain critical traction in the marketplace.

With the way that we're surrounded by tablets today, it's hard to believe that the personal device market was once thought a nonstarter. Apple CEO John Sculley actually brought the first one, the Newton, to market in 1993. The device was, in a way, the original iPad, but Steve Jobs later killed the project after returning to the helm of the struggling company, rationalizing that the poor design of the product and its ill-conceived stylus somehow characterized Sculley's poor leadership, illustrating this by famously remarking, "God gave us ten styluses, let's not invent another."[13]

In a slightly less glamorous but similarly ill-fated venture, tech hardware manufacturer and business software developer Cisco Systems, already pretty visible and present in the enterprise arena with collaboration and software solutions, decided in 2010 that it would be a good idea to marry the software with a dedicated B2B team-friendly pad called Cius—which you've never heard of, as it died a costly death just a year and a half later. "That's a great idea from Cisco that's about two years and one hardware project too late," wrote Kevin Tofel of the technology research and analysis firm Gigaom.[14] Whether it was an inability to keep in front of its customers' needs or a tone-deaf approach to a marketplace fully embracing Bring Your Own Device (BYOD), this failure demonstrates that Cisco lacked those leading-edge relationships—or wasn't having those ongoing conversations—that would have alerted it far earlier to Cius's mismatch with evolving market conditions.

Up until late 2015, robotics start-up QBotix seemed on track to establish its revolutionary solar tracking technology in the large-scale land-based solar generation space, with almost $25 million in funding from companies like E.ON and Siemens. Its key products, rail-mounted robots that automatically adjusted solar trackers to maximize output and minimize costs, had proof of concept, and demonstration projects raised interest from a few major players faced with the cost of replacing and installing failure-prone motors in traditional trackers. QBotix boasted that its technology would completely disrupt today's cost curve with an innovative tracking solution, reducing the cost of energy by 10–20 percent yet offering higher reliability and system intelligence.

Wow. Sounds great! But two things doomed QBotix, both key factors in adaptive innovation. First, the company should have known that the very "traditional" systems their product was disrupting were, at the same time, themselves being improved and redesigned, with fewer mechanical parts and higher reliability and reduced operating costs. Second, because they were concentrating so much on the tech end, they gravely miscalculated time to adoption. After all, utility companies are generally very large and conservative, and those with solar installations were simply more comfortable with traditional technology that they understood and were used to. It had not occurred to anyone at QBotix to talk to the utility companies first. That same year, their major start-up competitor, NEXTracker, with dramatically faster ramp (delivering 275 megawatts in 2014, and north of 2 gigawatts in 2015), was acquired by Flextronics for $330 million.[15]

As these examples show, when you build an innovation engine through conversations in every area of your business, integrating strategic stakeholders' experience directly and impactfully into the innovation process, your innovation engine emerges from its bubble. Now you are listening louder, creating the validation of critical assumptions, and constantly prototyping and piloting new facets of the business.

Adaptive innovation is never fixed in a point in time; it is never "one and done." It is ongoing, creating new norms through creative disruption of the status quo. And as I said in chapter 1, it has been proven that if you don't disrupt yourself, someone else will. I have seen through my consulting work with clients that this disruption often comes from an unknown or an underestimated competitor. Marriott was not disrupted by Hyatt—it was disrupted by three college dropouts who rented out an air mattress in their apartment. Now look at the market capitalization of Airbnb.

LISTEN LOUDER

The ongoing process of adaptive innovation requires leaders to anticipate and plan for factors in the environment outside of their organizations. That's where "listening louder" comes in.

Nourcabulary

Listening louder means expanding an organization's environmental scanning capacity to find an executive's astute ability to prioritize relevant information in guiding strategic planning, innovation, and marketing.

It would be overly simplistic to present listening louder as a synonym for environmental scanning, market intelligence, or market sensing. Table 2.1 defines these terms, showing how they relate and add up to listening louder.

Environmental scanning is a broad term, which includes gathering intelligence about competitors as well as social, cultural, technological,

Table 2.1: Components of Listening Louder

Environmental scanning	Market intelligence	Market sensing
The process of acquiring information about an organization's external environments to detect early signs of trends that may influence its strategic plans. Like adaptive innovation, environmental scanning should be continuous.	The information gleaned through environmental scanning that describes or gives insight into the behaviors of a target group of consumers.	The sum total of all the activities involved in gathering market intelligence and acting on that information.

ecological, economic, legal, and political intelligence about everywhere you operate in the world, whether as buyer (of raw materials or component manufacturing, for example) or seller. It promotes a forward-looking orientation among leaders, allowing them to be proactive in the face of constantly changing market dynamics. Its methods of data collection include monitoring the media, conducting primary and secondary research, and personal observation.

What is missing from this description? A pulse! While these are all activities that produce information needed to drive strategic planning, and each feeds the process of listening louder, they do not emphasize the active role of the entities being *listened to*. Listening louder allows organizations to transform customers, partners, and employees (strategic relationships, all) into active Co-Creators of value rather than passive consumers of value.

Listening louder to your strategic relationships also helps you discover information that your managers didn't think to monitor, that your data mining algorithms were not tuned to detect, that the media you follow hadn't yet become interested in.

Listening louder casts a much wider net than environmental scanning alone. It takes you outside your industry, outside your geography, outside the echo chamber of your internal relationships. What is that brilliant professor at that lesser-known university doing? What is that process consultant in that other smaller market doing? Why is a passionate JP Morgan Chase executive with deep domain expertise thinking about negative yield? What is that incubator start-up doing with Watson?

Listening louder is broadly about picking up signals and filtering out noise. But it's also about reading between the lines to discover what those signals are *not* saying. In a way, it's like reading body language. What might someone be holding back that in itself provides crucial insight?

Signals in the environment can be quantitative or qualitative, structured or unstructured. As such, organizations need one integrated system to gather signals from multiple data sources and synthesize them into coherent insight. They need a tool to test various scenarios, so that the result is not a static snapshot but a real-time conversation with the data.

To take it one step further, while traditional environmental scan-ning is by definition external to the organization, listening louder also takes you *inside* your organization. Remember, employees are a key stakeholder group too, and have insights and experiences at the edge of where value delivery happens. They can and should inform your adaptive innovation process. Listening louder across the organization helps you ensure that different sections of the organization see their various contributions as part of one company narrative. As a consul-tant, if I walk into a company and hear "us and them" while talking to one division about another, I know that company is not functioning optimally.

And finally, listening louder is a filtering mechanism that distills a huge quantity of information down to the most relevant pieces so that leaders can prioritize which signals to act on.

Amit Kleinberger is the thirty-five-year-old CEO of Menchie's, a frozen dessert chain with about 200 franchises in the United States and another 250 internationally. He joined the company in 2008, one year after it opened its first store, and was soon leading the franchising effort—first in Southern California, then across the country and into,

Figure 2.3: Listen Louder

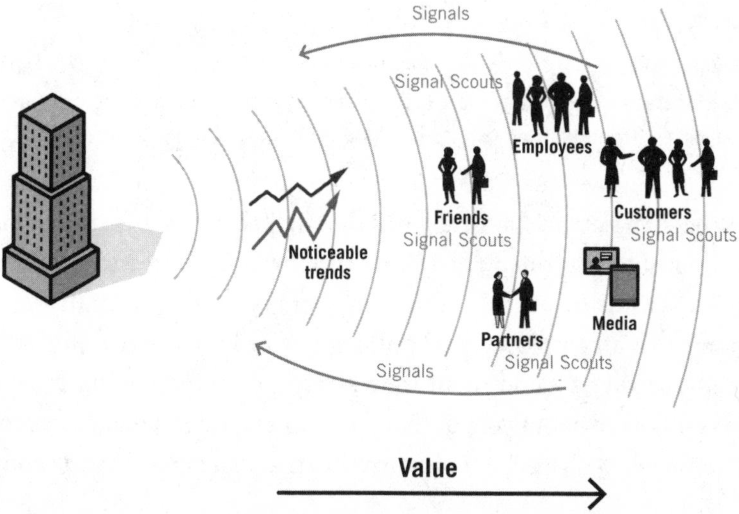

at last count, twenty-five other countries. With this kind of scope, the company has to perform excellently in both B2B *and* B2C roles. I was interested in how Kleinberger uses his network of relationships as listening posts. The company needs to know that consumers in Beijing prefer toppings like dragonfruit- and lychee-flavored gummies, while Bostoners are just fine with jimmies. And Menchie's also needs to know which region might change its tax laws, its labeling standards, or even its government at any time. Kleinberger uses his network of CEO peers both inside and outside his industry to create a circle of trusted advisors with unique expertise—people who will tell him what he needs to hear instead of what he wants to hear. He has intentionally developed that inner circle around his identified needs and goals. This group acts as his filter and prioritization tool.

DETECT FAINT MARKET SIGNALS

Environmental changes do not emerge without warning, but the earliest signs tend to be faint signals, not obvious developments. By the time the signals are strong enough to be readily observed, any possible first-mover advantage is gone. For this reason, it is absolutely essential that your company's "listening louder" mechanism be tuned to detect faint market signals.

Nourcabulary

Faint market signals are the emergent bits of information that offer organizations a means to detect trends or changes in environmental factors early on, thus offering a lead over competitors in adaptive innovation.

What can be classified as a faint signal? Think of it as a unique need or randomly mentioned pain point by a broad, often unrelated audience. It's masked as an interesting perspective by a really astute customer, or an employee that notices why or how you're doing something. It could be a comment that a partner company mentions that they've observed about you, or that you hear several times at conferences that resonates with you. An organization that can perceive and monitor these subtle streams of information can create extraordinarily powerful competitive advantages.

Strategically, faint signals are at their most valuable when they are subtlest, like the slight changes in animal behavior that precede an earthquake. But here's the rub—many of those faint signals will simply be irrelevant to your organization. You need a litmus test to detect which are relevant to you, to your market dynamics, to the strategic path between your present circumstances and aspirational future. If you hear something once, it could easily be an anomaly. If you hear it over and over again, pay attention. If you are hearing that rumble from people you like, you respect, you trust, then your strategic relationships are serving as your signal scouts. They are helping you identify faint signals in your market.

Retailer Nordstrom has found one way to validate signals from the exterior by monitoring—and acting on—social media posts. With 4 million plus Pinterest followers, the store began noticing users were creating virtual "wish lists," as one exec put it, on the platform. Nordstrom took the next logical step, curating individual items and then cleverly grouping them both in stores and online, a form of crowdsourcing fashion picks. And recognizing that "faint signals" in one place may be a shout in another, it set up a program for local stores to act on regionally popular Pinterest picks—what works in Arizona won't necessarily apply in Alaska.[16]

Early warning signs, or leading drivers (which I will discuss in chapter 6), convey advantage in the Co-Create economy if you develop the ability to separate invaluable signals from useless noise.

VALIDATE CRITICAL ASSUMPTIONS

When I suggest that you need a filtering mechanism to separate the signals that are relevant to the dynamics of your market from those that are not, I am inherently encouraging you to make assumptions about those signals. And wherever there are assumptions, there needs to be a system for validating those assumptions, or you are in danger of operating in an echo chamber—or, worse, in a land where the emperor has no clothes.

Behind your engine for listening louder and filtering faint signals, there needs to be a systematic process, the metaphorical equivalent of an assembly line, where you verify, validate, or void those critical assumptions.

What do I mean by **verify**? Basically, you need to fact-check your information. "Did thirty thousand people really demonstrate that behavior?" "Did two thousand companies really buy that?" "Did a thousand organizations really adopt that methodology?" If the answer is no, you know you'll need to do some more digging before acting.

What do I mean by **validate**? Validation is proving that you are framing the right question. Validating is applying rigorous processes to ensure that you are not misunderstanding or misinterpreting the facts you verified, and that they are relevant to your adaptive innovation. QBotix, for example, was too involved in developing its own technology, too focused on the actual product to understand the market it was trying to sell that product into. If they had incorporated a broader perspective into their overall process, perhaps by consulting with long-time industry experts with a C-suite view, they might have adapted their product accordingly.

What do I mean by **void**? You must find and abandon flawed assumptions. This step assumes that some of your assumptions are flawed, and gets them out of the mix.

At this stage, you should be approaching a verified, working set of assumptions. Say you've gathered fifty faint market signals, identified ten that are stronger than the others, and determined that these ten are highly relevant. Through a process of "verify, validate, or void," you identify three that have the highest potential for disruption to your business. Thanks to listening louder, you can now pursue them to disrupt your own company before your competitors come to disrupt you. Again returning to the QBotix example, it is very easy for innovation to be blinkered, especially in a start-up scenario. This is why you build in reality checks from the beginning. If this start-up had had a timely, rigorous review process from the start, it is very likely the product would have been more appropriate to the market.

While they had seasoned venture capital pros with experience in funding energy sector projects on board, QBotix mistook these investors for end users who would actually buy their robotic solar technology—the risk-averse, hugely regulated utilities that were content to stick with improved but familiar technology.

Validating, verifying, or voiding critical assumptions prepares a company to undertake pilots and prototypes—the final agile objective. As we will see, "agile" here applies to all aspects of the "fail early, fail often, fail cheap" product-development model. Don't overbuild in the early stages, make sure your core concepts aren't so rigid there is no room for adaptation, and design projects to consume the least resources in the early iterations.

DEPLOY PILOTS AND PROTOTYPES

Once you've filtered fifty faint market signals down to twenty-five and identified ten that are relevant, once you've performed the due diligence to verify, validate, or void that working set, then you will have winnowed a vast array of potential innovations down to a small handful, perhaps two or three. Then the question becomes, "now what?" At this moment, the dynamics of a start-up come into play.

Today, most successful start-ups adopt a "Lean Startup" strategy. Silicon Valley entrepreneur Eric Ries coined that term back in 2008 after his experience working in several high-tech US start-ups taught him that it was possible to drastically eliminate waste during the product-development phase by implementing a combination of business-hypothesis-driven experimentation and iterative product releases (i.e., pilots and prototypes). Following this methodology gives start-ups a better chance of success, at a more rapid pace, and with fewer resource requirements. The underlying question is, "How do I—based on the best assumptions I can make, based on the best data I can capture, based on the trends I can identify most accurately—validate my innovation?"

Arvind Gupta, general partner at SOSVentures and former design director of Product Development and Strategy at IDEO (ranked number 10 on *Fast Company*'s list of the "Top 25 Most Innovative Companies"), lives by the motto "Create, learn, repeat." To survive in today's dynamic markets, he argues, one must adhere to the first precept of mountaineering: "Speed is safety."[17] Case in point: G'Five, a Chinese consumer electronics company specializing in manufacturing mobile phones for developing markets, regularly gathers data on its Indian market, then produces prototype phones with new configurations of features suggested by that data in limited runs of five thousand. Based on the sales velocity of that pilot run, G'Five then determines what features and price point will work best in the near term before releasing to the larger market. This methodology has helped G'Five turn what is ordinarily a low-margin enterprise into a profitable business model almost overnight, proving that speedy deployment of pilots and prototypes helps narrow down potential innovations to those that are likely to gain the most customer uptake. The company is the sixth largest phone provider in India and gaining market share much more rapidly than mature brands like Nokia, Samsung, and Sony Ericsson. Having just broken into the top ten largest phone manufacturers worldwide, G'Five started developing facilities in Pakistan and hopes to test the markets for smartphones and tablets in South Asia and Africa using the same super lean methods that have made it a success since its founding in 2003.[18] Imagine climbing Everest with only your iPhone as a guide. Pretty soon, there'll be an app for that.

A good example of the value of pilots and prototypes can be found in Marriott's 2016 rollout of a mobile app for guests. The app enhances the guest experience by automating tech-driven processes like check-in/check-out and in-room entertainment. But it offers more: "On average, a quarter of our guests have a question or request during their stay. Mobile Requests gives them another touchpoint for communicating with on-property associates," said Marriott chief innovation officer (CIO) Bruce Hoffmeister in a 2016 *Wall Street Journal* interview. To ensure the app was intuitive to use and served its intended purpose, Marriott rolled it out to a pilot group of twenty properties. As with other technology deployments, Hoffmeister told *The Wall Street Journal*, "We tested three things before scaling Mobile Requests: customer adoption, technical complexity, and operational feasibility." From the app pilot stage, Marriott learned which services or amenities guests accessed through the platform most frequently, which allowed the developers to modify the app to reflect guest needs and preferences.[19]

Too few start-ups test their ideas for a product or service early enough. Unlike Marriott in the example above, they often fail to deploy pilots and prototypes before launching into a full rollout. The assumption that people want the value you are creating, whatever it is, remains unchallenged for months, sometimes years. Meanwhile, the founders tinker without inviting the intended recipients of that value into the conversation. This is a fundamental failure to understand Co-Creation. Is it any wonder that many of these products ultimately fail? When customers finally get an opportunity to communicate, it is most often through deafening silence.

I counsel my clients and mentees to instead follow a path of pilots and prototypes very early in the innovation life cycle. Build a version of your innovation that makes its value evident. You don't need a perfect working model; you just need something tangible that conveys how it eases a pain point or delivers a gain, how recipients of this value are explicitly better off because it exists. This takes a certain mentality: if you're not embarrassed to show it, you're too late. When you're 80 percent ready, move. The last 20 percent doesn't matter. Conversations around a prototype are the Co-Create economy version of focus groups. That prototyping is going to go through multiple iterations, each benefiting from the reactions, insights, and suggestions of the last.

Customers are not the only people who need to be invited into the conversation around innovation and value. Your employees are also crucial contributors to your innovation engine.

In January 2015, Adidas's new CEO Mark King—known for having built golf's TaylorMade brand into a powerhouse through lightning-fast product development and lean innovation—essentially asked employees company-wide for their best ideas to move the brand forward. Within months, nearly five hundred viable projects had been proposed and passed on to a special working group with the authority to narrow the projects down to just a handful. The final idea began as three small words, "Netflix for runners," and emerged almost exactly one year after inception as Avenue A, a super-premium athletic apparel subscription service. Every three months a very sexy box arrives at the subscriber's door. It contains collections of select running and training products for women, each curated by a leading-edge trainer or workout artist known for his or her personal style.

Avenue A is a *very* different business model for Adidas, so different that the company created a special—and separate—development team. As King told *Forbes* magazine, "This needed to be done outside the normal machinery."[20]

King, working with leadership innovation expert Gary Hamel, went on to institutionalize Avenue A through an online learning platform on which employees could put their ideas through the paces before presentation to an expert panel. Why? Polly LaBarre, a director of the business think tank Management Lab, told *Forbes*, "Simply put, you can't grow the innovation quotient of your company if you don't invest in employees' creative capacity. If you want to strengthen the creative capital of your company, you must make innovation an everywhere, everyday job."[21]

Too Often, Small Minds Squash Big Ideas

Today's challenging business environment and pace of change leave no room for mere incremental improvement. Companies and organizations of every size are required to constantly innovate or risk becoming irrelevant. Unfortunately, I am seeing a painfully pervasive trend across a multitude of companies: small minds are squashing big ideas.

Consulting for a long-established regional land trust, I was asked to sit in on the last round of interviews to fill a top strategic position. One candidate with a lot of marketing experience, though not in the nonprofit world, proposed a wholesale change in how the organization viewed its members, whose average age was trending upward—the wrong direction for healthy future growth. Specifically, the candidate advocated for two member–recruitment approaches, one more traditional and one specifically designed to involve millennials. She suggested using crowdsourcing for specific projects and many, many more hands-on, family-friendly activities instead of cocktail parties and sedate gatherings. She talked about creating opportunities that focused on the values of this generation, their respect for the environment and need to feel like they were making things better, their healthy lifestyle, and their need to see deep meaning reflected in the organizations they joined and to which they contributed. Small minds on the hiring committee saw her ideas as too radical and disruptive to "the way things had always been done," and ensured that she didn't get the job.

This type of organizational oncology, through which unique ideas are inoculated as if they were deadly cancer cells, happens all the time! First, somebody somewhere, inside or outside the organization, comes up with a truly revolutionary idea—the next iPad, the next Uber. It is an idea that fundamentally challenges the status quo within the organization, and potentially the whole industry. It calls for a radical reinvention of where the company's been, what it's done, how it's done it.

Then legal gets hold of that idea. Or heaven forbid, HR. Or worse yet, IT. What was once a groundbreaking idea becomes "Let's move this pencil from over here to over there." Meanwhile that company's leaders have just taken 100 percent of the wind out of the sails of everyone involved. Is anybody likely to recommend a new idea, or even think about having one, after that? Leaders reinforced that this is *not* a culture that welcomes bold thinking, is unafraid of retribution, or is willing to take prudent risk. They have in essence made the company's mission statement, "We are about incrementalism, not real innovation."

Am I advocating that you run with every harebrained idea that somebody comes up with? No. But there is a reason that companies like Google have their "20 percent time" policies that encourage employees to work on projects they find interesting. You don't have to have a Silicon Valley address to be comfortable with balancing performing and learning. Rather than letting small minds squash big ideas, companies that make innovation a core value are constantly nurturing multiple ideas so the best ones can grow even better.

Of course, every company needs a margin of safety. We all have to execute, drive results, grow revenues, and control expenses. But how do you set aside the corporate equivalent of what my wife calls "mad money"—that portion of resources, of money, time, and effort—to test new ideas and approaches? How do you ensure that you are monitoring and measuring the results of your efforts?

This is where dashboards showing real-time performance come in (which I'll discuss in detail in chapter 6). This is where a group of independent advisors is handy. You don't have to take their advice, but you do need outside perspective on what's working and what's not working to accelerate your learning and growth.

Here's a lesson in encouraging and inspiring employees—and building innovation into the heart of everything you do with some real, but measured, risk involved. After about a thousand employees had passed through Adidas's innovation academy—resulting in a thousand feasible ideas to boost the brand—and after employees company-wide had witnessed the great press surrounding Avenue A, the company announced a *Shark Tank*–like competition to choose another winning project. They brought in a five-star panel of A-list corporate and sports outsiders as judges, people like management gurus Polly LaBarre and Gary Hamel, noted venture capitalist John Hamm, the company's global creative director, Paul Gaudio, and, to add a real world sports touch, UCLA football coach Jim Mora. This was CEO King putting his money where his mouth was, while at the same time ensuring that the right risks were being taken and firing up employees around the world.

If we want to stop small minds from squashing big ideas, we need to learn from the leading edge of innovation. I'm coaching my clients, particularly the large ones in mature industries (where innovation is often a lost art), to go spend a day within a start-up incubator. Attend a hackathon. Send a small group to South by Southwest (SxSW) or one of the other innovation summits. Spend time watching people who live and breathe agility. Watch the nimble do their work. You should do the same. I predict you will find a culture tightly focused on getting tests into the market.

As Guy Kawasaki said, forget about the PowerPoints; focus on prototypes![22] How do we create a model of an idea quickly and get that in front of our target audience? Not friends and family—they love you, but they are not going to write you a check for your innovation (and if they do, it will be for all the wrong reasons). There is only one cure for small minds that squash big ideas: getting that prototype to an audience that will care, that knows the difference, that will recognize the value in what you are trying to create.

Pilots Are for End Recipients, not Your Mother-in-Law

Recall Andy Stanley and the North Point Community Church he founded, discussed in the introduction. He said, "Inviters critique the right way and inviters complain about the right things," because they are imagining the point of view of the unchurched. Innovation pilots must be deployed to the market they are intended to serve—not to the first twenty people in your Rolodex.

The goal is to work with the most targeted audience that will, at this early stage, help you truly appreciate the dynamics, truly understand what end users gravitate toward, truly start to understand some of the black-and-white borders that separate true needs from everything else that is either unnecessary or unnecessary at this point. This back and forth with stakeholders who either have to market the product or actually use it leads to conclusions like: "This product works phenomenally well in the northeast, but southerners just don't get it." "This works well in a manufacturing environment but not in distribution." "This works in professional services but not accounting, for some reason."

You probably haven't heard of Method Agency, whose website doesn't mince words: "We design integrated brand, product, and service experiences."[23] What does that mean? It means the NCAA asked Method to design its on-demand iPhone app for March Madness, a go-to source for tracking your bracket, following the games live and for free, as well as reading and watching background stories on teams and players. The NCAA app is an interface, a series of screens or pages that must have a logical relationship and navigation, sensible and useful links, and that must also give the user that recognizable, branded NCAA tournament experience—all on a tight timeline, since the roster isn't even final until just before the event starts. Time to bring in the CGI and pack this baby with content, right? Nope.

They started with low-fidelity prototyping, at this level some hand-drawn basics—with pen and paper—then uploaded the results with Keynote. This "clickable demo" tool led to remedying some early mistakes—missing states and interface elements, unworkable or misperceived end-user needs. Next came medium-fidelity prototyping, where designers began to define the parts more clearly using wireframes—digital line drawings that sketch the skeletal framework of a website—giving stakeholders something accessible to react to and allowing them to provide further feedback and with a quicker turn-around time: hours, not days.

Finally, the Method team entered the much more time-consuming, detailed, visually driven high-fidelity stage. Showing design directions as well as the interactive user experience, high-fidelity prototypes allow executives to clearly visualize a product or service and ask the basic questions. Does it do what it needs to do? What does the user actually use? How can it evolve? What further needs might it fulfill?

The most important thing is to keep your eye on the ball through all stages, to remain rigorous about not getting too fancy, not building in too many flashy features, not clouding that simple vision of what a prototype *should* be.

Leaders need to understand that prototyping is a crucial part of the adaptive innovation process. You want to get to the pilot-and-prototype stage quickly, but once you are there, you do not want to hurry.

Prototypes and pilots are an iterative approach to learning, and they require time to continue the iteration and modification that ultimately refines the product (that turns an Apple Newton into an iPad). The disruption lightbulb is going to light up during the pilot phase, and you'll see that "Wait a minute!" moment when a valid sample of the target segment actually uses that innovation, whatever it is, and it makes the status quo way of doing something obsolete.

This process whittles the small set of ideas that made it through the "verify, validate, or void" process down to one idea worthy of investing resources in to bring it to market. Expect to be surprised! It's been my experience that, more often than not, the one that survives won't be the one you expected.

Similarly, don't expect that the idea that succeeds will necessarily be the one that best fits your capabilities for production. It may, in fact, require you to build capacity in an entirely new industry or area of expertise. Under Armour was a clothing manufacturer before it purchased technology providers. Adidas's Avenue A project took them way out of their comfort zone as a sports apparel and footwear company and into curated, cobranded merchandising, where those curators do not work directly for Adidas but bring their own leading-edge brands to the table. Expect to be similarly challenged.

CONVERSATIONS ARE THE MEDIUM IN WHICH ADAPTIVE INNOVATION GROWS BEST

Collaborative Co-Creation requires real-time interaction, or as close to it as we can get. Social media conversations are a crucial channel, because they encourage near-real-time two-way communication. Within the organization, all functions should participate—marketing and innovation, obviously, but also strategy, finance, operations, and talent.

These conversations also take place outside the organization, of course. What about involving your suppliers? Or your media contacts? The point is, when you shine the innovation flashlight at different facets of the business, it's amazing what creativity is unleashed.

That said, the functions most closely tied to adaptive innovation are innovation and marketing. Peter Drucker famously said:

> Because the purpose of business is to create a customer, the business enterprise has two—and only two—basic functions: marketing and innovation. Marketing and innovation produce results; all the rest are costs. Marketing is the distinguishing, unique function of the business.[24]

This explains why innovation and marketing are the stewards and champions of adaptive innovation in any organization. Using adaptive innovation, companies create a "virtuous spiral" of new offerings that lead to increased adoption, Co-Creation, and evangelism.

NEEDS-BASED SEGMENTATION

Underlying every concept discussed in this chapter is the premise that, if you bring stakeholders into close collaboration in the innovation process, the outcomes will be what those stakeholders are looking for. This represents a fundamental switch from the push economy's ethos of "sell the stuff we develop" to the Co-Create economy's "develop stuff we can sell with the people we're going to sell it to." Developing stuff we can sell means designing goods to meet the current and anticipated future needs of buyers, which is where needs-based segmentation comes in. Opportunities for Co-Creation in a continual process of adaptive innovation can be discovered through segmenting customers on the particularities of their buying journey. (This journey is the focus of chapter 4.)

Far too many strategists segment their market based on their company's capabilities, falsely assuming that their capabilities are a good fit to market demands. Or they group prospective buyers based on demographic and psychographic characteristics, which just doesn't support a culture of adaptive innovation very well. In the past, segmentation frequently relied on grouping by shared traits, such as lifestyle, geography, or demographics. But many unmet needs cut across all kinds of demographic and even psychographic categories. One forty-year-old white male may make purchases very differently from another. One small or medium-sized company buys technology very differently than another small or medium-sized company, even in the same industry or geography!

The success of adaptive innovation is grounded in **needs-based segmentation**, the process of separating potential customers into smaller, more precisely defined groups based on fundamentally understanding the *needs* of an end user, not some characteristics or traits that describe him or her. Your focus must be on understanding how your customers and prospects live their lives, how they experience the situations that give rise to wants you can supply or desires you can gratify. The simplest and most effective means to do this is simply to invite them into the innovation process, where you Co-Create together.

Nourcabulary

Needs-based segmentation is about understanding your customers' journey and determining where you can outperform your competition in delivering the value they need at any specific stage in that journey. Product and service differentiation is crucial to success; in the Co-Create economy, stakeholders drive that differentiation so it reflects what they need or desire, both today and in the future.

Many organizations classify their customers based on some often arbitrary metric. I fly frequently with Delta Airlines, so I am familiar with their tiers of "Medallion" benefits—Silver, Gold, Platinum, and Diamond status, each step up conveying additional perks. It is all well intended and reflects the prevailing mindset that those who spend more deserve to be treated differently. This may be true, but it also reflects an inward-facing mentality. It is about what you do and how you do it—the Silvers get a seating upgrade twenty-four hours before departure, but the Diamonds get upgrades immediately after ticketing, for example. That approach is simply not attuned to the Co-Create economy. Different customers often have very different needs at different times, and the benefits these statuses confer may be totally insignificant to users, as often as not.

I learned from one of my former CEOs and Peppers and Rogers alum Bruce Kasanoff that in the fast-moving Co-Create economy, it is critical to treat individual customers as individuals, or you risk getting left behind. He and Michael Hinshaw break it down in their excellent book *Smart Customers, Stupid Companies* in terms of making "SMART" moves:

1. **Segment** your customer base by their needs and ask, "How do I cater to those differentiated needs?" This is where needs-based segmentation comes in. It will drive the next four steps.
2. **Modularize** your capabilities. When individuals can choose the offerings most relevant to them, their satisfaction grows. Can you offer ways to integrate modular technologies that are already in the lives of your customers, like "let me pay with PayPal"?
3. **Anticipate** customers' future needs. Use leading drivers like sentiment analysis to help you get and keep your finger on the pulse of what they are thinking, what's of interest and value to them moving forward.
4. **Reward** win-win behavior. Because it is extremely resource intensive to cater to all buyers, find opportunities to get employees as well as current customers who are passionate about the brand to step up, and engage them to get more involved in win-win behaviors. Create opportunities for your enterprise evangelists to make a difference (a topic I'll return to in the next chapter).

5. **Transform** the touchpoints where your customers' experience takes place into data-gathering engines. Intelligent touchpoints that capture data, analyze it, and benchmark it against others will produce actionable insights that allow you to learn from every interaction.[25]

Of course, this is easier said than done. When it comes to even the simplest segmentation by needs, I find that very few companies can give me a current, accurate profile of any individual client. This seems to be at its worst with membership-based associations. Can you tell me which event a member attended? What did she download? Whom is she connected to inside and outside the company on LinkedIn or other social media? How many chapter meetings has she come to? A 360-degree view of members' or customers' behavior gives you a window into their likes, dislikes, preferences, interests—all the factors that would get them and keep them engaged, or that could drive innovation to serve new needs as they emerge.

So what does this look like in action?

For a former client in the wholesale vehicle trade, our team built a knowledge base and a customer-needs assessment system designed to evolve continuously as learning took place. Our vision was to understand the core needs and motivations of individual customers (automobile dealers) much more deeply, to inform strategy development and optimize product development. We set out to explore the customers' relationship with Manheim, the world's largest auto auction company; for example, were the customers part of a franchise or independent? From there, we set out to develop **archetypes**—research-based representations of subsets of the customer base—to inform improvements in their customer experience. This created a foundation for sales, marketing, and communication strategies and fed into price/value research.

Nourcabulary

Archetypes are research-based representations of a target customer within a specific segment. This semifictional individual represents the "who, what, where, when, how, and why" of one type of buyer. The more detailed the persona, the more accurately you can intuit the motivations, values, and preferences of individuals in that segment.

We conducted research into perceptions about the industry and the client's brand; we studied transaction histories of current customers; we did a business-needs survey to identify not just needs but also behaviors and emotions related to those needs. We reviewed the competitive intelligence to discover what our client's customers needed that the client uniquely could provide, what customers couldn't get elsewhere. We assessed satisfaction specifically with the client's products and services— how well were we filling the needs customers sought solutions for? We pursued customers' ideas for innovation. And then the actual segmentation and modeling was performed. All of those inputs, all of those lines of inquiry were then combined into what we called "Insights to Impact." Then the strategy of modularizing capabilities could begin. The outcome affected strategies, activities, products, pricing, sales and marketing, communications, and, most important, customer experiences.

How Archetypes Drive Customer-Experience Strategies

As you develop these archetypes, you begin to understand what they need, but just as important, the development starts to drive your customer-experience strategies. "James represents our high-touch, high-care customer profiles. James needs a dedicated concierge desk he can call 24/7 to talk to Susie, who may not have all the answers, but can give him a pleasant experience while she helps him get what he needs. Buyers like James have demonstrated that they are willing to pay a premium for that convenience." And from that persona-driven insight, a customer-experience strategy is Co-Created.

An Accurate View of Customers from Sequestered Data is Impossible

Needs-based segmentation helps companies identify a group of customers with a unique set of unmet needs, and can even identify to what degree those needs are unmet. I'm amazed at how often needs are ignored. Why does that customer go to somebody else? Because they need something and their primary vendor either doesn't get it, or can't do it, or can't do it well.

And yet, too many companies can't agree on what those customer needs are, much less on which are unmet. Siloed data is often the culprit. Customers' purchase history is in the Oracle system, but the company merged with another that uses SAP software while their Microsoft Dynamic CRM is tied to their supply chain, and no one has made a priority of bringing that data together. Imagine me trying to put a jigsaw puzzle together—with pieces from different puzzles. That's what these companies are trying to do. You've got salespeople who talk to customers, marketing that understands the target market from a research perspective, management that follows trends and has the highest-level view of what's happening. You have business development accustomed to working with different partners to bring the value chain together. And meanwhile, engineering and R&D are trying to figure out the next innovation. Nobody said this would be easy.

Executives have argued with me, asking, "How can we possibly understand customers when their needs are ever changing? Or latent? Or unarticulated?" Despite the challenges of sequestered data and continual changes in every customer segment, we still must strive to apply that SMART approach.

Every Stakeholder Group Is a Candidate for Needs-Based Segmentation

It is easiest to see the logic of needs-based segmentation when discussing the relationships among buyers and sellers, customer and clients, and vendors. Employees likewise have a very specific set of needs. One segment might say, "I have young kids, I can't stay until seven or eight at night to work on a project." Another might say, "I live two hours away from the office. I can't come in for a seven o'clock meeting unless I get up at three a.m." If you look closely, you'll find a lot of segmentation among employees. During the 1996 Atlanta Olympics, area businesses learned the benefits of flex scheduling. When your city is host to an estimated 4 million people for a two-week period, you learn to adapt. Many local companies allowed employees to come in late or leave early to avoid the traffic. They equipped them to work from home. They found that the work still got done.

If you understand the needs of those stakeholder groups—your employees, suppliers, media relationships, and so on—you can identify segments and represent them with archetypes that make it possible to envision what they need, when, and how. Every facet of your portfolio of relationships could benefit from needs-based segmentation.

TOOL 2: NEEDS-BASED SEGMENTATION

Don't forget to download the Co-Create Toolkit PDF from CoCreate-Book.com and apply some of the key ideas you've just read in this chapter.

This tool prompts you to match the opportunities you identified in Tool 1 to your relationships' needs and desires that could be currently unmet.

Chapter Two Takeaways

- Adaptive innovation requires the alignment of a company's various organizational functions so that their decisions contribute to an improved condition for stakeholder groups.
- Listening louder to the environment expands an organization's capacity to find and prioritize information relevant to adaptive innovation.
- Faint market signals are at their most valuable when they are weakest. Therefore, it is important to detect them as early as possible.
- Rapidly validate critical assumptions about market signals to eliminate non-starters for innovation and identify emerging trends with high potential to disrupt your business.
- Moving forward with pilots and prototypes rather than full-blown launches allows you to evolve with more agility and efficiency.
- Innovation pilots and prototypes have to be deployed in the market they are intended to serve.
- Opportunities for adaptive innovation and Co-Creation are discovered through segmenting customers on the particularities of their buying journey.

THREE

CO-CREATE FORWARD: STRATEGIC RELATIONSHIPS

 In this chapter you will learn:

- How and why creation of the brand narrative has moved from the organization's marketing function to its customers, employees, and other stakeholders;
- How every organizational function must evolve to meet the demands of the Co-Create economy;
- How "enterprise evangelism" delivers a sustainable competitive advantage;
- How visualizing information can reduce miscommunication.

The Co-Create economy has radically reshuffled the concepts of "sales" and "marketing communications," making many traditional functions obsolete. However, this transformation is much bigger than a rethink of these roles. What it really requires is making the customer central to every function of the organization.

In the Co-Create economy, the concept of "customer" includes everyone who experiences the value your organization generates. That means employees, suppliers, investors, and media contacts, in addition to traditional consumers. In the Co-Create economy, everyone is a "customer" to be welcomed into the Co-Creation of your value, which brings me to the fundamental focus of this chapter—*when your orga-*

Figure 3.1: Customer Centric

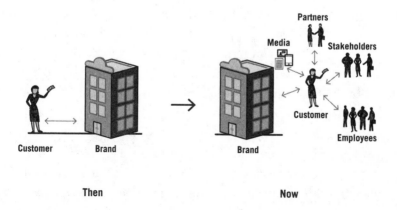

nization treats every stakeholder as a customer, your behavior has to become more relationship centric.

This chapter will explain how every function in your organization should refocus—on relationships. Every stakeholder represents a potential Co-Creator, advocate, and brand evangelist—someone who can help generate Market Gravity and attract the net-new relationships your organization needs to fuel growth. Relationship-building, which has always been the backbone of the sales and business-development functions, is now the name of the whole game. At the end of this chapter, you will perform a strategic relationship audit of your key groups and customer segments to determine where to put the most energy.

> **Nourcabulary**
>
> **Strategic relationships** are connections with individuals who make our efforts more effective, elevate our thinking beyond our current realm, and partner with us in Co-Creation of value. The concept of **strategic relationships** is the subject of my book *Relationship Economics,* which is a prequel of sorts to *Co-Create.* To learn more, visit this book's landing page—CoCreateBook.com—and download my free "Relationship Economics 101" PDF summary.

Digital communication channels (think social media, private online communities, and collaboration tools like Dropbox and Google Docs) have forced relationships to evolve from something face to face (or even voice to voice) to something virtual, available through any screen, at any time. This demands a drastically higher level of responsiveness from the organization if they want to maintain good strategic relationships. If your major client in Dubai tweets about a problem with your organization at 8:00 a.m. UAE time, you'd better have someone available with the responsibility and authority to respond at 12:01 a.m. ET in the United States.

Automating your service delivery can solve the problem—Apple's App Store, Amazon, and the Netflix website are excellent examples—but only if your recommendation engine is reliable and your delivery mechanism is equally intuitive. Across the business landscape, from the corner grocery to Silicon Valley to the biggest companies in the most mature industries, organizations are struggling with this question.

For an example of cultivating and leveraging relationships, consider Instagram, the social networking app designed around sharing photos and videos from mobile devices. Instagram has forged a beautiful relationship with the fashion industry. "Back in 2011, when the late Oscar de la Renta and his peers were Instagramming backstage at New York Fashion Week, the platform's involvement was pure luck," Emma Whitford wrote in *Fast Company*.[1] Since then, Instagram has worked diligently to develop a broad base of highly influential relationships with the help of leaders in the fashion industry and the art community. One example: hiring Kristen Joy Watts, who had been part of the launch of *The New York Times*' photo blog *Lens* (lens.blogs.nytimes.com). The highly visual blog shines its light on tastemakers, including fashion houses, models, professional photographers, and bloggers. With this strategy, Instagram has positioned itself as a powerful curator of popularity in this very visible universe.

The company invites Co-Curators in, starting in a ubiquitous space—everyone wears clothes every day—and many people, particularly women, have strong feelings about what they wear and their identity. Instagram provides the tools—and far better, easier tools to use than, say, Facebook—and the platform. Today, we have "Instagram chefs" and "Instagram models" and even "Instagram designers," all of whom have risen from obscurity to media prominence through the organic and authentic popularity of their Instagram feeds.

YOUR BRAND IDENTITY IS BEYOND YOUR CONTROL

This new emphasis on relationship-building has its roots in an essential reality of the Co-Create economy: your brand identity is now beyond your control. Brand reputation today is determined largely by what other people are saying about you. In a low-trust environment, the whole process of engaging and influencing has to be done in a Co-Created manner.

Your customers, employees, and other stakeholders create your brand's narrative, using the information they gather themselves. That information may come from any and all functions of your organization. It's the relationships you build with these partners and customers that will determine your impact.

Is this really true of every industry, though? Do commodity providers like gas stations and funeral homes, whose customer relationships are largely transactional, need to be concerned about the Co-Create economy? Is McDonald's worrying about building relationships with key stakeholders? In a word, yes.

Figure 3.2: Your Brand Identity Is Beyond Your Control

Then   Now

The funeral industry brings in more than $10 billion every year. And with a moderately priced casket going for more than $3,000 these days and 70 million baby boomers approaching the age of pre-need planning, one would think it's ripe for a spike in growth. Yet profits are on the decline. Why? Those same pesky baby boomers have disruptive ideas about how they would like their mortal remains put to rest. Entrepreneurs are responding with a whole new wave of products, services, and ideas that traditional funeral directors never conceived. Cemeteries are setting aside separate grounds where graves are hand-dug to reduce carbon footprint, with river stones instead of monuments, and where all maintenance and upkeep use organic substances. Green funerals for the ecologically minded mean no embalming or caskets, and often involve local, organic food and drink served graveside around a natural-dyed, hemp-shrouded loved one.[2] Esmeralda Kent, who founded Kinkaraco Green Burial Shrouds in San Francisco, now offers a line of burial wraps that come with pockets for mementos, as well as built-in biodegradable backboards and handles. "This is the last industry to be dragged kicking and screaming into the twenty-first century," she told *Bloomberg Businessweek*. "Myself and others like me are completely reinventing the business."[3]

Customers of all kinds are turning away from intrusive marketing messages that push products and services at them. In fact, for more than a decade, J. Walker Smith and the *Yankelovich MONITOR* (published by Kantar Futures) have shown consistently, year after year, that more than half of American consumers deliberately avoid buying products that overwhelm them with marketing messages. A full 70 percent of those surveyed are interested in software products that enable them to block out digital advertising that is not specifically targeted to them, and 55 percent are willing to pay to use ad-blockers.[4] Consumers and businesses alike are gravitating toward the companies, brands, and offerings that instead *pull* them toward collaborative relationships, Co-Creation of value, and partnerships that help them achieve their individual desired outcomes, goals, and objectives. The Co-Create economy has emerged as a result of this basic shift from push to pull.

Many people dye their hair. Until recently, there were essentially two alternatives: you could go to a professional colorist at a salon every month and pay about $170—sometimes well over that—or you could buy a commercially produced home-dying kit and do it yourself for $20. Enter eSalon, a 2014 start-up that began offering "Made for You" home-dying kits with a twist. First, you fill out an online survey, then make your color choice. Finally, you upload a photo of yourself that shows your current color, cut, and also your skin tone. A professional colorist reviews your survey and choices, together with the photo, and fine-tunes your color in consultation with you before the company ships you a specially formulated dye suiting your looks and needs. For a base price of $19.95 per package with subscription, you receive a beautifully designed kit containing everything you need to do the job and more: matching hair color, developer, color-safe shampoo and conditioner, non-latex gloves, stain guard, even a stain remover. Of course, there are upgrades: jazzy shower caps and professional hair color toolkits, for instance. Subscribe for recurring shipments—which apparently more than two-thirds of customers do—and you save 20 percent automatically. With expansion to Canada and Western Europe in 2015 and plans to open free-standing stores in select locations, eSalon has taken what anyone would regard as a mature industry and pulled that DIY customer into a personalized digital experience.[5] Even Nervous Nellies can chat with a professional who will talk them through the experience and answer any questions. This is one company that really gets Co-Creation, and their stylin' sales—north of $30 million in 2015—show it.[6]

Every potential stakeholder has greater access than ever before to real-time information when it comes to the marketplace. Prospective customers and employees are smarter. Suppliers, if they have been in existence for a while, have probably done business with your competitors, making them smarter, too. Your customers are out there doing their due diligence, and that means you have to start doing your homework, too.

For the past several years, there has been a bit of conventional wisdom circulating that the average B2B buyer is 57 percent of the way through the buying journey before ever engaging with a vendor sales rep. Logic would follow that by the time customers make their first contact with you, they don't need to be sold because they've already gotten themselves more than halfway there![7]

While it's true that the Co-Create economy is making many traditional functions of the sales profession obsolete, it turns out that these numbers aren't exactly what they seem. According to Forrester Research, 74 percent of business buyers do conduct more than half of their own research online before making an offline purchase. However, this magical 57 percent figure, while accurate, represents the average *aggregate trend* of all buyer behavior. The key to not mistaking factoids for actual facts is knowing *your* buyer.[8]

For instance, we now know that when making a major purchase, most older Americans tend to seek advice from friends and family, while millennials report that they are three times more likely to trust a recommendation from a stranger online than one from someone they know.[9] The companies that take the time to customize their message are the ones that are getting ahead.

Bain & Company reports that customer segmentation has the most growth potential among popular development strategies used by global executives. Although it was being utilized by only 30 percent of the companies in their 2013–15 survey, customer segmentation has the highest satisfaction ratings among those who do use it. In essence, companies that have figured out how to make customer data work for them are seeing results all the way to the bank, with 80 percent reporting that they predict growth in their respective industries over the next three years.[10]

Given the increased level of sophistication of these potential strategic relationships, organizations need different kinds of tools to create meaningful conversations. The advent of mobile technology now has your stakeholders buried in their digital devices. Therefore, you need to be there too. Each customer represents a potential Co-Creator, advocate, and brand evangelist—someone who will help generate Market Gravity and attract still more new customers. In this chapter we will examine how this move from push to pull demands that every function in your organization evolves its communications—not just what it says about your organization, but how it says it, and through which channels, to open two-way dialogue with its key stakeholders.

I will also introduce the importance of visual storytelling in the Co-Create economy. The idea of a "canvas" has become popular in business circles, stemming from Alexander Osterwalder and Yves Pigneur's popular 2009 book *Business Model Generation: A Handbook for Visionaries, Game Changers, and Challengers.*[11] A canvas is essentially just a means to visually represent the working parts of a larger concept—on one page—in a way that fosters conversations. We'll explore how to use a canvas to visually delineate an organization's different types of stakeholders, from potential employees to internal operational units, in a way that allows leaders to communicate effectively and thus drive the behaviors that develop strategic relationships with each key segment.

Just to give you the flavor for how conversations about employees as stakeholders might go, consider how important attracting talent has become for many organizations. (An extended example from the hospitality sector is coming up in the next section.) I have long believed that if you take care of your employees, they will take care of the customers. Therefore, attracting employees who will be evangelists for your company could be the most effective sales and marketing move you could make. Managed by Q is one great example. The office cleaning company foregoes heavy investment in sales and marketing and instead focuses on recruiting, training, and retaining the most effective employees. The excellence of the staff dramatically reduces customer churn by recognizing and leveraging upsell opportunities (the company does everything from replenishing supplies to reconfiguring walls and assembling furniture) and through their over-the-top great performance of their cleaning duties. The result? Customer loyalty and rave recommendations that make sales and marketing spend obsolete. Highly skilled, engaged employees are crucial to Managed by Q's business model.[12]

Given that your brand narrative is ultimately outside of your reach, the one aspect of your new business development that you *can* control is your strategic relationships, internal and external. The Strategic Relationship Audit tool in the PDF download from CoCreateBook.com is designed to help you differentiate positive from negative strategic relationships. Once identified, you can create strategies to draw these strategic customers into deeper relationships with your organization. Remember, every employee, partner, and interested observer is a customer, in addition to those who buy.

FOR CO-CREATION, EVERY ORGANIZATIONAL
FUNCTION MUST EVOLVE

As we discussed earlier, your stakeholders assemble their understanding of your brand from the bits of information they take in from a wide variety of sources. So it's critical to prepare every function to "sing from the same hymnal." Finance, operations, innovation, marketing, human capital, compliance—any division, or all, can and will have an impact on the brand narrative.

In this new paradigm, leaders must emphasize Integrated Marketing Communications (IMC), an approach that focuses on managing stakeholders' impressions of a company or brand over time. IMC brings your stakeholders' viewpoint into the communication process. Its goal is to integrate all management initiatives related to brand communications so that members of the target audience (potential employees, customers, the media, etc.) receive a coherent, consistent impression across all message channels. Successful IMC requires coordination across every business function. Internal resources must work harmoniously with external partners, from marketing firms (traditional and digital) to suppliers and partners. But achieving an effective degree of coordination among internal units, channel partners, service providers, and customers is not easy. It requires leadership, planning, and execution.

For some organizational functions, this is new. Executives in finance and compliance roles, for example, will likely never have conceived of themselves as having a role to play in "marketing communications." And yet, in highly regulated industries such as financial services or healthcare, both should be involved in communication with strategic stakeholders. For example, compliance officers might need to review marketing communications for alignment with the Health Insurance Portability and Accountability Act of 1996 (HIPAA) regulations.

Now, let's shift our focus from communications to the heart of Co-Creation—innovating new value that benefits all partners. True Co-Creation requires more than just passing that new innovation strategy through compliance or finance for review before deployment. Co-Creation engenders change, and the cost of that change can be better managed when finance has a stake from the start. Invite them to be part of the conversation that gives birth to those strategies! Every one of an organization's functions must evolve to see its role in the Co-Create Canvas discussion, which starts with the vision and strategy, then works through the priorities, organizational structure, and resources required. (This discussion is the subject of chapter 8.)

The senior finance professionals I've met have a degree of discipline and business acumen that would add enormous value to the collaboration process. The problem is that they aren't invited because of the perception that they are just "bean counters," not astute strategic thinkers. When the VP of finance is sitting in on the mobile-device strategy session and he brings up truly intelligent points about lessons learned from prior investments in mobile, the whole process of Co-Creation is stronger.

Compliance, too, is a division that belongs at the table. Typically, compliance gets called in only when trouble knocks. It would be much better to invite compliance to collaborate early in the process, not to inhibit creativity, but to give it the necessary legal and ethical guardrails. Yes, Co-Creation calls for thinking outside the box, but I'm a realist. At some point, you still have to function within the box. Finance brings stewardship of fiscal resources, and compliance manages risk and keeps innovation within bounds that can be operationalized.

Talent managers may only recognize "communication" in the context of "help wanted" ads. The CEO may simply never have considered that workers at the factory may be communicating the brand narrative through the things they think, say, and do, just as surely as the advertising department. (There is a good reason Ford incentivizes employees' car purchases.) This cultural shift is huge and will likely require extensive training, not to mention consistent leadership over time, supported by metrics that measure and compensation that rewards the right behaviors—behaviors that build consistent, positive brand associations in every conceivable communication channel.

The Evolving Role of the Chief Marketing Officer (CMO)

For one function—marketing—"customers" actually does mean customers: the people who purchase and experience an organization's products and services. One of the biggest challenges for marketers is keeping up with the dynamic, changing buying behaviors of a public driven by information overload. Marketers no longer exert complete control over the organization's public profile. B2B or B2C—it doesn't matter, most of your target audience doesn't believe your marketing and advertising; they believe and trust peers who operate within a network of shared values and likewise receive benefits from your products and services. Customers already hold most of the information required to make a purchase before their first contact with you, and they don't need to be "sold."

Self-described Silicon Valley "business romantic" Tim Leberecht characterizes your brand as "what other people say about you when you're out of the room." He points specifically to companies like outdoor clothing maker Patagonia, who appealed to their customers' desire to align with a brand that shared their values of authenticity, sustainability, and responsibility by urging their customers always to seek out secondhand clothing from online vendors before buying new Patagonia gear.[13] What began as a viral marketing scheme in 2011 had, by 2014, become a fully realized retail partnership with eBay in the form of an online store called Common Threads. There, US and UK customers can opt in, pledging to buy pre-owned Patagonia gear whenever they can, and in return gaining the privilege to sell whatever they no longer want or need in the store's online community. The innovative deal marries the brand's "ironclad" durability with eBay's first multiseller storefront, providing a platform where thousands of loyal customers interact in a virtual marketplace hosted directly on Patagonia.com, where the company can direct customers toward both used and new options of in-stock items. So far, more than seventy thousand people have taken the Common Threads Pledge and promised to reduce their environmental impact, and as a result, more than sixty thousand Patagonia items have found a second home in the United States and abroad since 2011.[14] You have to understand what motivates your customer to buy—especially how they evaluate potential purchases—and then you must help them buy, *even if it isn't from you!* It requires both an offensive strategy that takes your unique value into the market and a defensive strategy to manage wrong or competitive information.

The evolving role of the CMO also means being astute about Co-Creation of content and different channels of distribution for those stories, and the value they create from a peer standpoint. Think of multitiered distribution: a manufacturer sells to a distributor, who sells to a retailer, who sells to an end customer. At each stage, someone is marketing or co-marketing, and sometimes people who appear to be competitors need your cooperation toward a common mission or against a common enemy, such as fights over legislation.

High-end retail grocer Whole Foods has seen its stock suffer as competition in the organic and natural foods sector has grown enormously in recent years. Urban grocery delivery start-up Instacart has also suffered from a few missteps and growing pains, after raising its delivery and subscription rates significantly over time. Both companies needed to figure out how to compete more nimbly and intelligently. What about getting groceries to customers within a very narrow window, sometimes as little as an hour door to door (have you experienced Amazon Prime Now offering household items and essentials you need every day with FREE 2-hour delivery)? In urban centers like Los Angeles, San Francisco, and Austin, Texas, the one need most people have is for more time.[15] Instacart CEO Walter Robb began working for the company in 2014, and under his guidance the company got smarter, learning how to streamline their processes to hit that one-hour window as often and accurately as possible. The online tech business magazine *Re/code* reported that Robb told an investor meeting that "many" of the grocery stores are "seeing [Instacart] sales as a percentage of total store in the mid-to-high single digits."[16] This is why Whole Foods made a significant and strategic investment in Instacart in 2016, also signing a five-year delivery partnership deal. Instacart's success is Whole Foods' success, and vice versa.

Partners are proliferating in all different kinds of channels. Some simply want to be on the delivery side; others want to actually have a marketing agreement where you still deliver but market to very specific segments. Co-opetition and partner proliferation both demand understanding and a proactive response. The ecosystem of relation-ships that CMOs must manage is larger than ever, and still growing.

The marketing function is becoming more data driven by the year, with impact on two fronts: marketing automation and performance metrics. Most CMOs have integrated some kind of marketing automa-tion for lead management and media buying, simply because the tech-nology has come such a long way in creating business rules and what-if scenarios. But this isn't just about more effective push marketing. Tech-nology improvements are about more finely focusing the lens and ask-ing, where are we investing, and is that investment of time, effort, and budget the best possible use of our limited resources?

Finally, everyone needs good analytics, not only for general in-sight but also to help correct course when things go wrong. Today's CMOs must understand what data is needed, how to draw action-able insights from it, and how to work well with their CIO counter-parts to make changes on the fly. Analytical rigor helps avoid well-intentioned but doomed grand schemes before they go to mar-ket and creates pulse points along the way to understand what is or isn't working.

The leader who succeeds in the evolving CMO's role will be a mas-ter of data applications for marketing automation, measuring perfor-mance, and guiding tomorrow's marketing strategy.

Customers want a brand to look and feel the same whether they see it in an ad, kiosk, point of sale, or on a mobile device. There must be continuity in the way that they buy, not in the way that you sell. Unfor-tunately, several recent reports point out that one in five CMOs scores themselves below average in omni-channel attribution—the ability to measure media-buying effectiveness and correlate advertising to sales. When customers control the message (and it's so easy for customers to research and learn about a product or service), a CMO has to ensure that the message is available at the time of their choosing and on the device of their choice. Certainly there is a place for traditional market-ing channels; they just have to be seamlessly combined with digital campaigns, and the channels have to make sense for the company. The challenge for the CMO is to focus on the bread and butter (ads and tra-ditional media buys) while mastering digital acumen.

Figure 3.3: Time of Their Choosing and Device of Their Choice

Device of companies' choice   Time of their choosing and device of their choice

The Evolution of the Sales Function

Every sales executive in this country fundamentally understands that customers have become more sophisticated than ever before. They are more knowledgeable, more proactive, and they do an enormous amount of research before they ever reach out to a brand. Thus the importance of Market Gravity and how critical it is that your organization remains an object of interest. Once potential customers reach out to you, everything relies on how you respond.

Over the past two decades I have watched the sales function pass through several phases of maturity. When I began my first sales job in the mid-1980s, we talked about the basic features and benefits of our products. Then came the trend of "solution selling." Everybody wanted to be a solution seller, because it implied end-to-end coordination, seamless implementation, and of course "one neck to choke" if something went amiss. Besides, if you were selling fertilizer in an era of glamorous technology start-ups, it eased the sting a bit to see yourself as purveying a "crop-enhancement solution." More recently, the mindset has become "we're business advisors"—even the fertilizer seller is prepared to discuss business impacts with the farmer.

Not every sales rep can make the transition from one sales paradigm to the next. More important, there is a fundamental flaw in these models: they are entirely focused on filling a sales funnel with new customers. It would be better to focus on customer retention instead of constantly trying to go after net-new customers. If your company is B2B, you should focus on doing a better job of going deeper, having more of an impact on your current customers' business. If you're B2C, you should find better ways to help your end consumers achieve their desired outcomes, even outcomes they have yet to realize they want.

(After all, no one thought much about carrying bulky Walkmans for cassette tapes and CDs until mp3 players came along.)

The following examples should help you apply the evolution of the sales function to your own business.

THREE EXAMPLES THAT SHOW HOW FUNCTIONS EVOLVE

Let's put the evolution of how functions communicate with their stakeholders under the microscope. The following examples from my consulting practice show how:

- a hospitality industry giant communicates with its next generation of potential employees;
- a professional service firm communicates with potential buyers; and
- and a mature company in the construction industry communicates with a crucial supply partner.

Each example shows how functions innovate and evolve how they communicate.

Hilton Campus Conversations

In this example, we see Co-Creation of strategic relationships from a hiring pipeline standpoint.

Rod Moses is probably the most unlikely HR professional I've ever met. We got to know each other through the men's prayer group at my children's school. He was the head of global talent at Hilton at the time. I love how passionate Rod is about finding, developing, and elevating exceptional talent.

Rod read *Relationship Economics* then came to my home office where we talked about his business challenges. Hilton needs a continuous supply of talent for its corporate headquarters and its various properties. It was very clear to Rod that millennials don't want to walk into Hilton properties and see their parents, if not their grandparents, behind the front desk or carrying bags. To address this need for younger workers, Hilton recruiting had to do a dramatically better job of engaging, influencing, recruiting, and converting college students, primarily but not exclusively at fifteen colleges across the United States that have specialized hospitality programs. In its on-campus recruiting, Hilton had to create a compelling enough experience that students would want to continue their career journey with Hilton.

Rod introduced me to the HR director responsible for Hilton's campus recruiting efforts. We met, and I shared my early observations: Hilton had to come up with a way to build stronger, deeper, and more meaningful relationships with these students.

In a traditional model of campus recruiting, brands show up on campus and offer information sessions. These are one-way communications—in essence, brands tell students, "You sit there, be quiet, let us tell you how great our company is and what you can do for us." When I reviewed the Hilton presentation, it included comments such as, "We were the first brand with color TVs." "We were the first brand to offer room service." It was push communications through and through. Consider: if I'm a college student with a plethora of options from Uber to Yelp, Hulu+ to HBO Now, I probably don't remember the last time I watched TV or ordered room service in a hotel. It was a classic disconnect between the noise Hilton was sending and the signals the students received.

That meeting led to a consulting engagement with Rod and his team, and we embarked on a nine-month journey to transform Hilton campus recruiting. What we did exemplifies how brands can Co-Create forward, through a focus on strategic relationships—in this instance, with people who influence Hilton's search for millennial talent.

1. Start with identifying the needs of key customer segments. We did a needs-based segmentation of Hilton's customer base, where "customer" meant stakeholder in the employment pipeline. It is not unusual to have multiple targets.

One segment we identified was, of course, the students—juniors and seniors targeted for Hilton's internships and management-development programs. My first recommendation with this segment was: If you don't want a rotten apple, go directly to the tree. Let's start engaging them as freshmen. Even if we don't hire them, we build brand equity. They are going to travel, and when they do, hopefully they'll think of Hilton.

Another segment we identified was the university faculty, deans, and career office staff. If we build an emotional connection with that audience for Hilton, they are much more receptive to Hilton on campus, much more likely to recommend Hilton to student job-seekers, and more apt to proactively look for partnership opportunities with Hilton.

The third customer segment we identified was the general managers of Hilton properties. Regardless of location, if I'm a GM running a Hilton property, my success depends heavily upon finding and hiring that next generation of talent to work at my property, learn the business, grow with us, and work up to taking my job at some point. Hilton needs to give its GMs a solid funnel of qualified candidates.

Finally, Hilton Corporate is a customer segment in the talent-recruiting function, because there are specific opportunities at Hilton Corporate to bring interns and management-development opportunities into its McLean, Virginia, headquarters.

2. The closer you get to the customer base, the better. In the Co-Create economy, one customer segment will be the primary target, the center of the bull's-eye. In Hilton's case, that primary target was the students. Without them, there was no talent pipeline.

After conducting the needs-based segmentation, we started addressing the students with a proactive campus ambassador program. An old Chinese proverb says, "The mountains are high and the emperor is far." Hilton as a brand might as well be on Mars if I'm a student on a campus in the middle of nowhere, without some sort of flag-bearer to make its presence known. Hilton recruited fifteen students, one on each campus, to be that local liaison. Campus ambassadors become that link to that end customer. To prepare the students, they were brought to company headquarters in McLean for extensive training and development. We built a private, intelligent online community for them. The point of this step: the closer you get to your stakeholder base, the better.

3. Provide conversation enablers. After segmenting our customers and developing a strategy to engage the primary target, we provided the tangible supports that the strategy required. If campus ambassadors were going to engage students, they needed a way to initiate that conversation. We visualized the Hilton Campus Conversation engagement journey from the point of view of the students.

What do the students need? What are the top ten places around campus that you as a senior wish you had known about as a freshman? We created maps, called the "Campus #Trending10." We identified the best coffee shops to study in, the best places to people-watch, the best places to tailgate. We created fifteen unique physical campus maps featuring unique locations and branded it with Hilton. The campus ambassadors distributed them to freshmen both as PDFs and as hard-copy handouts. The maps gave our liaisons something authentic with which to start the conversation.

Branding isn't enough; you have to support it. The online community for students interested in Hilton was part of that. It created a private place where students could build affinity for the Hilton brand through groups, dialogue, forums, and discussions. Those ambassadors spend thirty minutes a day, every week, as online community managers. Another way that Hilton supports engagement with its target population is with a freshman "externship," where interested students spend a week at a Hilton property, working in different functions by day and staying at the property at night, getting the best of both sides of the experience as a staff member and a guest.

To further engage the millennial students, Hilton created a "Hospitality Olympics" at a national event sponsored in part by the company. Students from the fifteen college hospitality programs joined one of the Hilton teams as part of a mock Olympics, competing in job-related skills from folding bed linens to properly setting up a buffet.

Reinventing the campus recruitment program by creating engaging conversations generated dramatically enhanced results. Hilton saw an increase in student job applicants as well as an enhancement of the brand's visibility on campus. To measure the strategy's performance, we incorporated sentiment analysis (which is discussed in chapter 6). Students rate their experience of Hilton's campus recruiting. We are now getting some very candid data from those students that will help shape how this recruitment strategy evolves. To encourage this ongoing dialogue, we have created a Campus Conversation mobile app through which we can further engage students in real time. It includes news feeds from the hospitality industry, the Hilton brand, and Hilton at their respective universities. We made it relevant for students by

Figure 3.4: Hilton Campus Conversation Visualization

Campus Conversations Journey

Join us at the Campus Conversations Community

Favorite classes. Great friends. Sporting events. Social gatherings. Memorable moments. Résumé writing. Interviewing skills. Building relationships. All of these will contribute to your personal and professional growth. That's why we've created the Hilton Campus Conversations – to support your Journey. In the coming years, we hope you'll join us on- and off-line, on- and off-campus to **Immerse. Explore. Engage.**
Learn more at:

        www.HiltonWorldwide.com/USCampus
        #HiltonCampusConvo

"Engage"   INTERVIEW
Learn résumé and interview tips, techniques, and best practices through the online community and then interview with a Hilton recruiter.

"Explore"   INFORMATION SESSION
Informative half-day session including development workshops and classroom talks aimed at helping you assess your opportunities with Hilton.

"Plan"   CAREER FAIR
Sit, talk have a refreshment with us and review a Career Journey Map. Later that day, we throw a party at a fun local place and you're invited.

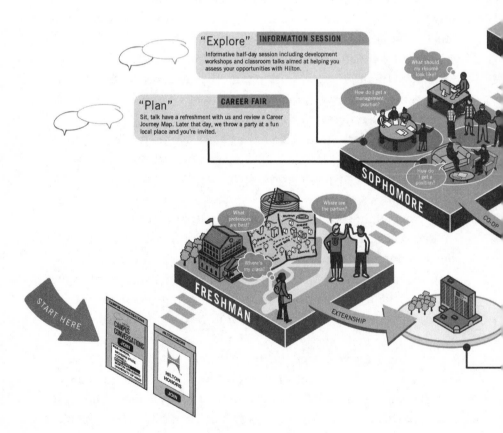

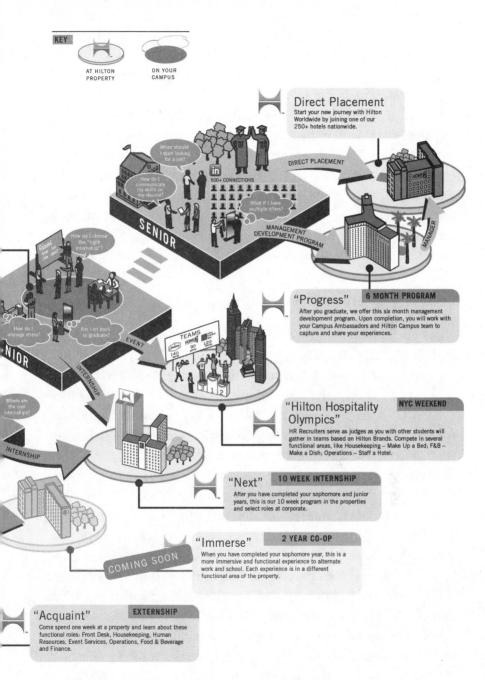

featuring a calendar of upcoming recruiting events, appointment scheduling, and more. Note the series of engaging touches, that funnel of pull drawing them ever deeper into a relationship that might become the foundation of a future job.

If millennial recruiting is your challenge, start with reinventing the way you engage with millenials. Make it about how they can help create value alongside you. As this example highlights, Hilton is now an enabler of hospitality students' journeys, starting on campus and, for some, leading to employment with Hilton. Identifying customer needs, getting closer to those customers, and providing the tactical support to create conversations with them helped Hilton Co-Create forward with those strategic relationships.

KPMG Anti-Bribery and Corruption Practice (KPMG-ABC)

Think about today's corporations. They have an enormous amount of complexity that potentially exposes them to risk. That risk is typically the purview of several stakeholders: the chief finance officer, the chief compliance officer, perhaps a chief risk officer, and the general counsel.

KPMG, in part through its Risk Advisory Group and within its Anti-Bribery and Corruption (ABC) practice, serves those stakeholders charged with managing corporate risk. Its forensic division offers a full suite of services that help organizations prevent, detect, and respond to anti-bribery and corruption concerns.

Here's the fundamental challenge with selling professional services—there's no product with a green button the client can push to see the lights come on. There is no whiz-bang product to demonstrate. Without the presence of a product with differentiating features and benefits, the fundamental differentiator becomes the relationship. If I'm the potential client, and you come in to pitch me—especially if you have KPMG on your business card—I am already assuming you are competent and capable of advising me on risk management. The fundamental difference between winning or losing my business, gaining my trust, is your ability to engage me and influence my thinking with an accompanying call to action. The only way to do this, as proven by the best performers within the KPMG-ABC practice, is Co-Creation of a solu-

tion that, in a very highly relevant manner, fits the immediate prioritized needs of one of those client stakeholders.

In my experience, stakeholders tend to be more focused on their
own agendas than on their interdependence. Compliance cares about
creating compliance-driven policies and procedures. General counsel
sees everything through the lens of legal exposure. For the sales function
at a firm like KPMG-ABC to go in and talk to compliance about something the CFO cares about is the equivalent of Hilton pitching its color
TV value proposition to university students. It's noise and completely
misses the point. For professional service firms, relationships are the
fundamental differentiator, so business development means, first and
foremost, focusing on the needs of the specific stakeholder.

As part of our ABC visualization engagement, we developed a series of templates, or canvases, as conversation starters to align the initial due-diligence process, the stated needs of that client, with the
capabilities of KPMG-ABC. "The purpose of the canvas is to stimulate
ideas, and create a better discussion with our client," Phil Ostwalt,
KPMG's Investigations Service Network Leader pointed out. "We
must avoid developing a canvas which could be interpreted as 'we
already know where your risks exist and how to address them.' That
answer can only be developed through an iterative process of discussion, research, and analysis with the client. The canvas is designed to
facilitate the process."[17]

Note that this is Co-Creation in its most fundamental state, with the
pull being an iterative process that begins with me bringing some unexpected value to the table. Even if we're wrong, we've come in with a
conversation starter.

"Visualizing risks," Ostwalt told me, "brings an entirely unique perspective to an area that has previously relied upon mounds of regulations and page after page of policies. The canvas allows clients to evaluate
its compliance program in an entirely new light, anticipate emerging
risks, and perhaps even uncover existing risk areas previously under
the radar."

So through that canvas, that visual storytelling, the Nour Group is
helping KPMG-ABC go to a prospective client with less of a pitch and
more of a relationship-centric conversation mindset.

Figure 3.5:

The Risks of a Global Organization

Organizations recognize that safeguarding their reputation for integrity is critical to success. Yet every day, that reputation is put on the line through a myriad of individual actions and decisions made by employees and third-party intermediaries operating across the globe.

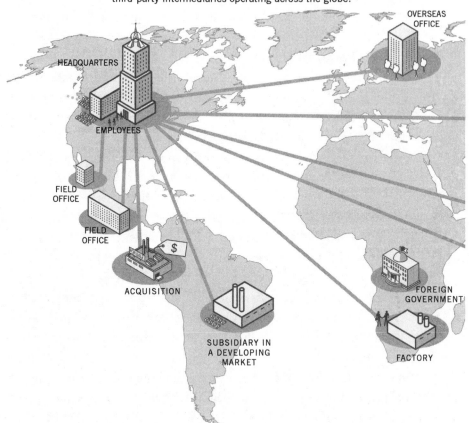

"Professional services organizations," Ostwalt observed, "have a tendency to lean on subject-matter experts to go in and tell their story, and talk through how they solved the problem before, and how they can help. The canvas is intended to depict issues on a page and will allow our subject-matter expertise to guide the client through a collaborative process to highlight the areas of greatest concern, and where the greatest opportunities for improvement exist."

What Ostwalt is describing is a dramatically different interaction; one characterized by intellectual rigor, candor, and an invitation to the Co-Creation of value.

So how does this work, what does it look like, exactly?

"Investing in compliance programs is akin to buying insurance," Ostwalt explained. "You may not know that you need it until it is too late. The canvas approach presents our client with a total view of the compliance risks which need to be addressed by a compliance program. Specifically, as it relates to anti-bribery and corruption, these risks will commonly occur internationally; therefore the start of our canvas is a global map on which we can layer in the company's unique risks which need to addressed."

Early feedback on this approach with KPMG-ABC is that clients appreciate that level of due diligence, as well as the more collaborative approach. No one, unless they are in professional baseball, wants to be "pitched" to. Before the new business team at KPMG leaves that visit, they have Co-Created—even if only conceptually—what the unique value could be to the client. It is very much the start of a "working together" relationship instead of a "working for" vendor transaction.

The lesson from KPMG-ABC for other professional-service firms is that the Co-Create approach to communication with potential buyers will be characterized by strategic relationships. These connections are the only effective means to differentiate a service firm from its competitors. The relationships must be relevant to the immediate prioritized needs of stakeholders, highly personalized and customized to each. Visualizations that present a supposition and ignite conversation—whether or not that supposition coming in was in fact correct—will tangibly illustrate the value the professional service firm will bring to the table if engaged.

ThyssenKrupp Elevator Americas

ThyssenKrupp Elevator Americas (TKE) is the largest producer of, you guessed it, elevators and escalators in the Americas, with more than 13,500 employees and more than 200 branch and service locations maintaining more than 1.1 *million* elevators on the continent. TKE sells elevators and escalators to new construction sites, and services as well as retrofits systems in existing buildings of all sizes.[18] If you are familiar with the construction industry, it's easy to see how this requires Co-Creation with a project's general contractor and architect—the individuals who spec out the TKE elevators for a project and install them.

The CEO of TKE US field operations engaged our team to address a specific challenge: a 1950s business model trying to cater to a twenty-first-century customer base. TKE benchmarks itself against Siemens and other global organizations, and it became aware that it was struggling against its competitive peers in several areas.

A critical area for improvement is communication among supply chain partners in order to improve the customer experience over projects that evolve from installation to ongoing upgrades and maintenance. As VP of US Field Operations David Holcomb told me, "The business was divided. There were 117 branches doing things 117 different ways."[19]

Here's why: The factory that manufactures the equipment is a separate business entity from the field organization that sells and services it. When the field organization takes an order from an end customer, the field has to then place an order with the factory, which triggers orders to supply partners. Between the time when the order is booked from the customer to the moment the customer is contacted to schedule installation, the order disappears. For weeks—or months—on end, no one can answer customer questions about what is going on, changes to schedule, delivery delays, etc. I started calling this the "TKE Bermuda Triangle."

In order to better serve end customers, TKE's Co-Creation of value has to happen between the field and the factory. When there is a "Bermuda Triangle" between when the field places the order, when the factory receives it, when the factory completes it, and when any of this is communicated back to the customer, there is an urgent opportunity to Co-Create a better process.

Under Holcomb's supervision with tremendous support from John Murnane, CEO of US Field, and Rich Hyssey, president and CEO of Americas, TKE is responding by building an innovative program called "Elevate" to address these issues while encouraging Co-Creation inside the organization. Whether the order is for a new installation or a mod-

Figure 3.6:

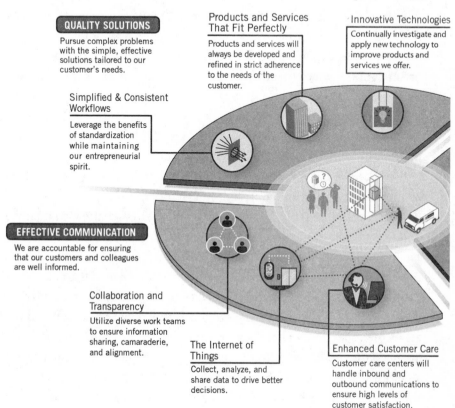

Our Path Forward:

We will exceed our performance objectives by focusing resources on providing the best customer experience in the industry.

This will be achieved by communicating effectively, solving problems with tailored solutions and providing our employees with an environment to grow and thrive.

QUALITY SOLUTIONS

Pursue complex problems with the simple, effective solutions tailored to our customer's needs.

Simplified & Consistent Workflows

Leverage the benefits of standardization while maintaining our entrepreneurial spirit.

Products and Services That Fit Perfectly

Products and services will always be developed and refined in strict adherence to the needs of the customer.

Innovative Technologies

Continually investigate and apply new technology to improve products and services we offer.

EFFECTIVE COMMUNICATION

We are accountable for ensuring that our customers and colleagues are well informed.

Collaboration and Transparency

Utilize diverse work teams to ensure information sharing, camaraderie, and alignment.

The Internet of Things

Collect, analyze, and share data to drive better decisions.

Enhanced Customer Care

Customer care centers will handle inbound and outbound communications to ensure high levels of customer satisfaction.

ernization of existing equipment, whether it involves field engineering or service and maintenance, it will live or die by that operational Co-Creation of value. It demands customer-centric standard operating procedures. It demands conversations between the field and the factory. It demands strategic relationships where individuals *want* to come through for each other. With "Elevate," the vision is to develop a global blueprint for Co-Creation of value through operational communication, efficiency, and effectiveness. "Elevate hones in on improving processes, tools and technology, better communication, and building the team," Holcomb elaborated. "These four rings are what we base our initiatives on and how we determine if something is worth investing time and resources in."[20]

In this paradigm, the factory has to work much more collaboratively with the field. It starts with the respective leaders of the two entities establishing a culture of Co-Creation, demonstrated to others through their behavior. TKE has created a new position, Head of Quality, and brought in an expert from GE whose job is to cascade through the organization the idea that quality, like safety and compliance, is everybody's job.

"The Elevate program," Holcomb explained, "takes those 117 different ways and turns them into one way: a standard operating procedure [SOP]. These SOPs are established by working with a group of pilot branches for several months vetting out best practices from around the country and forming one consistent way of doing business."[21]

TKE has the potential to be a great twenty-first-century company and is pursuing some very effective innovations. In addition to producing a monthly newsletter outlining "Elevate" progress and convening a quarterly town hall meeting, they have implemented two changes, relatively simple fixes, that directly bridge the divide between TKE and the customer. "We've provided all of our technicians with iPhones and all of our operations and sales personnel with tablets so that doing business day to day is not only more efficient for them but more efficient for our customer," Holcomb explained. On the customer side of things, the focus is on what TKE can do to improve the service they provide and overall customer experience. "We've launched a customer portal and e-mail notifications and have developed a customer experience team to focus efforts solely on each customer's unique needs."[22]

Another project on the Internet of Things front called "MAX" involves equipping elevators with controller boards that communicate with the cloud, performing predictive analysis and avoiding failure proactively. If a TKE customer operates a Manhattan high-rise with six elevator banks and we can prevent one of them from going out of service, that's a dramatically improved customer experience. Additional, measurable benefits include MAX's predictive abilities that avoid traffic jams and long wait times, as well as the added positive measure of better managing trip efficiency to lower energy costs, as elevators can consume 10 percent of a building's energy usage.[23]

Holcomb adds, "The efficiency we've gained comes as a result of SOPs and new enabling technologies. We've seen time savings from things like our automated booking process, DocuSign implementation, and system optimizations."[24]

By making visible the Co-Creation of value that must happen inside an organization to deliver an outstanding customer experience, TKE's experience highlights the gains to be realized by encouraging cross-functional communication.

Three Examples: Lessons Learned

As these examples have shown, Co-Creation is an opportunity to move your organization forward. The insights we should take away from them is that Co-Creation of value depends on three key attributes:

1. Focusing on needs-based segmentation of stakeholders;
2. Prioritizing effective communications through alignment of signals being sent with signals being received;
3. Replacing "pitching" with genuine dialogue, facilitated with conversation starters.

As we saw with Hilton, KPMG-ABC, and TKE, the bottom line is that functions must evolve. If every division in your organization recognized who the true recipients of their value were and treated them like customers, personnel would likely behave very differently.

USE INFORMATION VISUALIZATION TO STRENGTHEN STRATEGIC RELATIONSHIPS

My focus throughout this chapter has been on the need for organizations to evolve along two dimensions:

1. From the last-century "push" communication model to the "pull" modality of the Co-Create economy;

Figure 3.7: Information Visualization

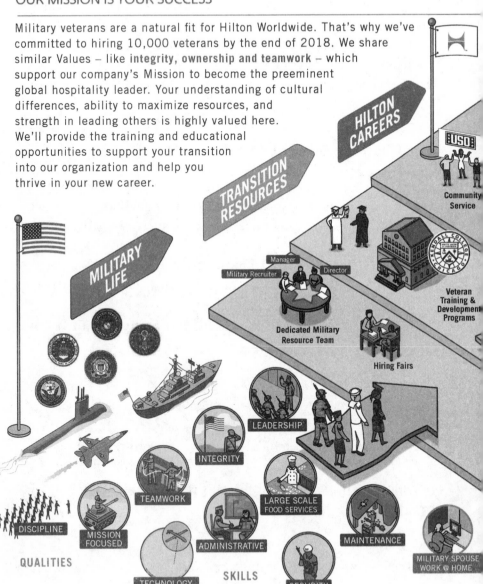

OPERATION: OPPORTUNITY
OUR MISSION IS YOUR SUCCESS

Military veterans are a natural fit for Hilton Worldwide. That's why we've committed to hiring 10,000 veterans by the end of 2018. We share similar Values — like **integrity, ownership and teamwork** — which support our company's Mission to become the preeminent global hospitality leader. Your understanding of cultural differences, ability to maximize resources, and strength in leading others is highly valued here. We'll provide the training and educational opportunities to support your transition into our organization and help you thrive in your new career.

Information visualization lightens the load of communicating complexity, internally and externally, across languages and cultures. Graphics can be designed in small formats for social sharing.

SALES

ACCOUNTING, FINANCE/TAX

REVENUE MANAGEMENT

HOUSEKEEPING

COMMUNICATIONS & PUBLIC RELATIONS

GROWTH OPPORTUNITY
General Manager
Hotel Manager
Director
Assistant Director
Manager
Assistant Manager
Supervisor
Team Member
Intern/Trainee

MARKETING

SPA, GOLF, HEALTH CLUB & RECREATION

ADMINISTRATIVE

CULINARY

BANQUETS, CATERING & SERVICES

INFORMATION TECHNOLOGY

eran Team Member Resource Group

GUEST SERVICES/ OPERATIONS

SECURITY

HIRED

Military Referral Program

PROCUREMENT & PURCHASING

FOOD & BEVERAGE

WORK @ HOME

UNIVERSITY OF PHOENIX

University of Phoenix

ENGINEERING, MAINTENANCE & FACILITIES

Special Recognition

litary er Site

CALL CENTER

Free Hotel Stays

2. From the view that only "sales and marketing" own customer communications to the view that every stakeholder is a customer, and every function is responsible for two-way dialogue with those customers.

What should be clear from the examples in this chapter is that corporate structure is getting more complex than ever before, and stakeholders are more inclined to do their own due diligence than ever before. This places heightened demand on every function's ability to communicate at a time when conversation skills—both in the everyday and in deeper, business senses—are diminishing. It is generally accepted that, with the expansion of technology, we're losing our ability to have genuine candid dialogue. As Sherry Turkle points out in her 2015 book *Reclaiming Conversation: The Power of Talk in a Digital Age,* conversation is becoming a lost art—and yet, it is critical in the Co-Create economy.[25]

One solution can be found in **information visualization**. We are a visual society. With visual storytelling, communicators can much more effectively align expectations. As functions interact across silos in our complex corporate structures, we make it easier to avoid miscommunication, misunderstanding—and the classic lost in translation between what was said and what was meant; we reduce instances of message distortion; and we bring to light where legitimately different views are held. This is the crucial element from which great conversation springs. When you show me an information visualization, it makes it easy for me to point out, "Here's where you've got it wrong," or, "That's what we need to focus on."

Nourcabulary

Information visualization is the visual representation of abstract data. These highly detailed illustrations are extremely effective at conveying complex concepts and thus helping individuals and groups quickly grasp what they need to know, internalize, and act on. In a world of information overload, people and companies who communicate with the greatest clarity have a tremendous competitive advantage.

A canvas is a form of information visualization in which there is more white space than information, because the whole point is to invite people to contribute. A canvas gathers people around a simple representation of an idea that is relatively easy to understand and discuss from any functional point of view.

A canvas is a tool that replaces intrusive "push" messaging with a seat at the table. It invites more "buy-in" than "buy." It allows strategic relationships to come together and Co-Create forward. If I visually represent what I perceive is happening, even if I'm completely wrong, it gets stakeholders to contribute. "No, we don't have that issue in Africa; we have it in Asia." "No, that third party isn't the real headache, it's the internal processes."

How to reclaim our ability to have meaningful conversations? Encourage everyone to bring their greatest candor, without fear of failure or punishment, to the table. Encourage them to raise provocative ideas based on solid due diligence to spark Co-Creation of value. Recognize that every function owns communication with its stakeholders. All this will happen much more easily when we use information visualization, especially canvases, to have those conversations.

TOOL 3: STRATEGIC RELATIONSHIP AUDIT

A friendly reminder to download the Co-Create Toolkit PDF from Co-CreateBook.com and apply some of the key ideas you've just read in this chapter.

Specificity drives credibility; this tool prompts you to select a population of key stakeholders to study—customers, employees, or investors, for example—and then to identify by name the individuals you sell to (either consumers, if B2C, or the purchaser, if B2B). A strategic relationship audit should differentiate positive from negative strategic relationships, allowing you to stop wasting time on the wrong (limited or unrewarding) relationships and manage a process to increase the value of the right (open-ended, promising) ones over time.

Chapter Three Takeaways

- Digital communication channels and automated service delivery make virtual relationships available on any screen, at any time. Stakeholders demand equivalent responsiveness in actual strategic relationships.
- Marketers no longer control brand identity. Customers, employees, and other stakeholders pull information from any (and quite possibly, all) functions of the organization to create an understanding of a brand narrative for themselves.
- Every organizational function must evolve to support Co-Creation of value and integration of marketing communications so that those messages stakeholders pull toward themselves are coherent across all channels.
- Enterprise evangelism promises to deliver a sustainable competitive advantage for the organization, one that can energize these passionate advocates through its attributes of "purpose, people, and experiences."
- Information visualization is remarkably powerful in reducing miscommunication, which will be crucial as organizations evolve to meet the demands of the Co-Create economy.

FOUR

CO-CREATE THROUGH: THE STAGES OF THE CUSTOMER EXPERIENCE JOURNEY

 In this chapter you will learn:

- The radical shift in objectives that the Co-Create economy demands;
- The six stages of the Customer Experience Journey;
- The requirements of recipients of your value as they move through those stages.

Needs-based segmentation allows organizations to modularize their offerings and sales/marketing approach. Customer retention—not acquisition—is the most sustainable source of business growth. Most businesses are still coming to terms with this counterintuitive truth, which lies at the heart of Co-Creation.

In the old economy, marketers were trained to follow a traditional "sales funnel" model, which narrowed a wide pool of net-new prospects to the point of *customer acquisition*. That model changed back in 2009, however, when *McKinsey Quarterly* used data from the purchasing decisions of twenty thousand consumers spanning five industries and three continents to show that customer loyalty looks a lot less like a funnel and more like a loop.[1]

The Nour Group's Customer Experience Journey model, building on that McKinsey looping structure, invites Co-Creation of value that deepens ongoing, interdependent relationships—the basis on which all Market Gravity is attained. In this model, *customer retention* supersedes customer acquisition as the primary objective of an organization. Let's examine how Co-Create companies make customer retention a strategy for growth.

DRAW OTHERS INTO DEEPER RELATIONSHIPS WITH YOU

Organizations hoping to succeed in achieving Market Gravity should replace the traditional sales funnel with a Customer Experience Journey that pulls customers through stages of increasingly deep and meaningful relationships with the organization.

Before we go deeper into this journey concept, let's remember that a customer isn't necessarily a purchaser. As explained in the last chapter, when you think of "customers," think about everyone who experiences your organization's value: employees, supply partners, investors, the media, and, yes, the literal customers who purchase and consume your offerings.

The idea of every stakeholder as customer in the Co-Create economy is key. If you have difficulty retaining employees or vendors or subcontractors or investors, you will expend a tremendous amount of resources just on repopulating those roles. It is unlikely your company has an internal process as developed as your sales funnel, ready to supply that drip (or flood) of new stakeholders that these other roles require. When your focus is on retention, your strategy becomes one of providing people with the support they need at each stage of their journey, so that they stay with you—not just through loyalty, but through an increasing sense that your best interests and theirs are bound up together. This is much easier when you invite your stakeholders into the process, and Co-Create your future together.

There are two distinctions that must be made clear before we delve into the Customer Experience Journey:

- In the Co-Create economy, it's not about you: it's about them.
- Therefore, you must be able to capture reverse perspectives.

In the Co-Create Economy, It's Not About You: It's About Them

For decades in the business world we've talked about "products and services" and "features and functions" (especially in marketing and sales). Notice how that conversation is all about *you*. This is a fundamental flaw in the push economy. Ideally, in a truly collaborative relationship, people enter and stay in a relationship with your organization because of the unique value you create together. If you have picked up anything from this book so far, I hope it is that Co-Creation is less about *you* and more about how your strategic relationships are better off because of you. Start by making this fundamental mindset shift.

If you believe that *it's not about you: it's about them*, then it should be apparent that your unique value can come into play at several different stages of a customer's journey.

First, that journey has nothing to do with your organization or its offerings. A person doesn't have to be looking for coffee to buy a mug. She may be thinking about drinking a cup tomorrow morning, but she might just as easily be shopping for a gift, or picking up a souvenir. Think how radically different those customer journeys are. Likewise, an organization doesn't have to be distributing a communications request for proposal (RFP) to learn about a new ad agency. An individual doesn't have to be looking for a job to join your firm. Customers very likely already have products and services that address what you bring to the table. They choose to engage with you because you somehow have a more compelling proposition or relationship.

Capture Reverse Perspectives

The journey is less about you and more about them, so you'd better learn to reverse your perspective. In fact, every individual whose contributions impact the customer—from the mail room to mahogany row—needs to be able to embrace and hold on to the reverse perspective.

In 2015, Mark Hoplamazian, CEO of Hyatt Hotels, spoke at the Skift Global Forum about bringing a new perspective to the hospitality industry. He described an insight triggered by a stay in a friend's century-old house in Connecticut. As the two of them ascended the old wooden staircase and walked down a long hallway past the master bedroom, he couldn't help noticing how loud the creaking of the old plank floor was. "By the time I get to this guestroom, I am seriously anxiety ridden because all I can think about is how much noise I'm going to be making while I'm in this person's house!" he told the audience.[2] I expect you've felt something like this when you've been a guest, scrupulously tucking your socks inside your shoes at night and attempting to stack your belongings in no more than six square inches of the hall closet. Holding your breath as you tiptoe down the hall to the bathroom at night.

Hoplamazian recounts a similar scenario: "At dinner I ask, 'So, what time do you usually get up? Do you go out for a run in the morning? Is someone coming down to make coffee?'" He described his efforts to best minimize his impact on his friends' household routine. "Here in this instance I'm the guest, they're the host, and I'm the one sweating what impact I'll have on them," he exclaimed.

For Hoplamazian, the experience triggered a profound shift in his perspective. For more than a century, the hotel industry has referred to its customers as "guests." It measures "guest satisfaction" and "guest metrics." It refers to its own role as purveyor of that guest experience with the term "host." But when your perspective on hospitality is reversed, Hoplamazian continues, "you realize that those of you staying in our hotels are not guests at all. The hotels are the guests in *your* lives. Lives that don't start or stop when you come through the front doors of our hotels."[3]

The hospitality business builds its infrastructure and services with the intention of being a part of their customers' journeys (literally). But those guests are people with a complex mix of routines, responsibilities, and emotions before, during, and after their stay. "The best thing we could do to care for you would be to tread lightly. To not interfere with your routine. To allow you to maintain your pace and not interrupt the cadence of your life. Because we're the guests in your lives," Hoplamazian concluded.[4]

And that, in essence, is reverse perspective: seeing the world through others' eyes, walking in their shoes, experiencing the customer journey as they do, so you can anticipate a need and fill it before it becomes a pain or foresee a desire and fulfill it before a competitor has a chance.

Remember, it's less about you and more about them—as seen from their perspective. These two fundamentals pave the way for a deep understanding of (1) what the Customer Experience Journey is, exactly, and (2) how to leverage it to build loyal-for-life enterprise evangelists.

THE CUSTOMER EXPERIENCE JOURNEY

"Anyone can play the notes; music is what goes on in between the notes," violinist Isaac Stern used to tell his students.[5] The Customer Experience Journey has its identifiable stages—the "notes"—but more important, it has its moments between the notes: transitions from one stage to the next. How these are handled makes all the difference between the customer who not only repurchases but also evangelizes and the customer who is an easy mark for a competitor with a similar or a substitute offering.

Seen in that light, it makes sense to first define the stages of the Customer Experience Journey, then to repeat the trip around that course and examine the experience of progressing from one point to the next with the benefit of an extended example.

Defining the Six Stages of the Customer Experience Journey

The purchase decision process has been described by generations of marketing pundits and professors, and each generation inducted into the profession has dutifully learned about needs recognition, information search, evaluation of a consideration set, the purchase decision, and post-purchase behavior. It has been understood that the process generally carries an individual in forward progress, but with pauses and backtracks caused by situational influences.[6] The push economy bias is evident in this model's underlying assumption that we—the sellers—are in charge of moving our prospective buyers through these mental tasks. Again, too much about us, not enough about them!

In the Co-Create economy, we take the reverse perspective. We prepare to meet prospective buyers where they are at each stage in a

Figure 4.1: Customer Experience Journey

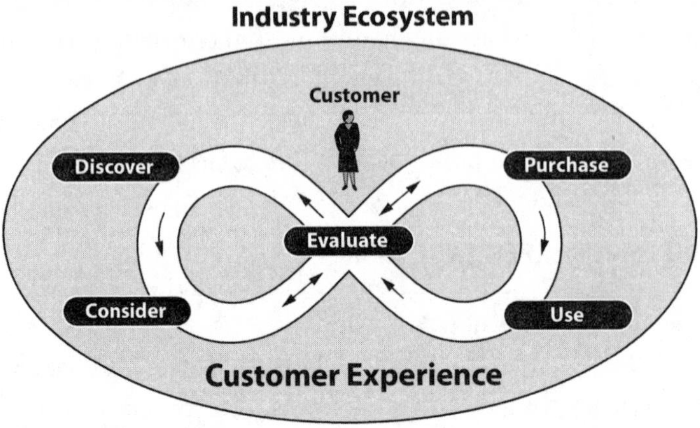

Industry Ecosystem

The Customer Experience Journey prioritizes Co-Creation of value so that relationships deepen over time, leading to customer retention and even evangelism.

journey designed to lead not down a one-way path (like that push economy sales funnel), but rather around the figure-eight course of figure 4.1 that conceptualizes the purchase as the start of a transformative relationship, not the conclusion of a transaction. Because the Customer Experience Journey is based on Co-Creation of value, relationships first deepen into habit, then evolve into loyalty, and next (in a perfect world) transform into evangelism. This is how customer retention, not acquisition, becomes a reliable, sustainable source of net-new business.

The six stages of the Customer Experience Journey are:

1. **Evaluation**: We engage in an ongoing process of evaluating the experiences of our lives. The journey begins when, motivated by a perceived want or desire, a potential customer starts to seek relevant options that might satisfy it.
2. **Discovery:** Increasingly aware of that perceived pain, gain, or series of tasks to be performed, the individual begins a discovery process. What options exist that might fill the need?
3. **Consideration:** Using criteria to evaluate what will meet or exceed the requirements of the solution, the individual deems some of those options better than others, and they become part of the consideration

set. The complexity of this stage varies depending on the degree of involvement the buyer feels in the process. Some buying decisions require deep involvement because of their impact on the purchaser's future experiences, or what the purchase will say about the purchaser. Others are relatively insignificant. This is the difference between choosing a college and choosing a café.

4. **Evaluation:** The customer journey leads back to evaluation, this central position where the loops of the figure eight meet, but now with a set of acceptable alternatives to consider and criteria to evaluate them against.

5. **Purchase:** An individual makes a decision to act. This can mean a literal sale, but it can also mean much more: "purchase" is the act of opting in, in any context.

6. **Use:** The individual is now in a "draft" relationship with the brand and the product or service, experiencing either satisfaction or dissatisfaction. Whether or not expectations are met determines if this cycle will be repeated.

As customers experience the utility of the purchased product or service and the nature of the relationship with the company or organization post-sale, a new phase of evaluation takes place. If the purchase—and the company that stands behind it—has performed well so far, this evaluation leads to expansion of the relationship. Like the infinity symbol, the figure eight of the journey that customers keep tracing is a loop of discovery, consideration, and evaluation, followed by a loop of purchase, use, and evaluation leading to the identification of related needs and desires to be fulfilled. The on-ramp into that relationship could be at any stage in the journey. Each successive trip around the figure eight deepens customer loyalty.

Now that we've defined the stages of the Customer Experience Journey, let's turn to the "music between the notes." We'll go around that figure eight again, this time examining what elements influence our prospective customers (and remember how broadly I use that term) and what we as business strategists can do to move those prospects into deeper relationships with our offering, our team, our brand as the journey takes place.

THE ECOSYSTEM SURROUNDING THE CUSTOMER EXPERIENCE JOURNEY

Think about the last time you traveled outside the country. (And if you haven't yet, make it a personal goal this year to get one immigration stamp in your new passport.) What comes to mind first? The places you stayed each night, or some fantastic experience during the day? One of the great values of travel is the opportunity to become immersed in an entirely new ecosystem. Likewise, there is an ecosystem around the Customer Experience Journey.

In any industry, there is an environment in which that journey takes place, an ecosystem where that experience is created. In this ecosystem, individuals exist in a constant state of assessing the experiences of life. During spare moments, we evaluate. At work: "I'm fed up with our copier because it doesn't duplex." At home: "This kitchen counter could really stand to be replaced." On your daily commute: "I wonder when gas prices will spike again. Maybe I should switch to an electric car." We are constantly evaluating different facets of our everyday lives.

A psychological driver of that evaluation is our need for personal and professional growth. It may be an unnamed yearning, an "Is that all there is?" feeling. Or it may be something more concrete: a personal commitment to learn and grow; a goal to develop, to the envy of others, fluency in a foreign language; a transfer or promotion to a new business unit; or it may be your jealousy at observing the sheer outdoor skills prowess of another dad. You begin to ask, am I creating a better life for my kids? Am I improving the way I work with others? Even if we don't state it, intuitively, this kind of evaluation is going on in our subconscious.

That's where we as consumers—the recipients of others' value—live. That is the center of the figure eight. Now, what happens when we decide to act, having realized through evaluation that some aspect of our life is falling short or could be improved?

From Evaluation to Discovery

When that constant state of evaluation leads to awareness of a want, a need, or a desire, feelings of motivation to act on that desire will frequently arise. This propels individuals from evaluation into discovery. Let's consider the hypothetical journey of the IT manager of a regional retail chain. Kristen K. has a dilemma. She's conscious that her company's point-of-sale (POS) machines are last generation, and she has a budget to replace them over the next year. She begins to research online, talking to colleagues inside the company and others at the annual industry conference. She also finds herself taking notes about her experience as a customer, as well as spending time on the sales floor at several of her own stores to find out how employees use the present system and what they would like to see in an upgrade. So far, so good.

As discovery begins, it is important for your organization to be top of mind. If you are not on your customers' radar, then you are not going to be on the short list when they form their consideration set.

So how do you get on the radar of someone who may not even be in the market for the value you offer? The only strategy you can actually control at this point is to "listen louder" (discussed in chapter 2) to identify when an individual initially enters the discovery phase. What can you do to create inbound inquiries? What can your organization do to invest in ways to be more visible, more "findable" by individuals (in B2B or B2C settings)? You have to be visible, ready to be a useful Co-Creator of the value your customers seek everywhere they go across all media, at the time and on the device of their choosing. This is the ideal opportunity for you to create compelling content, highly personalized and relevant to your target audience. Help them learn and discover new approaches, challenge their assumptions, but above all, lend a hand in their discovery process. In our experience, creating a unique perspective to test, touch, feel, or otherwise gain an initial impact is most beneficial.

From Discovery to Consideration

Discovery is a **due diligence** process. Buyers winnow the possibilities down to a set of acceptable alternatives, which means not only identifying alternatives, but also defining what "acceptable" means. Whether in a B2B or B2C environment, the buyer tries to align needs with wants.

What's a "must-have" and what's a "nice-to-have"? "Must-have" is reliability in a car. "Nice-to-have" would be leather seats. The more your content addresses both their known and unknown "must-haves," the more your brand is seen as a leading choice in their due-diligence process. Keep in mind that third-party validation, such as social media feedback or testimonials from others at the same stage of their journey, is the gold standard of credibility and authenticity here.

Nourcabulary

Due diligence in its strictest sense means the steps taken by a person in order to satisfy a legal requirement, especially in buying or selling something. But I prefer a broader definition: the comprehensive appraisal undertaken by a prospective buyer, especially to establish potential assets and liabilities related to that purchase.

Different people perform the transition from discovery to consideration in different ways. Some seek out peer reviews. Others really want the experience. They'll go straight to a test drive instead of browsing testimonials.

Once your offering has been "discovered," the conversation begins. In that conversation, you uncover a potential buyer's process. Against what criteria will they measure alternatives? Since there is no "one size fits all" answer, you will need to identify buyer profiles, then develop the ability to be responsive to each unique segment. In chapter 2 I talked about needs-based segmentation. It is relevant here, in context of the needs of each stage of the journey, but even deeper segmentation is possible—for example segmenting a group of individuals, all at the same stage of the journey, into several unique buyer profiles.

During this movement from discovery to consideration, the most compelling way to offer Co-Creation is to put the buyer in touch with others who have made the same trip. People don't want to be sold. If I'm considering buying an electric car, I want to go for a ride with a friend in his Tesla and have him talk about what an amazing machine it is. The Tesla sales rep isn't in that car with us. Tesla's brochure isn't in the car.

So, triggered by her searches, various companies have begun

contacting our IT manager, Kristen K. Most send reams of technical information and want to make an appointment. One invites her team to a group presentation in the conference room, a three-hour slog during which she feels very much "talked at" and which features too much technical detail without any real focus on her company's aspirations. (She knew it was a mistake as soon as she saw the forty-seven-page capabilities handout.)

The interaction with another purveyor, POS Pro, however, goes a little differently. The rep asks what she has found on her own so far, and gets a handle on her general ideas about what she wants as opposed to what she really needs. He then offers to put her together with a customer currently using POS Pro's system in a similar business setting, suggesting an on-site shadow to see how the system performs both on the floor and as a source of customer information for accurate inventory, sales tracking, and real-time trend analysis.

To Co-Create value, become a purveyor of relationships. Introduce multitudes of customers to one another. Introduce repeat customers to prospective customers and then get out of the middle. When you create a customer advisory board or an annual customer summit, you create these opportunities to nurture relationships. Here is some #CrazyTalk: Why not invite great prospects to your national sales meeting? Why not put a broad range of customers on a panel at that sales meeting to share what they've experienced with your team?

From Consideration to Evaluation

Because everyone approaches the journey from everyday evaluation to discovery to consideration very differently, it is critical to "hardwire" customization strategies into your organizational approach. Remember, we are not talking about merely keeping a new-customer funnel filled. We are talking about every "silo," or self-contained operating unit, within an enterprise. I often advise client companies to look at each of those functions from a reverse perspective.

How can companies stand out during the transition from consideration to mutual evaluation of the potential relationship? For years technology companies have managed the consideration phase by providing what they call a "proof of concept." At no cost to the prospective buyer, the company comes in and installs the software to simulate how a full-blown deployment would perform. At this stage, your competitive differentiation and value proposition must be crystal clear. Therefore, you must find ways to invite customers to a "tryout," allowing them to Co-Create that value.

One recent study from the Corporate Executive Board really crystallizes the power of that differentiation for me. In a survey of over three thousand B2B buyers across thirty-six brands and seven categories, researchers found that just 14 percent of B2B buyers perceive any real difference in supplier offerings. That means that a full 86 percent of your customers aren't making their decisions based solely on a perceived value to their business—there's something else there, a special feeling of affinity. CEB calls this special feeling "personal value," and according to their survey, 71 percent of B2B customers who see personal value in a transaction will purchase a product. In fact, personal value is more than two times more influential in B2B transactions than business value, and 68 percent of B2B buyers who see personal value are willing to pay a higher price.[7]

Here's an example from a customer's perspective. Last year, my wife and I were trying to select a new school for our children. The schools in our consideration set partnered with us in various ways to help us decide. Each offered a "shadow day" where our son and daughter spent an entire day in the classroom they would be joining. Although my wife and I would make the final decision, the children's experience was an important factor in our family's discussion. "How were the other kids? How were the teachers? What was your experience like?"

One school we considered "got" that we were on a Customer Experience Journey. They didn't leave us in the dark after those "shadow days." Rather, they invited us back to a Friday night football game. Think about it: you're in a high-energy environment; you run into some people who are evangelists for this school; and suddenly one school rises above the others in your evaluation. They also invited us to a school play and to a lunch with the headmaster. Our entire decision process was in many ways Co-Created, an acknowledgment that both sides were auditioning and choosing to deepen the relationship.

Kristen K., meanwhile, has made some discoveries. Her shadow started on the sales floor, six hours of sales, returns, special ordering, generating sales and stock reports, punctuated by a lunch during which she and her shadow manager, mid-career herself, talked frankly about the merits and negatives of POS Pro's system, which would likely not, in its current configuration, work for Kristen's company. But, the other manager pointed out, POS Pro was able to customize many features, something she'd learned while working closely with them during their recent installation of the new system. The installation phase, she reminded Kristen, is where the rubber meets the road. Get it right, and you're a rock star. Get it wrong, and you're fired. Kristen goes home sore of foot but much the wiser.

Only when a company understands what its customers experience as they move from consideration to evaluation will it be able to help them choose among several options.

From Evaluation to Purchase

As potential customers come closer to deciding to purchase, the question is, which option? Yours or your competitor's? Finally, they make that commitment, but how did they get there? According to philosopher and neuroscientist Antonio Damasio, at the end of the day, no matter how much of the initial fact-finding mission might be driven by logical evaluation and consideration of the product choices, we all end up making our final decisions—which ultimately means our purchases—with our guts. In his book *Descartes' Error: Emotion, Reason, and the Human Brain*, Damasio argues that it is fundamentally our feelings and not our thoughts that make us who we are as humans. Emotion, it turns out, is a critical component in nearly every decision we make, and Damasio goes so far as to demonstrate that people who have suffered damage to the cerebral cortex, the emotional center of the brain, find it nearly impossible to make even simple decisions. Even while being able to recognize perfect logic, these patients simply don't know how they feel about the matters at issue, so they can't make up their minds.[8]

Observable features and benefits drive our consideration set, but emotions drive which option we put into the shopping cart. Purchase can mean joining your company, or wanting to partner with you, or desiring to invest in some small way in your vision, your effort. Purchase is the first definitive proof that your prospect believes you, and believes *in* you, as you begin to validate the key assumptions in the outcomes their selection produces.

For Kristen K., the journey to this point has been one of information gathering and field testing, so to speak. What she didn't expect to learn in the process came from her shadow manager, who impressed upon her how important the implementation of the new system was. Almost, in fact, as important as any particular attribute. Kristen has since contacted two other, larger chains that use POS Pro's system, and she learned that POS Pro has a very good reputation, with an experienced team dedicated to on-site installation and training. They also propose to do a single-store trial for a small, fixed fee before her chain has to fully commit. This commitment not only to providing "proof of concept" in a customized tryout phase but also to providing personal value to Kristen K. by investing in her success as the lead on implementation here is key. Being a decision-maker in any enterprise is an inherently vulnerable position, but POS Pro's low risk trial helped Kristen K. avoid the inaction faced by 48 percent of B2B buyers annually who want to suggest a new workplace solution but don't speak up for fear that a failed launch will put their jobs at risk.[9]

From Purchase to Use

Whether in a B2B or B2C environment, making a purchase, on some level, feels like Christmas. The buyer can't wait for that product to show up. Once people make a decision, they want to get busy doing— addressing the need, want, desire; performing the job that led to the first half of this figure-eight journey. Much like how my kids tear into packages at birthdays, businesses are eager to get started, eager to install that improved technology, eager to bring that individual through on-boarding and into full productivity, eager to put supply partners and internal teams together to begin experiencing that new value.

Psychologically, something interesting happens in the space between purchase and use. One example: of people who book travel through TripAdvisor, 20 percent return to the site after booking all the details of their trip, some returning multiple times. Perhaps they come back to enjoy pictures of the place they'll be visiting; perhaps they simply want to daydream about their upcoming vacation; part of the value proposition TripAdvisor provides is this virtual escape. "I think of TripAdvisor as being in the happiness business," Barbara Messing, CMO at TripAdvisor told the authors of *Happy Money: The Science of Smarter Spending*. "I believe that people derive as much pleasure from that [planning] phase as from the trip itself. It's the dreaming phase, the fantasizing phase, when they think about how great the tapas and the sangria are going to taste."[10]

And according to narrative psychologists, in terms of maximizing loyalty, capitalizing on this impulse to connect early in the process is key for building loyalty and brand connection. "Narrative processing creates or enhances self-brand connections because people generally interpret the meaning of their experiences by fitting them into a story," writes Jennifer Edson Escalas. Narrative processing generally maps new experiences and these "imagined narratives" onto existing memories of past experiences. And because these new stories tend to "focus on goals, actions, and outcomes" and further because "stories in memory are likely to be self-related," Escalas notes, "self-brand connection may be formed based on these perceived psychological benefits."[11]

Consumers want to move as quickly as possible from the purchase phase to the use phase. In that use phase they start to experience the alignment between expectation and experience, real satisfaction that justifies all the energy they put into making the choice. Ideally, use leads to feelings of *that was useful, that was pleasant, that solved my perceived need, that was exactly what I was looking for.*

Companies can make the transition from purchase to use a positive experience for buyers by meeting their need for help and support. Buyers need validation that the solution is what they perceived it to be. They form a great deal of their opinion about the value of that investment as they begin to use the purchase, and with that narrative scaffolding firmly in place, they begin to write the story of their customer journey, with themselves in the starring role.

You want to increase mindshare? You want to increase wallet-share? Improve the use phase! This is where customer service becomes crucial. You must find dramatic ways to exceed customer expectations. "Wow, I called that company and I got a live technical support person on the first ring." "Wow, the instructions for assembling that furniture were perfectly clear, and just as promised, I didn't need any special tools or skills." "Wow, those guys were there for after-the-sale service as much as they were before, during the configuration and proposal and recommendation phase." The wow factor in the use phase is critical to customers' willingness to continue, and can accelerate their delight with your brand.

During the single-store demonstration install, Kristen K. learned an awful lot about successful implementation. POS Pro used the opportunity to build buy-in and deepen personal investment with employee "learning lunches," one-on-one interviews, short online questionnaires asking what was going well and what needed work, and even a Facebook page and regular Twitter and Snapchat updates. These varied touches at points throughout the process addressed issues particular to the chain's products while honing overall training for the full rollout. Mid-level managers rotating in teams through the demo store had the chance to use—and get excited about using—the new program and machines, sidestepping the resistance to change that can occur when basic systems are altered dramatically.

Consider the transition from purchase to use in other functional areas of the business. Hiring a new employee? Use the onboarding phase to provide the alignment between expectation and experience that will help individuals become productive members of their teams more quickly. Reengineering a supply chain? Ease the transition for the new supply partners by anticipating and supporting their needs. They will be new to your culture and communication styles, so pair them with experienced vendors.

From Use to Evaluation—and Deepening the Relationship

The journey has now come full circle through the figure eight back to evaluation. Knowing what they now know, would those consumers repeat the journey? Would they make the same decisions? If the relationship has become mutually beneficial, the answer is often a resounding yes.

Now, the opportunity to deepen the relationship begins. A perfect example is maintaining a view of the customer's activity. In this age of transparency, I'm finding more and more customers expect that you can answer questions like, "What was it that we bought last October? That worked out well." "What is New York buying that LA needs to know about?" "What pricing am I getting in Minneapolis that I'm not getting in Miami? We've got to get on the same page, because I'm looking to issue a blanket PO for what we need for the next six months for the entire US." Some companies are creating customer portals to allow access to all that information. As consumers, we've grown accustomed to this from our experiences with companies like Amazon, and we now bring that expectation with us everywhere. When a single provider like Amazon becomes the sole channel through which many goods and services flow, that interface is a huge creator of loyalty—with an emotional component as well. For many of us, the sight of that brown box with the big black arrow triggers an "Oh, yes! It's here!" moment. A little bit of Christmas every day.

The last part of Kristen K.'s journey is that she realized that her purchase was not in fact the last step. POS Pro contacts her regularly to check in with her and check up on the system. They have asked her, as a trained expert with experience of the product, to join a customer feedback group and online troubleshooting forum, to sit on industry event panels, and to help train their trainers for ever-more-painless installations and implementations. She's proud of the fact that they've asked her to be a potential customer's shadow manager. This evolution embodies Co-Creation, with each partner giving to—and taking from—the value they've created together. From another perspective, ask yourself what the product is in this example—you'll realize it is as much or more about the relationships and not a single physical POS system in a single retail chain.

The real opportunity in the Customer Experience Journey is being able to discover how you can Co-Create throughout the stages. When you get every iteration of that Customer Experience Journey right, you create an army of evangelists. They are not casually talking about you—they are speaking passionately and with conviction. They want to influence and persuade others to join the same journey and grow together in the process.

This is the fundamental reason that, in the Co-Create economy, the focus must shift from customer acquisition to customer retention. When loyal customers become evangelists, finding the next customer and the next no longer absorbs the lion's share of an organization's resources. Evangelists do that work for you.

BEYOND ACQUISITION TO RETENTION

Retention done properly deepens loyalty by providing new value customers may not have even discovered they want or would like. Consider the example of HBO GO and HBO NOW.

HBO has been around since 1972, producing scores of hit shows like *Sex and the City*, *The Sopranos*, and *Game of Thrones*, as well as spawning the American basic cable and satellite television channel Comedy Central, whose *The Daily Show* with Jon Stewart is largely credited with reinventing the late-night comedy show. The company sits on a library of thousands of original movies and documentaries as well as sporting events. While the company has a vast library of content to offer, CEO Richard Plepler reasoned that the pipe through which the content could be delivered was limiting consumption. "I had a hunch that there were a lot of voters out there," the visionary Plepler told *Fast Company* in 2015, "who were undecided because they didn't fully understand the range or the value of the brand."[12] Hence the birth of HBO GO, whereby subscribers can access all that content on DVRs, tablets, phones—any digital device. That was in 2014, not coincidentally HBO's best year ever in terms of new subscribers. (Today, HBO is in roughly one-third of American homes.) Interestingly, sometimes when you create so much value, others can't help but want part of the pie. In this case, telecom provider AT&T U-Verse began bundling HBO GO with Amazon Prime for $39 per month.

The next year, Plepler blew up the subscription model with HBO NOW, a platform through which the viewer—any viewer—can order shows à la carte with no monthly fee. And talk about inmates running the asylum, he also began licensing some original content, such as "The Sopranos" and "The Wire" to Amazon as well.[13] HBO's strategy appears designed to achieve transformational company growth with a value proposition that is "too good to pass up" for new subscribers who help the company achieve the customer acquisition goal. Once in the door, those customers very quickly realize that the value is "too good to let go," helping with the retention of that growing customer base.

Must a company choose between prioritizing acquisition or prioritizing retention? Not necessarily, as the HBO example shows. An organization that makes a successful transition to the Co-Create economy can either continue to pursue a growth strategy through new customer acquisition—essentially adapting the push model to include more of the Co-Creation of value consumers now expect—or pursue a less-is-more business model that replaces quantity with quality of relationships as the goal (which I'll describe later in this chapter). The former is necessary if growth goals are so ambitious that deepening relationships with current customers simply cannot produce the desired transformation. But I frequently find myself recommending the latter. A closer look at these two strategies follows.

For Transformative Growth, Relentlessly Focus on Changing Market Conditions

To retain customers requires adaptive innovation. You must stay attuned to changing market conditions. This means calling on everything I discussed in chapter 2 about listening louder, monitoring faint market signals, validating critical assumptions, and proceeding with small-scale pilots and prototypes before full-blown execution.

You can't argue with success—and if you are seeing increased customer retention through Co-Creation of value throughout the Customer Experience Journey, you are succeeding. But success can also be quicksand in the making. Changing market conditions constantly erode even the most solid ground.

I recently met with several executives from a billion-dollar business unit of a Fortune 50 company whose execution formula is absolutely rock solid. They know what works and how to do it. They have a team of thirty-year-plus veterans working the system. The business unit becomes the kind of well-oiled machine where all they have to do is turn the crank. Even so, they called me based on a referral from another business unit executive our team had worked with for some time. Curious, I asked, "How can I help?" They realized that their market was declining. That their "machine" will soon be less proactive. They've built an execution engine in a tight box, but now they must find ways to extend, expand, or even blow up that box and reinvent their business model if necessary.

I have several observations about what has contributed to their success and the challenges forcing them to change.

1. Approach to sales. This business unit has a tremendously sales-driven culture. Here's a quote from our first meeting: "The sale starts when the prospect says no!" Their sales team gets hundreds if not thousands of "Nos" a day, but the BU still generates over a billion dollars a year in revenue at very healthy margins, which gives you some ideas as

Figure 4.2: Execution Engine in a Tight Box

"We've built an execution engine in a tight box."

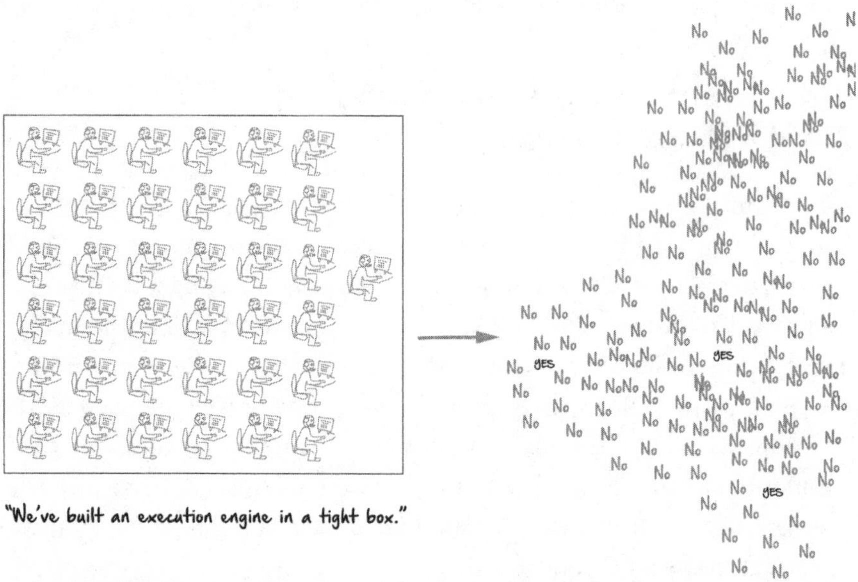

Typical high-pressure sales engine box in a push-model faced with exponentially negative market feedback

to the scale of their operation. The challenge: The company's customer base is becoming more sophisticated. They have more options than ever before. Recent research tells us that consumers are doing 57 percent of their due diligence before they ever contact a company. When customers don't look to you for information, you have to change your selling model—how you engage them.

2. Approach to product innovation. This BU's product portfolio is its core competency. It is unique, and it continues to bring in revenue. In short, it works. The challenge: the market now demands much more agile, customized product development. The company had become accustomed to building a new product over two or three years before bringing it to market; its competitors can do the same thing in five to six weeks! They need to shift from a long-runway, asset-heavy production cycle to become dramatically nimbler.

3. Approach to customer acquisition and retention. Part of this BU's past success stems from repeat purchases that present opportunities to cross-sell and upsell. They have a captive audience, about which they have reams of sales data. The challenge: the source of their prospective customers is changing. If consumers stop making the initial purchase, that highly profitable cross-sell and upsell revenue stream dries up as well.

This BU, while a solid success seen from today's vantage point, would appear to be resting firmly on quicksand when examined through the lens of coming disruption. And yet, their goal isn't just maintaining that $1 billion performance: they want to get to $3 billion. To do that, they must not only reinvent their approach to sales, product innovation, and customer acquisition; they must also fundamentally change their business model. The conversation has always been about them: their strength, their focus, what they've done well. But solid performance in the future will be won on customer experience and engagement.

4. This company must change its conversation to focus on the Customer Experience Journey. This business unit has never captured what their customers go through as they become aware of a need the company can satisfy; as they discover solutions for consideration; as they evaluate, purchase, and use that solution; and finally, as they evaluate its utility and, if pleased, expand the relationship

Figure 4.3: Evolution of the Organization's Business Model

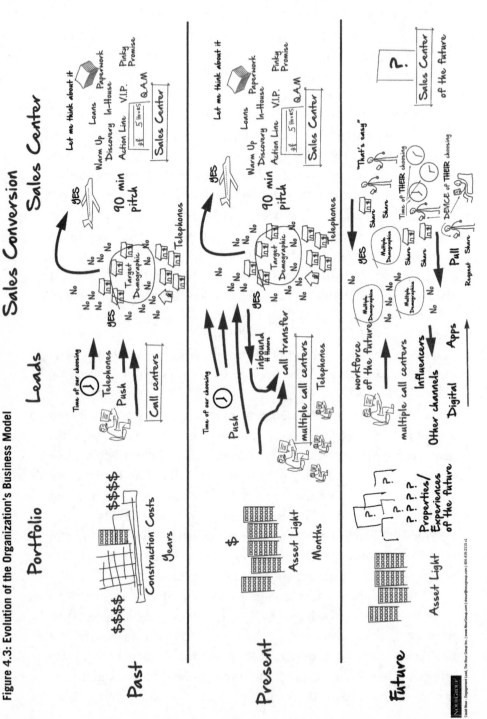

Fundamental need to evolve business units with a strategy visualization depicting the organization's past, present, and future

Figure 4.4: Refocused Organizational Priorities

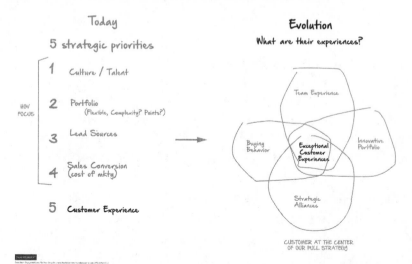

With the evolution of the organization's business model, its strategic priorities will need to shift to align with delivering exceptional customer experiences.

with uptake of more of the company's value. This journey has never been documented. This company doesn't even have a CRM system! They have an incredible system for tracking sales leads through the funnel, up until they become customers, but do nothing about engagement afterward.

The real opportunity here is to put the customer experience at the center of the approach, from sales, to product innovation, to customer retention. The company must completely change their mindset from selling ("push") to buying behavior ("pull"). They must optimize the organization to segment and support customers at each stage of that journey. Their old sales model will need to be completely reimagined, with interdisciplinary centers of excellence coming together around each step on that Customer Experience Journey.

A successful business can turn out to rest on quicksand. But by building relationships with customers throughout their experience journey, you can cross that quicksand to reach new, more market-ready solid ground.

Now, let us turn to the other strategy—where the goal is deeper relationships with a smaller customer base.

The "Jerry Maguire" Business Model

Certain movies become iconic for capturing a certain time, place, or ethos. A few invite the public into the C-suites and boiler rooms of business, like *Glengarry Glen Ross* and *Wall Street*. One in particular offers an enduring snapshot of values-first entrepreneurship: *Jerry Maguire*.

Can we work with fewer clients and create greater impact in their lives, without going broke? The Jerry Maguire business model says it is not just possible, but advantageous, to thrive at a small scale.

In the 1996 movie, a young sports agent starts living by the motto of his mentor. (No, not the "Show me the money" quote—that was the motto of his first client, Ron Tidwell.) I'm referring to Jerry quoting his mentor's famous manifesto, *"The key to this business is personal relationships."*[14]

I am becoming weary of companies treating me as if I don't merit a relationship. My business is not an interchangeable unit in their plans for scalability. I have no interest in being serviced by robots with canned pitches for standardized packages. Their "work with as many people as you can and offer everybody the exact same thing" approach may be a functional formula for short-term efficiency, but it is also a recipe for churn. It leaves no room for personal relationships.

In the shadow of the towering "standardize and scale" business

Figure 4.5: The Jerry Maguire Business Model

Shallow and wide   Deeper and narrow

model, a niche opportunity appears for the firm that operates on the Jerry Maguire business model and allows it to flourish. This model requires just two components:

1. put clients first, and
2. recognize that a certain level, although not absolute peak performance, really is enough.

It's that simple. And it's worth a closer look.

Put clients first. The Jerry Maguire business model says you see yourself as directly responsible for your clients' enduring and evolutionary success. From this moment onward it is all about relationships. If you believe that notion, then by definition you have to create genuinely customized solutions.

It is tempting, especially in the start-up phase, to put your own interests first. Everything is about you and what you need—that next sale to meet your growing payroll or that high-profile client who will give you bragging rights. It is terribly hard to be candid about both your prospective client's best interest and your own, and then put the client's best interest above yours. But that's what Jerry Maguire would do.

Recognize enough. A while ago I spent a few days with a mentor, an extraordinarily gifted consultant who coached me in public speaking. (Yes. Even though I have been presenting before large, sophisticated corporate audiences for years, I still recognize that the truly effective speaker is the one who strives for continuing improvement—in diction, in delivery, in body language, in using the stage.) During one of our morning walks, he said something that really resonated with me about how often he had to travel: "I knew when I reached my limit, I would know it." We all know there are only twenty business days in an average month. A professional speaker could book an engagement for every one of them. But my mentor said, "I wanted to speak a maximum of eight times a month." He didn't want to travel more than that so he could spend quality time with his family. He calculated that financially, at that scale his earnings would be enough.

If you recognize your "enough" and respect it, your focus shifts from going after the never-ending more business. Instead, you truly focus on making your existing clients dramatically more successful. You put your strategic relationships first.

Know your right-fit client. In the Jerry Maguire business model, it is essential to know your ideal relationship profile. A clear target, with a clear sense of how you create value for them, leads to a sustainable business model at any scale.

Where most of us run into trouble is that we lack confidence, that if we put clients first, enough will be enough. The Jerry Maguire business model teaches that if you have five clients, and you are directly responsible for their success, and the arrangement compensates you abundantly, then your business is a success. At some point, too many of us run into the poverty mentality. We live in fear, "If I don't get that sixth client I'm going to lose it all!" We get stuck in permanent sales mode, chasing too many clients.

Never forget the satisfaction of a business based on a manageable number of deep, long-term relationships. Never forget the rewards of being able to balance work with friends, family, faith, and fun. And don't forget to see a good movie about business once in a while, like *Jerry Maguire.*

Whether a company decides to focus on transformative growth through new customer acquisition (without losing focus on retaining those customers once acquired) or opts for a "Jerry Maguire" mode of focus on deeper relationships with a smaller customer base, the journey is essentially about drawing others into a deeper rela-

Figure 4.6: Deeper Relationships

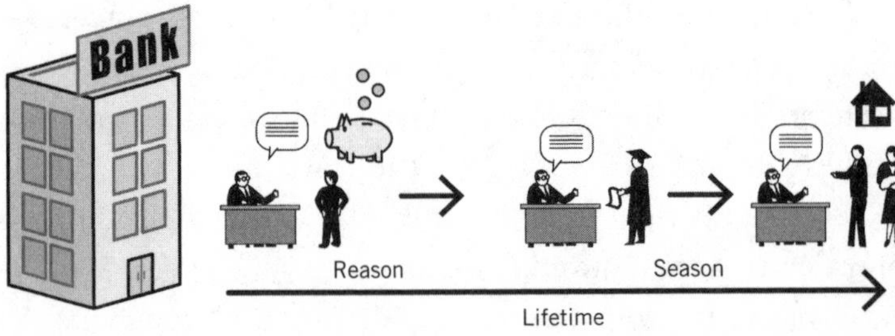

tionship with you. I learned years ago that there are three types of business relationships: a *reason,* where you think transactionally about why two entities work together; a *season,* where you put several reasons together over some period; and a *lifetime,* where you continue to find mutual value, heightened respect, and deepened trust in the relationship. Which ones are you intentionally, if not strategically, nurturing?

SEGMENT AND SUPPORT AT EACH STAGE OF THE JOURNEY

In chapter 2 you learned about needs-based segmentation, which supports the premise that if you bring stakeholders into Co-Creation to innovate new value, the outcomes will reflect what those stakeholders want. In terms of a company's offerings, different customers will need very different features and benefits. Needs-based segmentation allows a company to modularize its offerings so individuals can choose the product or service most relevant to them. In the process of segmenting needs, certain archetypes or personas emerge that put a face on those unique groups within the company's customer base.

So let's apply chapter 2's insights about needs-based segmentation to supporting your buyers and prospects throughout their Customer Experience Journey.

On that journey, individuals in different segments take different paths at different speeds. One segment may be organizations that use RFPs as part of their purchasing process. Any corporation doing business with the federal government knows this—and that significant dollars are involved. Depending on how you define "spending," government contracts comprise from 20 to 35 percent of the US gross domestic product (GDP). A company that is bound by an RFP stays in the evaluation stage much longer than a company that can make quick decisions and move on to the purchase stage.

A company planning a technology-based purchase will need to see a proof of concept. The NCAA needs to know that their March Madness iPhone app is fully functional and won't crash the moment

Figure 4.7: Needs-Based Segmentation

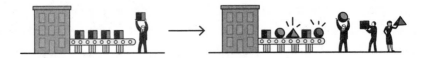

a million fans download and start using it. The organization's discovery phase is going to be longer than the other stages because they are trying to build an example of what this deployment will look like.

Those are organization-driven needs; individual psychological needs also factor in. The "fear/uncertainty/doubt" buyer (or "FUD") by temperament needs to read blogs and visit customer review sites, which influence him before he makes a purchase. By contrast, an impulse buyer sees it, likes it, and checks the price in one or two places before making a purchase. It's still the same journey, but the length of time spent in each stage, the acceleration through each stage, the actual steps in each stage are dramatically different for different needs-based segments.

Needs-Based Segmentation Example: Intalere

The Nour Group performed a needs-based segmentation consulting engagement for Amerinet (now known as Intalere), a group-purchasing organization (GPO) serving the healthcare industry. A broad base of healthcare providers become members in order to save money on supply purchases and to access data analytics, executive development, and specialized consulting. The company serves close to ninety thousand member companies.

If you think about it, a clinic has very different needs than a long-term care facility, which has a very different set of needs than an ambulatory surgical center.

We segmented the company's members by attributes, including the benefit they sought from Intalere, their purchasing sophistication, characteristics of their decision-making process, and the percent of Intalere's revenue they comprised. We then recommended modularizing

Intalere's product and service offerings to meet the needs of those different segments. As well, we recommended a strategic mix of marketing communication channels and sales and marketing involvement based on identified goals for each segment, and we designed a system that would grow each member toward deeper loyalty and purchase volume by making them partners in their own growth. An abbreviated view of this needs-based segmentation is illustrated in Table 4.1, where segments defined by buyer evolution are addressed with different strategies. Buyer segments range from Stage 1 (ignorant of GPOs) to Stage 6 (so expert they could run a GPO themselves).

In addition to its group-purchasing service, Intalere developed a suite of consultative offerings that are strategically designed to cascade the best practices of its most sophisticated, successful segment down to its other segments.

You may be thinking, "How can needs-based segmentation work in my company?" It's true that the implementation won't always look the same across industries and firms of varying size. But no matter who you are, how you define customer needs in the Co-Creation economy must change. Every action must be judged in terms of its probable outcome. From a customer's point of view, what would help them achieve the outcome they're after? If you use those outcomes to segment that market and start grouping customers who share similar unmet needs, you will discover the reasons those segments actually exist. Then modularize your capabilities. Finally, anticipate what they will need next.

TOOL 4: CUSTOMER EXPERIENCE JOURNEY ASSESSMENT

The Co-Create Toolkit PDF, available to you to download for free from CoCreateBook.com is intended to help you apply some of the key ideas you've just read in this chapter.

In this chapter I discussed the ecosystem surrounding the Customer Experience Journey and the advantages to shifting from a focus on acquisition to a focus on retention through deep relationships of mutual benefit. These tools prompt you to assess that journey and develop a strategic plan based on what you learn.

Table 4.1

Buyer Evolution Segment / Description / Purchasing Sophistication	Largest Benefit from Intalere	Primary Marketing Strategy/Tools	Sales and Marketing Involvement
Stage 1 Entry level buyer. May not know they have any other option. Minimal.	Awareness of options.	Advertising. Create awareness through immersion.	Low. Visited by field rep to connect to Intalere, then passed to inside sales. Account then becomes "self-sustaining."
Stage 2 Know what a GPO is. Still trying to figure out what to buy from where. Minimal.	Confidence in purchasing decisions.	Advertising. Sales collateral.	Low. Moving toward outside sales involvement.
Stage 3 Utilize GPO(s) and have some tier interest. Sourcing starts to become a recognized function. Basic.	Effective purchasing process.	Inform and lead to best conclusion. Sales collateral.	Medium. Outside sales lead.
Stage 4 Utilize multiple GPOs, often through distributors. Moderate.	Education and quality programs.	Inform and segment. Sales collaterals.	High. Primary targets for first-line sales.
Stage 5 Leveraging GPOs to get better deals for self-contracting. Self-contracting to avoid fees. High.	Ability to create custom programs.	Segment and show success. Success stories.	High. Multiple levels of sales leadership engagement.

Stage 6 Extremely sophisticated buyer that utilizes all options and actively pursues new opportunities. Substantial.	Data and tools that increase efficiencies.	Show specific value and success that could not be achieved on their own. Be able to showcase the "wins" of the account itself. Have to know they are with others "in their class." Success stories, opinion leader engagement.	High. National accounts and major affiliates.

Chapter Four Takeaways

- In the Co-Create economy, the objective shifts from customer acquisition to customer retention.
- The six stages of the Customer Experience Journey are awareness, discovery, and evaluation; leading to purchase, usage, and again, evaluation.
- Support and help recipients of your value as they progress from one stage of the journey to the next; make each transition a positive experience.
- Needs-based segmentation allows organizations to modularize their offerings and sales/marketing approach to fit different Customer Experience Journeys.

FIVE

CO-CREATE AHEAD: LEADING THROUGH PROVOCATION

 In this chapter you will learn:

- How the Hollywood Talent Model benefits the Co-Create organization, and what it requires;
- How the Hollywood Talent Model can be relevant for more traditional and mature, even manufacturing, companies;
- How to lead teams of passionate evangelists; and
- What the organizational structure of the future will look like.

To sum up what we've discussed so far regarding an organization's evolution toward a business model attuned to the Co-Create economy:

- The success of any organization relies on an excellent portfolio of product and service offerings, driven by deep understanding of customers' needs, desires, and experiences.
- That inherent quality and fit should be assured by inviting customers and key stakeholders into the adaptive innovation process, where they become essential partners in research, development, and prototyping.
- Since this process involves all key stakeholders, not just customers, all of an organization's functions—not just sales and

marketing—must learn to develop strategic relationships with stakeholders.

- Through a process of shifting your organization from an inwardly focused "us-centric" structure to a customer-focused "you-centric" structure, you transition from a push economy model to a Co-Create model.

Now let's explore the kind of leadership required to spearhead a culture of Co-Creation today. What challenges might you encounter in the rapidly changing workplace, where many "employees" might in fact be freelancers, contractors, or consultants bringing their expertise only to specific projects or to achieve particular goals?

Leaders at every level must promote passion and evangelism—the same passion and evangelism that the organization wishes to inspire in its customers, employees, partners, and investors (as well as other key stakeholders). To rouse employees from their functional silos, purposeful, provocative leaders must use the five strategies we'll learn later in this chapter.

In chapter 1 I defined purposeful, provocative leadership as a mindset that balances organizational learning with performance, welcomes prudent risk-taking, doesn't fear failure, and encourages a relationship-centric culture—as illustrated by the example of Kevin Plank of Under Armour. My goal in this chapter is to prepare you to exemplify that role in all that you do. But first, we need a foundation to build on, a sense of the organizational structure. Let's examine the new work reality that has become known as the "Hollywood Talent Model," then move on to explore the role of passion and evangelism in great teams.

THE HOLLYWOOD TALENT MODEL

A 2016 *Fast Company* article proposed that the future of work will look a lot like Hollywood—a place where the "free agents" of Free Agent Nation (to use the term coined by Tom Peters and popularized by Daniel Pink in a book of the same name)[1] have long come together around specific film and television projects to Co-Create under the leadership of an executive producer—before moving on to the next project.[2] The

Figure 5.1: Free Agent Nation

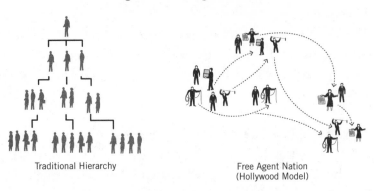

Traditional Hierarchy

Free Agent Nation
(Hollywood Model)

rest of the business world is quickly discovering the advantage of this mobile human capital strategy.

To summarize those advantages: From the employer side, sheer size is inefficient in terms of both payroll cost and operational agility; great talent may only be available on contract; business needs are seldom predictable enough to keep a team fully productive 100 percent of the time.

From the employee side, fewer people are interested in long tenure with one company. The "security" of such jobs is questionable at best, and ultra-talented workers tend to become increasingly undervalued over the course of a long tenure. The days of thirty-, twenty-, and even ten-year anniversaries are behind us. More professionals are freelancing, by choice or by necessity, aided by the emergence of digital talent marketplaces like Upwork and Guru that help contractors and companies find each other.[3] These trends have set the stage for the Hollywood Talent Model.

Interestingly, you might think that the GEs and Rolls-Royces and Caterpillars and Bechtels of the world—capital-intensive manufacturing industries whose products (ships, jet engines, bridges, mining machines) require more formal, traditional corporate structures and defined, dedicated employee roles—would be immune to this kind of redefinition. But even they are adopting the "distributed talent" model, albeit in other ways. LEGO's flat, team-based, management structure—almost absent traditional hierarchy—looks a lot more like groups of high-talent, empowered freelancers than a bunch of suits in silos worried about their boss, who's worried about her boss, etc. Contract manufacturers like Hospira, a privately held Chicago-based company providing biopharma production for major drug companies, represent a Hollywood Talent Model approach that enables agility that would otherwise be hard for large manufacturers to achieve.[4]

Whenever I watch an award show like the Oscars, I am reminded of the incredible range of effort that goes into creating a feature film. To make it a financial success, its producers must bring together and leverage the skill, knowledge, and experience of an exceptional team (both in front of and behind the camera). Today, it is very rare for any of those team members to be permanent employees of the studio.

Clarity of Intent: The Senior Leadership Team and the Storyboard

Let's consider a typical movie production. Franchises aside (Batman, Superman, Marvel Comics, Transformers, James Bond, etc.), very few films originate inside the big studios. Instead, much smaller production companies—many belonging to established stars—receive pitches and scripts on spec and then take the best to those larger studios, who choose an executive producer from inside their ranks to "quarterback" the project. In an organization, the board and the investors who hold fiduciary responsibility are the equivalent of the studio, and the CEO is the equivalent of the executive producer.

The future is not nebulous at this point. Before the studio decides to greenlight a project, it has to conduct significant research and market analysis. Clarity of intent informs the selection of the screenplay and the leadership team to produce it. The studio and executive producer bring in a director who has the vision, the skills, the knowledge, the background, and the experience to execute that screenplay.

Likewise, CEOs, boards, and organizations that are consistently successful begin with clarity of intent. The screenplay is the vision that everyone who has signed on so far has agreed upon, the shared understanding of what they're making, how the outcome will look, how it will perform.

Before production can begin, this initial leadership team must plan the production in terms of its scenes, visual effects, and schedule in order to determine its talent requirements. In most cases, storyboards—

graphic, shot-by-shot representations of the screenplay—are the medium for that planning, helping the director and others see how the vision will come to life. (The film industry's reliance on storyboards illustrates the importance of strategy visualization, which I discussed in chapter 3.) We're a visual society. Storyboards—whether in movie production or business initiatives—help people see what leaders have in mind. You might also think of storyboard panels as the equivalent of slides in a PowerPoint presentation or the wire frames of web design we saw with Method's March Madness iPhone app in chapter 2.

In the studio model, once the screenplay (strategy) is in place, the question becomes talent: Who's going to be a good director, second director, casting director, cinematographer, and head of visual effects? These are the studio equivalent of an organization's C-suite, and the human capital choices at that level will drive decisions about every additional team member, from best boy to stunt coordinator.

Sourcing the Cast and Crew

With the clarity of intent the storyboard brings, the next step can begin: lining up the talent for the cast in front of the lens and the crew behind it.

The success of any initiative hinges on the team's ability to understand the vision and execute it. And here's where the Hollywood Talent Model comes in. If I go down the list of all the people on a movie production, none of those people are employees of one studio. As Hollywood shifted away from the studio system it perfected in the 1930s, it adopted the free-agent talent model, which—just like in professional sports, which gave us the term—signifies independence from any single company or contract. It is high time for organizations to ask why we continue to rely so heavily on an employment model. I can hear you saying, "But David, we use contractors and consultants all the time." I understand, but in my view, far too many companies use contractors in a highly transactional way. The shift to the Hollywood Talent Model is driven by the rise of "knowledge work," a term coined in the 1950s by management guru Peter Drucker, who suggested "the most valuable asset of a 21st-century institution . . . will be its **knowledge workers** and their productivity."[5]

Nourcabulary

Knowledge workers are individuals whose main capital is between their ears. The term applies to anyone who "thinks for a living." Knowledge work is characterized by the problem-solving capacity it requires. Knowledge workers must be able to analyze, assess, connect, see trends, and create.

The message for organizations in this: You don't have the market cornered on intellectual property and those who create it. There is no reason to assume knowledge workers should be managed the way an industrial-era workforce was managed, and every reason to assume these workers see themselves as at-will. If you want the best and brightest talent in key strategic areas of your business, you need to inspire them to come together around a common mission, vision, or enemy. Let's consider the impacts of this new talent strategy on your organization.

What would the Hollywood Talent Model do to the human capital dynamics of your organization? What would that do to your expense line for sales, general, and administration (SG&A)? What would that mean for your physical plant—would you cease expecting people to come into the office every day? What would that do to your talent management approach—would managers still review their reports, would peers be expected to complete 360-degree reviews, would there still be career paths? What would that do to strategic relationships internal to the organization?

I may sound like I'm making the argument that there should be no employees, but that's not the case. Every company needs a stable core to assure its sustainability. In the Co-Create economy, that stable core will be surrounded by a vast, flexible ring of "gig workers" that changes periodically to meet evolving needs.

When I consider the implications of the Hollywood Talent Model and the ubiquity of on-demand platforms for matching buyers and sellers, it seems clear that individuals will compete to win a role in a new initiative, even at the highest executive levels. When casting suggests a lead male role, they don't suggest just one name; they ask a number of actors to audition. If the director didn't like the sound

technician she used on the last production, she gets another technician for the next.

Of course, there are implications for your own professional development, your own investment in your skills and knowledge, your hopes of
remaining relevant in competing for key parts. As a free agent, you are
forced to take personal responsibility for your ongoing employability.
But believe me, this is a good thing.

Let me take the implication one step further. Encouraged by the
convenience of on-demand platforms like Uber and Airbnb, we are
becoming increasingly accustomed to people competing to serve us. I
believe talent management will also evolve to where individuals have
to compete based on ratings. Look at Upwork, Guru, TaskRabbit, and,
for the web industry, specialty platforms like PeoplePerHour and
Freelance; these are all real-time talent exchanges in which individuals' success is tied to confirmation of the value they deliver, since recipients of that value leave feedback that affects future hiring decisions.

If you own a home, you might use Angie's List or Yelp to find service providers in your area, like a plumber to fix the leaky faucet or the
lawn crew to deal with landscaping. If you own a company, particularly
a small company, you likely outsource your payroll to a firm like ADP,
which specializes in this area. If you're interested, they can also do
everything from administering your benefits plans to writing your
employee manual, allowing you to step away from all parts of the HR
function.

Figure 5.2: Ongoing Employability

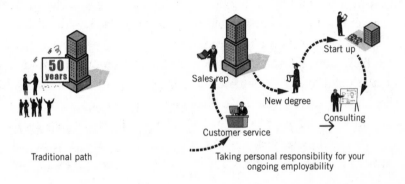

50 years

Traditional path

Sales rep

Customer service

New degree

Start up

Consulting

Taking personal responsibility for your
ongoing employability

So let's outsource part of our company's innovation function. Really? Yes. I'm inviting you to recognize that, in certain situations, it makes more sense to engage outside talent for specific needs. Researchers at MIT's Sloan School of Business identified several circumstances where this approach is most effective. First, when one company acquires the rights to a complex process or product with which they may be unfamiliar. This is common in the pharmaceutical industry, where product development is so attenuated and specialized that adding new products often means outright acquisition rather than in-house efforts. Others relate to early stage product development. For example, Health Care REIT, Inc. (the United States' largest nonprovider owner of senior living properties) has turned to MATTER, an incubator for healthcare-related technology innovations, to develop solutions that facilitate communication among patient care teams.[6] Another circumstance might be a situation where intellectual property isn't well protected, making it difficult to commit to a serious investment in R&D, as in consumer fads like Razor scooters and hoverboards where knockoff manufacturing led to a number of patent lawsuits.[7]

And if you think your company is too large or your project too specialized or complex to hand any part of it over to outsiders, consider that Boeing outsourced production of many of the prototype parts for both its Joint Strike Fighter and Phantom Ray spy planes, sometimes using specialized suppliers to produce and test thousands of parts in molded plastic before actual production.[8]

The Hollywood Talent Model says, fundamentally, "We believe that the intellectual requirements of our enterprise are changing and will continue to change. We want to design into our organizational structure the flexibility to continually adapt to those changing conditions." This might call for new roles, such as a freelance talent manager. It might call for more emphasis on strategic relationships, to encourage greater loyalty among free agents who have no overt allegiance to the company.

It might call for groundbreaking hiring approaches, like Heineken's HR campaign that rivals the "cool" of any of its consumer advertising. In 2016, the brand began to invite candidates to view a manifesto and then respond to a dozen questions.[9] The resulting profile is submitted electronically to Heineken along with a résumé. The interactive video is witty and eccentric, and neatly customized to localize it to any of Heineken's markets around the globe. After taking the interview quiz, applicants have a clear sense of whether they would fit as part of the Heineken team or not. And Heineken's HR team has a fine-tuned sense of where to deploy the individuals it hires based on their profiles.[10]

Just as talent will be constantly competing for the next gig in this model, so too will ideas compete to become future strategies. Consider how networks and other content platforms almost always ask production companies for pilots before they commit to a longer-term TV series idea. In the new norm of the Hollywood Talent Model strategy and the organizational culture of Co-Creation, how do you measure success, how will you apply what you learn from workplace equivalents of pilots and ratings and award nominations? What feedback mechanism rates those prototypes like the value-recipient feedback rates talent?

One more plug for what business can learn from Hollywood before I leave the topic: Look at the diversity of thought that comes together in the entertainment industry. An Italian director works with a Portuguese producer and a Nigerian actor on a Canadian production. Forget nationality; you are bringing together an enormous diversity of thought to the table. And diversity of experience: all these people have worked on different teams before. Knowledge of best practices from around the globe is part of the intellectual capital they bring to each subsequent engagement. To apply this to a business, it might take the form of job-rotation programs among the core staff. Put the leader of your Korean division in charge of the Brazilian operation, or move a leader from Nigeria to head up Asia-Pacific. You'll give your next generation of leaders a broader perspective and enhanced strategic relationship development skills. If your organization is not multinational, consider how you could replicate this kind of broadening through other talent-deployment strategies. Simply instituting a job-rotation program increases the diversity of experience that employees bring to their next team assignment, even if the enterprise is no larger than the local credit union.

To summarize what this shift means for you: Look to how Hollywood makes movies for a model of your organization's human-capital approach in the Co-Create economy. Successful films find clarity of intent before assembling the team, then bring together individuals with diverse experiences and outlooks who are the best fit for this production.

REQUIRED: A CULTURE OF STRATEGIC RELATIONSHIP DEVELOPMENT

Today's leaders need to recognize two phenomena that, if not managed successfully, will create disruption when they collide. The first is the Hollywood Talent Model I've been discussing, and the second is a pervasive lack of skill in strategic relationship development. Organizations need access to talent with strategic relationships, but individuals are not being mentored or trained in the mindset of how to acquire the necessary skills or how to use them.

In the open-talent economy, people have replaced capital, real estate, and raw materials as the essential assets of any business. Knowledge is the chief competitive advantage.

Today, leaders must assemble the smartest people and facilitate their knowledge acquisition and sharing. In a globally connected workplace, those people may or may not be traditional employees (in fact the Hollywood model predicts that they will not be), and they may be anywhere in the world—an evolving mix of full- and part-time employees, independent contractors, ex-employees, and individuals with no connection to the company other than their web of socially enabled relationships. Today, the quality and scope of your talent's network may be your chief competitive differentiator, because those networks help your people build collaboration teams, solve problems, and execute initiatives.

"That sounds great," you say, "but the people in my organization aren't yet equipped to immediately engage in the way you describe. What should I do to provide training, modeling, or mentorship to help them develop fundamental skills in identifying, nurturing, and sustaining strategic relationships?"

One way to begin is to recognize that those skills are nowhere better exemplified than in start-ups, where a handful of people on fire with an idea hire out all but the core functions of their project. Creating and communicating an organizational culture of Co-Create can take the form of small groups of employees, chosen for their leadership skills and inspired to create a new product or venture, being sent to work alongside actual start-ups at co-working sites off premises where the coder is at the next table and the designer is down the hall, and where a 3D printing class is given every Friday. These groups can come back to the company to spread this new way of working in an intentional way.

In the realm of retail, a pop-up store or shop embodies the pilots and prototypes concept we've been examining. A pop-up by definition is small in scale, temporary in both location and time span, and often a place to try out prototypes and to fail fast and cheaply. Pop-ups also generate a form of ratings in their ability to spur visitors to buy or consume—and to engage in relevant social media about their experiences. Remember Market Gravity?

Even mature companies are engaging in this kind of experimentation. Chobani and Nike, for example, have opened stand-alone stores in hip neighborhoods.[11] The goal? To expose not only innovation teams but also key personnel to experimentation with different product mixes and merchandising, and even to allow cobranding partners, brand ambassadors, and local influencers to stimulate new thinking and learn new ways of working.

And then there's Kola House, a hipster cocktail destination that opened in New York's Meatpacking District in the spring of 2016. It boasts storied mixologists behind the bar, and hopefully soon a buzz and offerings to match. Behind this venture you might expect to find a restaurant group power chef like Danny Meyer or Mario Batali—and you'd be wrong. It's Pepsi. Yes, PepsiCo, whose products will only be loosely associated with Kola House. (The company did work with an experienced NYC hospitality group, The Metric, to help bring the project to life.) This mature company—whose sales of sugary beverages have dropped alarmingly in recent years—wants to find inspiration for new products way beyond the focus group and tasting lab, and with the product developers taking the form of quaffing consumers and the folks behind the bar creating those products. Guess what? They're also out to harness the power of social media to get the good word out in an organic, authentic way to attract attention to existing Pepsi products—

as well as to new products that might result—one Tweet, Facebook post, or Instagram image at a time.[12] Every impressed customer out there in the wired universe becomes a brand ambassador, a tiny but crucial cog; the best partners in the Co-Create economy are intentional participants evangelizing the impact of your unique product or service.

Travelport: An Innovation Through Co-Creation Case Study

Think a company in a mature B2B industry would have difficulty applying this advice? Consider the example of Travelport. This $2 billion (NYSE: TVPT) travel commerce platform provides distribution, technology, payment, and other solutions for the travel and tourism industry, with roots going back to 1971. The future would appear uncertain at best for an operation like this, given the disintermediation occurring in the travel industry. Consumers are able to purchase directly from online ticket agencies, skirting distributors. But businesses still need to manage their workforce's travel, and they have fiduciary responsibility that you and I as consumer travelers do not. And on the consumer side of the market, more choice means that planning vacations can be a very complex process, leading many consumers to utilize travel agencies. In fact, recent studies indicate that millennials are significantly more likely to use a traditional travel agency than either boomers or Gen Xers.[13] Travelport provides the platform that enables corporate and leisure travel booked through travel agents and travel apps.

The company's leaders believe the travel industry, valued at $7 trillion, is ripe for disruptive innovation, and they'd rather eat than be eaten. The company launched the Travelport Labs Accelerator two years ago, creating a start-up lab within a mature company. "What you get from your internal programs tends to be 80–90 percent incremental, only 10–20 percent innovative," Nathan Bobbin, senior director of product innovation at Travelport, said. "It is very hard for a well-established company to even get out of the box enough to think about disrupting themselves. Who does that really well? Start-up companies."[14]

The Travelport Lab Accelerator uses the "Lean Startup" methodology, focusing on passionate founders ready to address the needs of the travel industry and able to create a minimal viable product (MVP) ready for pilots and prototypes. It graduated its first cohort of industry-relevant disruptive start-ups in spring 2016.

"We recognize there are talented start-up teams looking to innovate in the travel and tourism space," Bobbin said. "By working with these start-ups, we have a better chance to reach customers and achieve growth in a mutually beneficial way. They get a lot of support to get started, and we help to launch innovations that improve travel for everyone in the value chain."

Travel start-ups run through the program alongside internal teams during two sixteen-week programs each year, with benefits to the internal and external innovation teams and the company itself. "It's eye-opening for people who have been in a multibillion-dollar company their whole careers to see that you can move very fast with very little budget; you can learn a lot by building very little in a very short time," Bobbin said. When you fail in sixteen weeks with twenty thousand dollars, it's not a failure; it's a win because you learned something important. People soon shift from worrying about the effect of a "failure" on their careers to a willingness to embrace risk.

External teams benefit from Travelport's domain expertise and relationships in a complex industry. "Access to people who understand the intricacies of this market expedites the learning curve for these start-ups," said Bobbin. Note the strategic relationships component: "We can make warm introductions, which is very important if you are a three-person start-up in business for eight months trying to get a senior-level executive at a major airline to return your phone call," Bobbin said.

The benefit to Travelport itself is the close relationship with the disruptors of the future, outside the industry establishment. By being part of the disruption, Travelport is well positioned to take advantage of merger and acquisition opportunities, and participates in corporate social responsibility as well. "We want to be judged solely by the success of the start-ups that come out of the lab. Travelport may not directly benefit in any measurable way from the teams coming out of our program. The idea is, what's good for travel is good for Travelport. The only way to be successful is to improve travel for someone in the ecosystem, and that's the intent of this initiative," Bobbin concluded.

I find the place of the Travelport Lab Accelerator in the larger organization intriguing: in the org chart you'll find it under global marketing rather than as a standalone or part of strategic planning. The company's leaders recognized that marketing has the substantive knowledge about market trends, where the pain points are, and how different segments of travelers move through their experience journey. Marketing leaders are in the best position to evaluate potential opportunities and to support getting the most viable ideas off the ground. Tying an innovation lab to the marketing function creates a perfect environment for Co-Creation among strategic partners, inside and outside the company.

Why Executive Buy-in Is a Must

Of course, top-level corporate leaders also need to have drunk the Kool-Aid. They need to spend a weekend at a hackathon or whatever South by Southwest–type conference is relevant to their industry—or even not relevant!

In the Co-Create economy, talent and ideas will constantly compete; recipients of that value will use something like a ratings system to leave feedback either overtly in the online world or in the form of choosing whether to reengage with you or your company. This system rewards people who are comfortable with collaborating, with the give-and-take of ideas.

Think about what all this means for your organizational structure: What will your strategy be? How will you prepare to lead the transformation to that new strategy? How will you communicate this evolution to all stakeholders? It will take purposeful, provocative leadership for organizations to leave the "command-and-control" structure of the industrial past for the Hollywood Talent Model of the Co-Created future.

TEAM PASSION AND EVANGELISM

I believe evangelism is a business model evolution that is essential in the Co-Create economy.

Evangelism consists of passion and conviction based on deeply held beliefs that compel the evangelist to influence others. For reasons obvious and less so, there is sustainable competitive advantage in having an ecosystem of enterprise evangelists internal and external to your organization. In this chapter on leading through provocation and creating and communicating an organizational culture of Co-Creation, I apply that view of evangelism as a competitive advantage.

You are probably most familiar with the term "evangelism" in its religious context, where it means the promulgation of the teachings of Jesus Christ and his apostles. But the term can also mean missionary zeal applied outside the framework of religion. Evangelism at its root is really about a desire and intent to persuade others, to influence them, to summon them to take action because the evangelist believes wholeheartedly in whatever it is that inspires him or her. This is the aspect of evangelism you want to leverage on your organization's behalf.

Evangelism is driven by passion—an earnest, authentic, compelling emotion that says, "I'm wild about this and I want you to be too." Constructive passion is credible. Positive passion is infectious. Impactful passion is persuasive. Don't be afraid of passion; don't write it off as "zeal" of the kind that springs from closed minds and leads to confrontation instead of collaboration. Yes, people can be unsettled by passion: they will say things like "This person is a zealot" or "He's a hot-head." No, many are simply really passionate about what they're doing. Rather than fearing evangelical passion, learn to put it to work to drive your organization's evolution.

Evangelism in the Co-Create business model allows you to focus on fewer customers and make them more successful, have more impact on their lives, and, thus, create passionate advocates who do your selling for you. Likewise, evangelists can connect you with employees you would never have found through a recruiter; investors who would never have taken a second look at your prospectus; media coverage you could never have won on your own. Evangelism is the net return on impact. Evangelism is the tangible reward for being amazing at identifying needs and delivering value to key stakeholders.

Leaders regularly undervalue passion as an asset. Passion motivates us to learn, to recover after a mistake, to find inspiration, and to apply it in ways that cross-pollinate and spark innovation. When you see a good idea at the grocery store and you think, "How could that apply at my business?," that's a sign of passion. For example, young people are absolutely passionate about craft beer these days, and small breweries are proliferating all over the country. Traveling in the northeast recently, I walked into a chain supermarket and saw something very appealing and very smart. While my Atlanta store has a local beer section where six-packs are all gathered in the case, here there were shelves selling individual bottles of twenty-five local brews, with a handy rack holding the slotted carrying cases in a clever design. You had to buy a six-pack for a fixed price, but it could be six different beers, eliminating the fear of buying a whole six-pack of something you end up hating. The business takeaway: maybe there's a way to switch up your offerings to appeal to more clients or uncover unusual but valuable partnership opportunities.

Where Does Passion Come From?

I am genuinely curious about where passion comes from. The word itself derives from the Latin root *pati*, meaning "to suffer," which highlights the fact that passion moves people to persevere, to push through pain or difficulty. Recent studies on concert pianists in Stockholm have built upon work with long-distance runners in the United States, demonstrating that there are measurable physiological responses in parts of the brain during motivated activity (the ventral striatum and amygdala). Yes, there is solid neuroscience behind that "flow state" you enter when you are passionately engaged in something you find meaningful. And what's more, the greatest increases in blood flow and activity in the brain seem to be in areas connected with creativity.[15]

I wake up every morning feeling blessed that I am able to do something I'm passionate about. When I travel as a speaker and consultant and find myself in the fifth city in a week, it's not energy drinks that keep me going—it's passion. When an entrepreneur is told "no" by one hundred potential investors, and the one hundred and first says, "Yes, I believe in you enough to back this," that's the result of passion. When I watch former San Francisco 49ers Hall of Fame wide receiver Jerry Rice on ESPN talking about how he learned his incredible work ethic from his bricklayer dad, I see passion for the game of football. I am not certain that every individual has that spark of passion inside him. However, since we all have a ventral striatum and an amygdala, I want to believe we all have the potential to feel it—if we can just find whatever it is that lights up our hearts *and* minds.

Successful brands tap into that passion. Ducati comes to mind for its attention to performance with style, and Apple has intense commitment to product aesthetics. Before you conclude that passion is only for B2C, consider the Silicon Graphics, Inc. (SGI) subsidiary Alias|Wavefront, a company I worked for in the mid-1990s. Alias had a truly world-class animation and 3D-modeling software product that industrial designers loved. People became such evangelists of Alias|Wavefront that if they left one firm, the first thing they would do in their next was to ask for Alias|Wavefront software and SGI hardware. As a result, SGI invested little in trying to gain mindshare from industrial design firms; the industry workforce was an active army for its products. Products that create evangelists are marketing hacks that can elevate a brand far above competitors. All you have to do is make a product so phenomenally great that its users can't imagine life—or work—without it.

Evangelism is something felt at the individual level, but it can be contagious. Provocative leaders encourage that passion at the level of the team, division, and business unit. There are several ways leaders do this, such as sharing their own emotions openly. This triggers a mirroring reaction in those around them at both a primal level ("monkey see, monkey do") and a social level ("we're all in this together"). Aligning individual, team, and organizational goals is also likely to enhance the spread of passion for the brand by making those goals more meaningful.

Leading Passionate People: Three Insights

Passion is something deep and primal; leading those who are passionate can be challenging. Passionate people have more zest, more drive, more energy, but that can also mean that they make snap judgments or have blind spots. Three requirements for leading individuals and teams composed of passionate people are:

1. Direction;
2. Specificity; and
3. Outcome focus.

Passion needs direction. You need to make sure your advocates understand what they're evangelizing, and make sure they're promoting the right attributes. The headmaster of our children's school told a group of parents, "If you are going to recommend us to others, please recommend us in the right way." I was really curious, so I asked him what he meant. He replied, "No school is perfect. Absolutely, highlight the things you are excited about. But rather than avoiding mention of our flaws, talk about areas where we can improve, and be sure to include what we're doing about them." By directing those who are fueled by passion, you create effective evangelists.

Passion needs specificity, because specificity drives credibility. I'm passionate about Ritz-Carlton properties, as you know if you read chapter 1. I have experienced a level of service from that brand that makes me want to share my story—not just with a statement like, "I recommend the Ritz," but with specific, detailed anecdotes. Arm your evangelists with the right ammunition to intelligently tell your story—specific examples that highlight your successes and demonstrate your integrity by being frank about your growing edges as well.

Passion needs to be outcome focused. Evangelism needs to be transmitted in terms of the outcome for the recipient, not a feature or benefit of the product. If I say, "My new iPhone has a stabilization camera," I'm being specific. But am I moving you to want one? Probably not. But if I showed you crystal-clear low-light images and a video of my daughter's soccer goal? Now that's more believable. My passion is more persuasive because I've helped you see how something I'm evangelizing can help you achieve outcomes you seek.

To keep your evangelists singing from the same hymnbook (so to speak), lead with these three insights mentioned above. Then direct team members to speak about your brand with specificity and a focus on outcomes.

Evangelism Must Be Credible and Relevant

For evangelism to have the desired effect, the source must be respected and trusted. Recipients of that evangelism must form an opinion that the source is someone who is knowledgeable and credible and who brings a broad base of experiences that gives their evangelism context. An industrial designer talking about how Alias|Wavefront's animation makes designing speedboats easier means much more to me than a sales rep's praise for that feature. How many other design tools has he tried?

Evangelists need to be able to defend their position, not just regurgitate it. If I ask you for specifics and you have no answer, your evangelism just went out the window.

For an example of how this kind of credible, relevant evangelism factors into a business model, consider Airbnb. In a TED talk about the origins of Airbnb, founding partner Joe Gebbia recalled the hurdle that establishing trust between individuals presented to his innovative idea for app-enabled home sharing. As a design student, he knew that "design is much more than the look and feel of something—it's the whole experience." He posed the question you will face as you activate your army of evangelists—how do you design for trust in the experience between that army and the recipients of their evangelism? A well-designed reputation system was the key for Airbnb: once users (hosts and guests) accumulated ten reviews, acceptance rates for bookings increased. A joint research project with Stanford revealed that the right amount of disclosure—not too much ("creepy!") or too little ("Yo!") is crucial to building trust in a system that relies on reputation created by accumulated reviews. How did Airbnb operationalize this insight, designing its interface for just the right amount of disclosure? Gebbia said, "We use the size of the box to suggest the right length, and we guide them with prompts to encourage sharing." This is an example of directing evangelism through software design. It is also an example of team passion on display, as the design students and Stanford researchers worked together to discover the best possible solution.[16]

By directing evangelism to be specific and outcome focused, you recognize each evangelist's role in the Co-Creation of that message. You invite them to talk about what matters to them—with great specificity—but to couch it in terms of outcomes for other recipients of that value. This invites the recipient of the evangelism to Co-Create new value through engaging with your brand, your organization, your mission. Leaders should recognize the diversity of thought on their teams. Individuals may be equally passionate about the team's common mission, vision, or enemy, but for different reasons—and that's okay.

Leaders who make passion and evangelism contagious will always reap its competitive advantages.

THE ORGANIZATIONAL STRUCTURE OF THE FUTURE

Co-Creation has to become part of your evolution as a firm. This requires a more proactive approach in identifying and developing those individuals who can carry the water, with less left to chance.

Unfortunately, I see too many companies "doing HR" in outdated ways. In the organization of the future, trust and track can replace command and control if senior leaders are confident that five key facets of their human capital approach are functioning as they should be. (They should also be confident that day-to-day performance does not require their direct involvement. This frees the senior leaders for more strategic pursuits, most important attention to key relationships.)

The five facets of an organization's human capital approach are:

1. Strategy
2. Talent
3. Culture
4. Brand
5. Metrics.

While new start-ups can design themselves around the organizational requirements of the Co-Create economy, and agile and small companies can adapt (if not easily, then at least with some effort), this shift will be difficult for mature companies. We have to elevate more people away from the minutiae of "human resources" (traditional HR) to a strategic focus on human capital as a critical business asset.

As a blanket example, we'll consider an international logistics company, let's call it Acme Facilities, with a burgeoning new business in infrastructure project management. The company was originally founded in the American oil patch to provide on-site housing and other facilities for oil and gas drillers. They discovered, with the construction boom in Canadian oil sands, that the same skill set for Texas worked equally well on more remote, weather-challenged building sites in the far north. As they began working farther afield, they also moved away from owning and leasing actual modules to outsourcing that function while developing their management services beyond just installing and building. They needed fewer crews of riggers and carpenters and electricians and truck drivers; they needed more people who knew how to manage and coordinate those crews.

It all begins with *strategy*. If your job is casting the film, you need to know the screenplay backward and forward. If you are responsible for hiring, it is important for you to be able to dissect the strategy as envisioned by the CEO and the board. To deeply understand that strategy, you have to challenge and defend and push back, in candid give-and-take with that board and CEO. (And if you fear reprisals for your candor, consider finding another employer more suited to you. Your company may very well not be ready for the Co-Create economy.) Just as the screenplay drives all subsequent decisions in a movie production, the strategy drives the talent needs of the organization. With Acme moving more toward project management, the implications run from C-suite hires, who come from that very specialized world of international construction and infrastructure and thus have top-level contacts, to the location of new workers as Acme becomes decentralized.

Thus, the next question becomes the *talent* portfolio. Senior talent managers must identify the roles that are critical to the success of that company's vision and strategy. What will those roles require, not just today, but in eighteen or thirty-six months? What do we anticipate those roles will look like? Where are the individuals who can fill those roles? There are three possible answers:

1. We have them already and can immediately slot them into those roles.
2. Right-fit individuals work for us but they are in other parts of the organization, so they must be transitioned to the roles.
3. We have gaps and will need to find talent to fill them.

Too often, unfortunately, I've seen traditional HR plug any warm body into a role, which is a shortsighted "inventory management" approach, not the long-view "quality assurance" approach needed. A talent QA approach asks, "Do we have people with the right skills today, who also have the right ingredients to expand those skills to meet the needs we anticipate for this role in the future?" The uncertainty of that future demands that we select talent based on willingness to learn and grow. In Hollywood, they talk about an actor's range. The same attribute is critical for talent in those key positions. Acme, given the boom or bust nature of the oil industry, had always been run lean, with even mid-level managers taking on multiple functions. One hurdle for the head of HR hired by the new CEO was that the board and half the top executives didn't get the new direction memo and were leery of both lots more employees and new hires who don't necessarily come from the industry but have up-to-date skills.

Now we can move on to considering what *culture* will support that talent and strategy. The culture infuses Co-Creation throughout the organizational structure. There are enormous opportunities for Co-Creation involving culture.

For example, I consult with several clients in very mature companies in very mature industries. Think manufacturing, industrial controls, construction. They have known for years that brain drain is taking place. Older workers are retiring, from individual contributors to senior leadership, and not enough new people are coming into the industry. The companies should take responsibility for introducing, training, and developing the next generation, and yet I see very little of that.

One particular company—an $8 billion multinational—brings its offering to the marketplace through a dealer network over which they have no hierarchical control. As such, Co-Creation is its only path to align the dealers' vision and strategy with that of the manufacturer they represent. These dealers are "mom-and-pop" shops, with all the risk inherent in small business, and yet they are this company's lifeline. Could some of the talent at the manufacturer coach those mom-and-pops on best practices, perhaps even create a trade association of dealers that would give them unparalleled access to a community of peers and vital industry knowledge?

For Acme, it was up to the CEO to help realign his teams to the new strategy going forward and demonstrate that it was here to stay with carefully chosen top-functioning talent paid from an increased budget and deployed in this new growth area. Some spoke different languages and were from different ethnic backgrounds, also aligning the company to better perform in different countries and cultures with a more diverse, multicultural workforce.

Film studios support film schools because they realize that's where the next generation of directors and producers will come from. Across broad swathes of the economy I hear complaints about talent shortages. Here's a Co-Creation strategy: instead of complaining, get much more active in creating opportunities for newcomers to learn. Why can't professional service firms—the KPMGs and Deloittes—loan their retiring partners to high schools and colleges to teach the next generation? Some of this happens serendipitously, but it has to become part of the evolution of industries and organizations. To thrive in the Co-Create economy, supporting successive generations of workers has to be part of your culture. Identifying and developing that talent cannot be left to chance.

In many ways, culture becomes the *brand*. An organization that intentionally creates a culture where employees feel passionate about their roles is much more likely to see that reflected in a well-received brand. Customer experience (created by interaction with frontline employees or what behind-the-scenes employees have produced) is the fundamental test of your culture. Passion for a job well done on the part of those employees increases your likelihood of passing that test and enhancing your brand's reputation. Every day, Acme's human capital—both the workers in the field and the managers in the office—affect the Acme brand. Brands benefit when strategy, talent, and culture align.

The fifth facet of human capital strategy I want to touch on is *metrics*, which drive compensation. In the Co-Create economy, we must start talking about metrics and compensation in terms of outcomes. It doesn't matter to me how you do what you do; what matters is the quality of the result. Too much of how organizations manage metrics and compensation is outdated, from annual performance reviews to 360-degree reviews, where I've seen anonymity give rise to unnecessary nastiness. (I also have yet to meet anybody who enjoys either getting or giving such reviews.) We are trying to measure an organization's future needs in terms of talent and culture with inadequate and flawed tools of the past.

If metrics and compensation were focused on outcome instead of input, more people might focus on the core value their work creates for others. We would in fact breed more "intrapreneurs" who innovate new and better ways to achieve the outcomes their internal customers want and need. I have already mentioned rating mechanisms on talent exchanges. What if as a company we rated our peers on the quality of their outcomes in a system that was available to others, like Airbnb's host and guest ratings? If you're like me, you'd feel motivated to keep your score high so others would want to work with you. Exciting opportunities would be more likely to come your way.

Of course, compensation also drives behavior. Companies have for far too long been asking for "A" but measuring and compensating "B." Similarly, pay grades are a broken concept. My question is, what are we doing to measure our talent's progress, their impact, and their contribution up, down, and across the organization? If we want more Co-Creation behavior inside the organization, we should measure and compensate that behavior. The Ipreo case study that closes this chapter shows that it is possible to replace last-century HR practices with dramatically more effective ones in the Co-Create economy.

Some changes are here already in terms of core benefits—vacation and maternity/paternity leave being two of the most important. Market intelligence provider Ipreo, alternative credit start-up Zest Finance, smart-data company Umbel, ad agency Paper G—these are just a few companies that don't have fixed vacation policies. Employees take what they need. Must be a West Coast, start-up, small-company kind of thing, right? Well, if you consider Netflix and GE small, sure . . . Netflix also offers paid unlimited maternity leave, while Etsy, Microsoft, Google, and Adobe all have extended leaves with pay far beyond the traditional month or two.

Now we must ask what the organization chart of this Co-Create economy company would look like on paper, this enterprise where the leaders' focus on strategy, talent, culture, brand, metrics, and compensation drive the team formation, as well as individual contributions.

From Hierarchy to Customer Centricity

I detest organizational charts because of the hierarchical "command-and-control" assumptions on which they are based. I encourage you to throw out your rows-and-columns org chart and replace it with something new. Something more acutely attuned to your company's value chain, more customer-centric, more talent-centric in recognizing that your employees are stakeholders, as crucial to your growth as your customers are. I can envision a diagram of concentric circles, with a needs-based customer segment, as discussed in chapter 4, at the center, and surrounding it a ring representing your customer segment team. These are the customer-facing individuals. The outside ring contains the people who support the customer-segment team. To envision how this might work, consider the example of Intalere discussed in chapter 4. Table 4.1 summarized buyer segments differentiated by their purchasing sophistication and described different levels of sales/marketing involvement for each.

Cast this way, you can better assess the resources and data they need. You will likely end up changing the corporate infrastructure to better reflect those needs. In this way, the entire culture lives in an eco-system of customer centricity. Buyers at Stage 1, entry-level with minimal purchasing savvy, were assigned to inside sales teams, as opposed to buyers at Stage 2 and beyond, where outside sales becomes involved. These customer segments can have a geographic component. If that customer-facing team serves Kansas City, the next ring is a regional structure that supports Kansas City. And the outer ring becomes a combination of corporate and external resources responsible for serving the teams that serve that customer segment. Undergirding this model is a philosophy that resources should be as close to the end consumer of that value as possible, with those employees empowered to make real decisions. Do more in the field, less at the corporate headquarters. Put field engineering, customer service, all these functions closer to the end customer who needs them right now, where those functions can immediately address that end customer's needs quickly and completely.

Where customer segmentation on income/value/budget size is driving strategy, elevating customers from one segment to another can be part of the metrics and compensation of the customer-segment team. We did this at Intalere, the healthcare group purchasing organization presented in chapter 4 as an example of needs-based segmentation. The basic value proposition is to use Intalere members' combined purchasing power to save money for individual hospitals and clinics. Within their membership are different needs-based segments. (If I'm a small, one-location clinic in the small-business market segment, I have very different needs and buying behaviors than a multilocation clinic. The medium group has very different needs, and as such requires different resources and capabilities from Intalere. Part of the compensation for the small-market segment team would be a bonus for each customer they elevated to the medium-size segment. Now they have a vested interest in helping their customers grow. In addition, they get rewarded for smoothly passing that baton.)

Another opportunity for Co-Creation of value is account planning sessions. During this annual planning meeting, you can talk with your client about their strategic plans and issues, as well as ways you've identified that lead to growth. Think about how much more relevant and meaningful that relationship becomes. Now you have customers saying, "We couldn't have done this without your team." This isn't "crazy talk." IBM has done this for years; banks have organized around customer segments for some time.

I believe the organizational chart of the future will look like interdisciplinary centers of excellence, not siloes. Such is the case with Ipreo.

IPREO: A CASE STUDY IN LEADING THROUGH PROVOCATION

I don't usually get excited about working with HR executives—benefits, vacations, etc., just aren't my area of expertise or a field of opportunity for me. When I met Ronnie West, chief people officer of capital markets data provider Ipreo, I recognized a truly visionary executive who just happens to work in the HR sector.

Ipreo is a Manhattan-based private-equity joint venture between Goldman Sachs and Blackstone that consists of sixteen acquired companies operating in fifteen different countries. Ipreo wooed Ronnie off a European beach where his success with the credit card unit of the British bank Barclays had landed him, after six challenging years. "It was time to decompress," Ronnie recalled, so he and his partner set out on a two-year vacation. "But then I met Ipreo's executive team. Three factors—the charisma and passion of the leadership team, a business ready to pivot, and acknowledgment that the people agenda would be key in generating future value—actually drove me to leave the beach six months early."[17] Before long Ronnie had exchanged his vacation villa for an office in Ipreo's midtown Manhattan location.

Ronnie's résumé included eleven formative years at Unilever, followed by a position on the executive committee at Barclaycard where, during his tenure, profit before tax (PBT) doubled in five years, despite saturated and highly regulated markets. Ronnie's focus on people made a major contribution to those results for Barclaycard, and Ipreo wanted this MVP for its own team.

Ronnie exudes a caliber of intellect I rarely see in typical HR functions. He's brought to Ipreo a lens through which he sees a fundamentally different paradigm regarding human capital. In a meeting to explore how we might work together, he laid out his approach. (By the way, I practice what I preach: when Ronnie e-mailed me that he was ready to explore opportunities, I didn't default to a phone call. I paid for an airline ticket and flew to Manhattan to meet in person.)

Earlier, I identified five facets of a company's approach to human capital: strategy, talent, culture, brand, and metrics. In our meeting, Ronnie walked me through a board presentation encompassing a triangle of strategy, talent, and culture. "In the middle is the client or consumer," he explained.[18] His fundamental premise is that *people* carry a company toward its goals. It is possible to build an ecosystem that leverages that human capital to help the company *exceed* its goals. But how?

It starts with *strategy*—specifically, a people approach that is intrinsically entwined with the business vision. Ronnie's presentation to Ipreo's board succinctly articulated a clear strategy, and he supported it with visuals and organized it into a narrative of the company's past, present, and future. It was aspirational, yet believable. It laid out a pivot to a new business model that would take Ipreo from a loose construct of local, independent entities to a future state where those loose teams are tightly woven into a global, integrated way of working.

You would expect pushback from such an evolutionary strategy; one of Ronnie's first tasks was to gain the buy-in of his three senior stakeholder groups—Ipreo's executive committee and representatives of its two owners, Goldman-Sachs and Blackstone. After a few months on the job—time enough to solidify his credibility with some deliverables accomplished—he presented a business review of his people agenda in a series of meetings with the three stakeholder groups. "I began by talking about the financials, showing them how HR could occupy a more strategic space than just 'comp and bens,'" Ronnie said. "Then I showed a vision of how, if you get the people agenda right, HR can add incremental economic value—profit, revenue, EBITDA—in its own right."[19] Ronnie got the response he sought: a solid buy-in from both Blackstone and Goldman.

Next, we consider *culture*. To assess a company's HR culture attributes, I will often ask about its dress code, its approach to hiring, and its vacation policies. When I asked Ronnie about these things, he ticked off the changes he was bringing to Ipreo: Dress code? A once-massive policy reduced to "You're an adult. You know your diary. Dress appropriately." Hiring? Most companies take the traditional route of job descriptions, advertising vacancies, interviewing, and so on. Ronnie said, "We are working to dispense with that. We no longer look at résumés for certain groups. If you're interested in working with us, send us a five-minute video." Vacation? Ronnie's perspective is, "Take whatever time you need to come back reenergized." He is passionate about keeping the focus on outcomes, not on how much time people clock on the job. In his view, "what matters is that you deliver exceptional re-sults."[20] Step by step, Ronnie is fundamentally changing the culture through provocative, purposeful leadership.

Which brings us to *talent*. This is where, under Ronnie's leadership, Ipreo is blowing up the traditional organizational structure. Ronnie showed me the scorecard he presented to Ipreo's board, a scorecard de-signed to force a deliberate dialogue around Ipreo's transformation to the global, integrated brand the strategy calls for.

He also revealed a completely fresh way of looking at how work gets done in an organization. "We usually draw organizations with boxes and reporting lines, and it is very much concerned with the seniority, status, and experience of individuals and the roles they occupy," Ronnie said. "At Ipreo we asked, what if you put the work at the center?" This led to what Ronnie terms "the Weave," an organizational chart that depicts market segments partnered with technical specialists, shown in figure 5.3. "Where the two intersect is where work happens," Ronnie explained.[21] Reporting lines are becoming irrelevant. Technical exper-tise has been liberated from its various silos. The result is a holistic, integrated structure that empowers key talent.

Figure 5.3: Ipreo's Customer-Centric Organizational Chart

Note how different the structure shown is from the typical pyramid-of-boxes orga-nizational chart.

Other transformations of Ipreo's talent strategy include:

- revamping its practice areas to bring together common skill sets, with a focus on internal mobility, career progression, and communities of practice;
- implementing new, simplified corporate grading to enable structured career progression;
- developing the Ipreo Academy, which incorporates all of its previous training assets into a structured, long-term approach to investing in talent development; and
- introducing Project Praxis, a central knowledge repository to reduce key person risk—the "brain drain" of institutional knowledge now held solely by individuals. By internally branding the project and creating energy around it, he has made an initiative "cool" that otherwise would have generated little interest.

But perhaps the most revolutionary of Ronnie's initiatives is a fundamental shift toward getting the right people in the right roles, where the match of challenge to capability enables them to work in a state of flow (a concept pioneered by Hungarian psychologist Mihaly Csikszentmihalyi[22]) in which they feel neither too much anxiety nor too much boredom. Ronnie has led Ipreo to identify the top twenty roles critical to helping the CEO outpace the strategic outcomes for which his board of directors holds him responsible. Then his team asked: What individuals do we already have in the right jobs? Who do we know with the right characteristics to be plugged into some of those twenty positions? That leaves the positions for which Ipreo must recruit.

With this talent approach, Ipreo makes sure that the efforts of all individuals align with the CEO's strategy, and that strategy cascades down to every employee, with appropriate metrics and compensation. "There is often a huge disconnect between a company's vision and how people in the business understand their contributions to the bigger goals," Ronnie said. He replaced Ipreo's convoluted approach to goal-setting with a simple formula: against the entity-level scorecard, each individual creates six objectives: three business outcomes, two personal goals, and one values objective. The three business objectives directly link to the Ipreo scorecard. "As a result, every one of Ipreo's over one thousand employees knows how his or her work contributes to Ipreo's financial performance and achieving its vision," Ronnie said. The two personal goals give individuals space to drive dialogue about what they need from the organization, which could be related to the business or to other aspirations. "This doesn't mean we will assess and set bonuses on personal goals," Ronnie was quick to clarify, "but to let our people say what they want out of the relationship. People have really embraced it." The values objective recognizes that individuals' behavior and outcomes must be aligned with the company's overall values.

Ipreo is reengineering everything from how it runs its executive committee to its company-wide compensation structure. Business performance reviews increasingly focus on a dialogue about risks and resource allocation, so that everyone can get the help they need to mitigate that risk. Recognizing that metrics and compensation drive behavior, the executive team's annual bonuses are tied to Ipreo's overall performance: one-third tied to EBITDA, one-third tied to revenue targets, and the final third tied to the executive team's delivery of results. "We do this in order to force the trade-off discussions—resource allocation, prioritization," Ronnie explained.

Ronnie's approach is unorthodox. Would it work in every company? That depends on the caliber of its current talent. I would rather see organizations clean out the talent that would hold them back from this kind of evolution than see them miss an opportunity to Co-Create value through leadership.

TOOL 5: ORGANIZATION EVOLUTION SCORECARD

The Co-Create Toolkit PDF, available to you to download for free from CoCreateBook.com is intended to help you apply some of the key ideas you've just read in this chapter.

This tool prompts you to assess your organization's strategy, culture, and talent to discover what elevates your company's human capital function to a driver of financial performance. As part of an off-site strategy session with your senior leadership or board, this tool—and the exercise of iterating through it as a group—is an excellent jumping-off point for global vs. project-specific discussions.

Chapter Five Takeaways

- The Hollywood Talent Model, where people come together around specific projects, will become the norm, requiring clarity of intent and a culture of strategic relationship development.
- Teams will be comprised of passionate evangelists; leaders must direct them to evangelize with specificity and a focus on outcome.
- The organizational structure of the future will put customers at the center, with resources aligned around them via interdisciplinary centers of excellence.

SIX

CO-CREATE UPWARD: THE SPIRAL OF GROWTH

 In this chapter you will learn:

- The importance of leading drivers in making strategic decision-making nimbler;
- The role of sentiment, reputation, and engagement, as well as other external and internal leading drivers;
- The application of Key Performance Drivers (KPDs) to anticipate and respond to customers' emerging needs;
- Ways to become more proactive using evolutionary performance dashboards; and
- The role of "SMAC" (Social, Mobile, Analytics, Cloud) in challenging technology to become more strategic.

The right metrics, at the right time, with insights in the hands of the right action-oriented individual—these are critical enablers of strategic, profitable growth in the Co-Create economy. And the best way to gain access to the right metrics is with a real-time dashboard that tracks key performance drivers, or KPDs. Please pause and read that again, because this is the mission-critical message of this chapter. If you take nothing else from your reading, please remember this: in the Co-Create economy, your growth depends on getting the right customized, forward-looking KPDs in the right hands, up, down, and across your organization.

These performance drivers can't be the same old reports from last week, last month, or last quarter; those are key performance indicators (KPIs) and many are *lagging indicators*—results of your past performance. For organizations in the Co-Create economy, the far more important set is comprised of *leading drivers*—of customer intention toward buying products and services. You can track harbingers of anticipated growth by paying attention to the following metrics, all of which we will examine in detail in this chapter.

- **Sentiment**—How do customers feel about their experience with our brand in all stages of their buying decision?
- **Reputation**—How are we perceived in customers' hearts and minds?
- **Engagement**—When, where, and how do customers prefer to be engaged by us and our brand?
- **Buying-Cycle Alignment**—How can we increase our efficiency and effectiveness at meeting buyers along every stage of their Customer Experience Journey?
- **High Performers and High Potentials**—Who in our organization consistently behaves above and beyond expectations when it comes to engaging and influencing the thinking and motivation of our customers? Similarly, which individuals show a stronger level of commitment, work ethic, and eagerness to learn and grow with our brand?

In my view these are the most important performance drivers you can have. Now, how will you get them into the hands of the right action-oriented individuals at the right times? That's where evolutionary dashboards come in.

The concept of dashboards has been around since data warehousing began in the late 1990s. These data visualization tools allow users to drill down into complex information and improve decision-making. The main appeal of dashboards is the visual interface that makes them so easy to use. (Think of the experience of being behind the wheel of your car.) One of the simplest dashboards is your business's weekly LinkedIn page update, which shows how many people you've engaged, likes you've accumulated, shares of your posts, campaigns you've announced, etc.

But **evolutionary dashboards** take that idea further by being available on all mobile devices, with data as close to real time as possible, reflecting leading drivers, and customized for specific roles in the organization.

Nourcabuary

Dashboards are visual information displays that keep relevant key performance drivers (KPDs) readily in view. Distinct from most current dashboards are those I call **evolutionary dashboards,** which are specifically engineered to drive adaptive innovation. These must be based on data as close to real time as possible, feature leading drivers, and be tailored to specific roles, such as sales, talent management, or production.

In the Co-Create economy, Co-Creation of value extends to the KPD dashboard, which is customizable based on individual functions, creating maximum engagement by demonstrating individual impact on shared objectives. Going from micro to macro (as shown in figure 6.1), our need for information is driven by our roles:

- **Individual contributors**—How are my efforts making a difference in the larger vision for the organization?
- **Managers**—Do I have my finger on the pulse of what's happening at the edge of our business where current and prospective customers live; where skills, knowledge, and changes in our behavior can have a real-time impact?
- **Group or business-unit leaders**—Are we agile enough to anticipate changing market demands, so that we can make appropriate course corrections and always offer a competitive value proposition in the eyes of our stakeholders?
- **Executives**—Is our strategy and vision for the next eighteen to thirty-six months—which is the Co-Create economy's strategic

horizon, a departure from the traditional five- and ten-year plans—sufficiently adaptable? Does it have the right balance of brand equity and human capital assets and culture to meet those shifting market demands?

- **Fiduciary stewards**—Are we asking the right questions of senior leadership to mitigate risk, sufficiently understand disruptive technologies and business models, and anticipate appropriate shifts in market direction with our current governance model?

Figure 6.1: Roles and KPD Dashboards

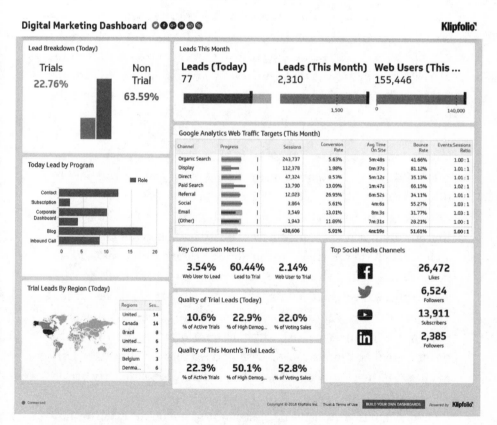

Sample Klipfolio Digital Marketing Campaign Performance dashboard. Note how data starts top left with today and presents a nutshell graphic view of spend, conversion, and other metrics. Online, a hover permits click-through to ever more granular and historical layers of data.

Each role is assigned its own KPDs, displayed to individuals on a dashboard matched to their specific roles, so each can clearly see his or her impact on outcomes and, thus, align individual and team efforts to achieve those outcomes.

An upward spiral of growth in the Co-Create economy depends on whether your organization is: 1) registering as an authentic object of interest to its most highly valued customer segments; 2) helping prospective customers and clients with their decision-making process; and 3) fueling their urge to tell their friends and business networks about their experiences. Customer evangelism, as we learned, can dramatically reduce customer-acquisition costs, freeing up resources to aim for delivering exceptional customer experiences and further creating greater Market Gravity. Evolutionary dashboards can help every function in the organization operate more effectively. Data from these evolutionary dashboards can also be used to increase an organization's speed-to-market factor by anticipating new customer needs, allowing the organization to strategically drip new iterations, if not innovations, into the market.

By now you are probably getting curious: Where do these dashboards come from? Aren't these "soft" drivers extremely hard to measure? How do I pin "sentiment" to a point on a scale? I will address these concerns. But first, let us explore the terrain.

Throughout this chapter, keep in mind the Customer Experience Journey discussed in chapter 4, because we build here on key insights about that journey. I will show you how the right dashboards can keep every function in an enterprise attuned to customers' evolving, and ever-rising, expectations and needs, especially those not yet sensed. This enables adaptive innovation, which leads to increased customer retention, which can be the basis for either transformative growth to scale or for a smaller, more strategic base of deep relationships (the "Jerry Maguire" business model). That is the promise of evolutionary performance dashboards.

Let's begin by getting my deepest concerns out on the table: the fundamental ways organizations undermine their efforts. Without solving these challenges, no dashboard can show you the way forward.

Figure 6.2: Framing

CHALLENGE: FLAWS IN FRAMING

To understand and drive the evolution of your growth, you must frame the right challenge. Not based on gut feel or intuition. Not because you've been in the industry for thirty-five years. Rather, your framework for data-driven decision-making must be based on a clear understanding of the outcomes you are trying to achieve and the problems that stand in your way.

Consider the following exercise, which I often use with the teams I work with.

I tell them, "You are hiking in the North Georgia Mountains when you come across a cabin. There are several dead people inside. Your job is to figure out how these people died. I will answer any yes or no question you ask me."

Ten out of ten times, the audience begins to ask very logical questions. "Can you smell any fumes?" "Is there any sign of animal attack?" "Is there blood?" "Do you see any kind of weapons?" They start to discern what exactly happened in this cabin.

A few minutes go by in this question-and-answer activity. Then, I typically ask one of the participants, "Can you see in your mind's eye what this cabin looks like?" Let's say I call on Bob. Bob says "yes," and I ask Bob to come up to the front of the room and sketch an image of the cabin. Bob begins to draw a structure—four walls, windows, a door. Maybe he includes some damage, or a fire. In a few moments he has produced some iteration of a physical log cabin structure.

I gain consensus by asking, "Does everybody believe this is a representation of the cabin?" I'm not asking for world-class art here, or forensic evidence. But structurally, does this audience believe this is what the cabin would look like?

And then I flip the page, and I draw the outline of an airplane. Because what they came across was in fact an airplane cabin that had crashed. Yet when I say "cabin," unconscious bias leads that audience to envision a cottage in the woods.

My point is that if you frame a challenge or opportunity based on assumptions, it may be flawed. You can waste time and resources going down the wrong path because of a faulty definition. To this day I am amazed at how many leaders, teams, and organizations are thinking about "the wrong cabin." That's why forward-looking, collaborative decision-making based on verifiable data is so important.

Starting from the wrong frame is one challenge to an upward spiral of revenue growth. The other is lack of analysis.

CHALLENGE: NO ANALYSIS OF PAST PERFORMANCE

I would estimate that more than 80 percent of my clients don't do any kind of win/loss analysis on their new-business efforts. They don't understand what wins them business, and, more alarmingly, they don't understand why they're losing business. If you ask the sales rep, the reply is typically something like, "Well, that buyer had a brother-in-law who works for one of our competitors." If you ask the customer the same question, you hear, "They really didn't understand where we are trying to go." Bad information leads to flawed assumptions and, thus, framing the wrong challenge.

If you don't understand the key drivers of your growth, the speed of that upward spiral, the cost of that growth, the elasticity of that demand, you'll never know which levers are under your control and which are not.

You may think you have a great idea that's working very well, until suddenly it's not. Rent the Runway (RTR) is a clothing and accessories rental site founded by two Harvard Business School grads in 2009. By the end of 2015, it had raised more than $120 million in venture capital and was valued around the half-billion-dollar mark.

It has over 110,000 Instagram followers and 380,000 Facebook "likes"—who could resist a selfie in that stunning Badgley Mischka? Nevertheless, *Fortune* magazine reported in 2015 that RTR had yet to make a profit and had lost seven top executives in the span of ten months, perhaps due to what former staffers told the magazine was the company's early days of cliquishness and *Mean Girls* corporate culture.

Scroll down through the Facebook comments, too, and you see just how steep their spiral was—and just how poorly they had initially anticipated how to scale their concept. "When we launched," CEO Jennifer Hyman told *Fortune,* "we got such great PR that it looked like an immediate boost, but it didn't sustain itself. It was a false positive."[1] Expanding their special events rentals to include an accessories offering was a failure. Those initial skyrocketing sales also revealed some weak areas in their execution and business plan, like getting the right sizes to customers and even having basic stock available either online or in their showrooms to offer some kind of consistent choice. "I think the hardest thing is that you're continuously doing a job you don't know how to do," Hyman revealed to *Cosmopolitan.* "Nothing can prepare you to learn how to be a leader while your business is growing so quickly. . . . I try to be humble and learn from my mistakes."[2]

As my teenage daughter has been known to say, when a girl needs a dress, a girl needs a dress, but the bashing that the company is still taking on social media all these years later is a testament to the importance of consistency over quantity in customer satisfaction. As a hypothetical, imagine that a company informs you—in mid-May—that those ten bridesmaids' dresses you reserved in January for your June wedding won't be available. Well, the internet has lots of places built on spreading that bit of unhappiness far and wide.

Since her first successful meeting with Diane von Furstenberg back in 2008, however, Jennifer Hyman has had a key contingent of backers in the fashion industry who see RTR as an ideal venue to connect their older brand to a younger demographic. And despite the problems with customer experience, RTR's recent addition of a subscription model for business and everyday wear has apparently been successful—so far. Hyman is counting on radical changes in leadership and attention to leading drivers to remedy that shortfall. "The first core value we have is that everyone deserves a Cinderella experience," she told *Fortune*. "And I looked around at the team that I had, and thought that we needed a very different team to scale us."[3]

What that new team discovered when they started listening louder was that the future of RTR wasn't so much in renting prom dresses but in giving women greater access to that Cinderella feeling every day. "How life-changing would it be to have access to hundreds of thousands of designer pieces and be able to have a new outfit every single day?" Hyman asked *Cosmo*. "It's a vision we were not able to launch until we built our company and nurtured our relationships with designers. To convince women that they should have a rotating closet of unlimited options that they can wear to work, on the weekend, *and* at parties is a much bigger, much bolder idea."[4]

Rent the Runway, by only monitoring social media rather than performing more rigorous analytics, missed early faint signals of coming missteps. In the first years when Hyman's vision was so narrowly focused on growing their initial business model, the company lost sight of improving metrics key to any service business: have what you offer in stock and in excellent shape (materials stretch, buttons go missing, a minor stain goes unnoticed), ship the correct product on time and to the right place, and make the customer whole when things go awry. The moment RTR began to address issues like these was also the moment a new management team was brought in and a new business model was launched that responded more effectively to customers' needs. Paying closer attention to early wins instead of losses could have allowed for more agile responses as strategies revealed weaknesses.

These two challenges—framing the wrong problem and failing to analyze past performance to drive future decisions—far too frequently undermine organizations' growth goals by depriving them of an actionable view of the road ahead. This is where leading drivers come in.

LEADING DRIVERS VS. LAGGING INDICATORS

How can we start looking ahead as far as possible to give us the time we need to make course corrections? Begin by focusing your radar on leading drivers rather than lagging indicators. In boardrooms across the globe, leaders meet and discuss reports that are obsolete before they hit the table, because they draw on lagging indicators, everything that is past. KPIs related to financial performance, like profit, revenue, and costs, are results of past activities of the team and the company. They are all lagging indicators. Likewise, an improved customer satisfaction measure (such as an NPS score) shows the result of initiatives taken in the past, not how well you are satisfying customers today.

Unless you're the Fed chairman, the economy isn't within your control. But access to economic drivers is. How and where we choose to invest, how we behave based on that information—all of this contributes greatly to organizational growth, or lack thereof. In the Co-Create future, not just acquiring but agilely manipulating data will make a fundamental difference. Movies like *Moneyball* (2011) and *The Big Short* (2015)—based on Michael Lewis's caustically hilarious examinations of, respectively, professional baseball and the recent housing bubble—have shown us how data analytics can separate winners from losers. Those who can draw actionable, real-time insights from the data gain a dramatic advantage over those who cannot. That's why, in the Co-Create economy, we need more roles like Insight Architects who can structure massive data collection, warehousing, reporting, and analysis so it becomes a real-time, insights-driven environment.

Of course, reviewing where you've been is essential—as exemplified by the win/loss analysis just discussed. But in the Co-Create economy, leading drivers of growth are the signposts we use to navigate. Leading drivers highlight the activities that are valid predictors of increased revenues and profits.

It's easy to measure lagging indicators, but it is very hard to improve upon them, or even influence them. Leading drivers, on the other hand, are often difficult to measure, but easy to influence. I think we can all relate to the experience of trying to lose a little weight. Stepping on the scale is a very clear lagging indicator that's easy to measure. You can't do anything now about what you ate in the last few months that led to the numbers on that scale. The way you are going to reach a diet goal is through the leading drivers of calorie intake, burn, and consistent exercise regimen. That's where data collection comes in, hence the popularity of wearable fitness devices, which ultimately make it easier to both measure and influence the leading drivers and make decisions accordingly. As in, put down the bacon burger, and run that extra mile.

Frankly, too many managers—and even senior executives—find it hard to believe that leading drivers can directly and immediately impact their business. They can. Leading drivers are measurable, they occur before you set your strategy, and they will highlight a particular pattern or trend, allowing you with a high degree of accuracy, and thus confidence, to predict the future and adjust your efforts and resources. (I am referring to personal, team, and entire organizational growth.)

There are general leading economic drivers that typically change before the economy as a whole changes. The Conference Board publishes its Leading Economic Index (LEI) that signals peaks and troughs in the business cycle for major economies, including the United States. The Organization for Economic Co-operation and Development produces the Composite Leading Indicators (CLIs) designed to provide early signals of turning points in business cycles with a focus on qualitative rather than quantitative information about short-term economic movements. If you listen to the business news, you are constantly hearing talk of such drivers, such as new business starts, building permits in the housing market, employment outlook, and stock market dynamic forecasts.

These are valid and highly respected, but in my relationship-centric view, you also need to identify specific leading drivers for your own business that measure the depth, breadth, and potential of your relationships with customers, talent, partners, investors, and other key stakeholders.

Figure 6.3: Leading vs. Lagging

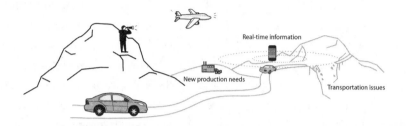

Real-time information

New production needs

Transportation issues

The Canyon and the Curve Ahead

When we learn to drive, we are taught early on to look as far ahead as possible, because it gives us more time to make necessary course corrections. As a motorcycle rider, I know that the sooner I understand the curve dynamics, see the potholes or other potential risks on the road, and observe the hills ahead, the more smoothly I can find reference points for my entry, apex, and exit points and thus the safer my ride will be. And yet, from a single point of view, only so much of the road ahead is within my view.

This is where Co-Creation reveals one of its strengths. Imagine you are in a car, driving through a mountain range. One of your partners, or perhaps a customer, is sitting on top of a mountain with binoculars, looking down at that stretch of winding road. They may not see the potholes, but they certainly see what's around the corner better than you can. Now, imagine you have a partner who's flying above and can see the entire landscape, and an employee of yours in a car who just traveled this route an hour ago. Now, imagine you all have Waze, the Co-Creation traffic and navigation app on which drivers share real-time traffic and road information. Through Co-Creation, you can monitor leading factors that affect your experience of the journey and your ability to reach your destination safely and without potential delays. An improved experience often leads to profitable growth.

Leading drivers are crucial to understanding what is ahead.

Co-Creation makes available certain leading drivers you wouldn't be able to monitor on your own.

Leading drivers must be outcome oriented. When an organization like ThyssenKrupp Elevator tries to improve its compliance with service level agreements (SLAs), the outcome that matters is the resolution of service issues within committed timeframes and expenses. Therefore, key leading drivers that could be shown on a dashboard might include the number of incidents reported, the percentage of open incidents older than two hours, the percentage older than one day, and the average backlog of incidents per agent. By monitoring these outcome-based key performance drivers (KPDs) every day, managers can work on identifying problem areas, improving them, and thus improving SLA compliance.

Will this require a culture shift? In some cases, certainly. But the payoff is a greater degree of confidence in the decisions made and more lead time to craft those decisions. Leading drivers are not one size fits all; what outcomes are worth monitoring on a dashboard will vary by function and by role.

To summarize: leading drivers are critical to organizations' upward spiral of growth because they give decision-makers longer runways—more time with more real-time insights—in which to make strategic choices. Of course, some are skeptical that leading drivers can ever be reliably identified and monitored, but I refute that view. General economic drivers are available, and it is possible to identify specific leading drivers in your own enterprise, as we'll see. The goal should be deployment of evolutionary performance dashboards displaying leading drivers in real time, customized to the needs of individuals and teams in a variety of roles.

EXTERNAL AND INTERNAL LEADING DRIVERS

Earlier in this chapter I listed the leading drivers I find most valuable: sentiment, reputation, and engagement. These are leading drivers of stakeholders' experiences external to an organization, but they also impact its performance. We will consider these first, then move on to two that are internal-facing leading drivers—those concerning buying-cycle alignment and human-capital development.

SENTIMENT

Can an organization measure how people feel about it? Yes. By listening louder, as I discussed in chapter 2, an organization can produce a meaningful metric comprised of the polarity of sentiment (positive, neutral, or negative) and the degree of fervor with which that sentiment is felt. Sentiment analysis is most easily applied to social media channels, where blogs, review sites, discussion groups, etc., collect the views expressed by "ordinary people," creating actionable data.

Sentiment analysis makes it possible to capture nuances that are too often lost in more traditional customer satisfaction surveys or NPS® scores. I recently flew from Atlanta to San Francisco. Gates? Might as well be a cattle call. The inflight Wi-Fi (that I pay $500 a year to access) was not available on that five-hour flight. The fourteen announcements over my headphones were often repetitive and way too loud. Yet Delta keeps sending me stale customer satisfaction surveys that ask, "How were the flight attendants?" They were fine! It was the rest of the experience that had me gritting my teeth. Delta is surveying me about the wrong thing! It's the "wrong type of cabin"—flaws in framing—all over again.

In digital conversations, consumers focus on whatever feature of the product, service, idea, or experience is bugging (or thrilling) them at that very moment. In late 2015 in the United Kingdom, Barclays Bank launched Pingit, a mobile payment service available as an app, which created lots of initial social media buzz because it made sending money to someone as easy as knowing their phone number. Using data analytics from Our Social Times to decode every post, tweet, share, like, chat, and text, they realized they had miscalculated how useful the app would be to one group of users—parents wanting to transfer funds to their minor children. They quickly added this functionality so that even younger kids with Barclays accounts could benefit, and thus captured the good feelings of a group of customers who would have been otherwise dissatisfied.[5]

Sentiment analysis can tease apart distinctions in natural language. Cognitive computing (which I speak about in the next chapter) will accelerate that capacity. This opens up the possibility of a more finely grained understanding of consumers' perceptions, feelings, and potential to influence others' calls to action.

REPUTATION

As the demand for transparency increases in the Co-Create economy, the impact of reputation becomes even stronger, affecting one's intention to buy from a company, join a company, or invest in a company. The higher the dollar amount of the investment, the more importance and priority the unmet need is given, the more reputation matters.

Particularly in purchase decisions, reputation matters a great deal (as it does in any kind of strategic relationship). When I look at Glass Ceiling.com to consider you as a potential employer, or I do my due diligence on your investment prospectus, your reputation is a critical facet of your value proposition.

In the digital world, reputation is oxygen. You cannot influence others without it. Klout developed its social media analytics platform, which ranks its users according to their perceived social influence, because of the importance of reputation. Each user is assigned a "Klout Score" with a value between 1 and 100. Individuals use Lithium Technologies' Klout services to improve the impact of their social activity and measure the value of their earned social media reputation, while brands use the Lithium platform to reach influencers and design user experiences for maximum social engagement.[6] I'm uncertain as to Klout's accuracy (if I drink coffee every day and tweet about it, does that make me a coffee connoisseur with a respectable Klout score in coffee? On the other hand, I've been a student of business relationships for over two decades, write and speak extensively on the topic, and my Klout score is 65 out of a possible 100!) and thus long-term viability, but it is an interesting perspective.

ENGAGEMENT

Engagement is a critical leading driver, because it is the closest approximation we have of mindshare. If you are not getting mindshare, it is highly unlikely you'll get wallet-share.

Online, engagement is largely about measuring interaction with content: clicks, bounce rates, time on site, downloads, page views, likes, shares, posts, reposts, tweets, comments, etc. Offline, engagement is about inviting consumers of our value into active involvement and relationship with the brand, then measuring the frequency and fervor with which those invitations are accepted.

Lithium Technologies actually goes a few steps further than just managing reputation and reaching influencers, for they help companies—large and small, tech, retail, and B2B—create authentic online communities where there are spaces for more interactions—and the growth of reputation through engagement. For Best Buy, the $45 billion electronics and tech product retailer, they built the "Best Buy Community," where customers can communicate directly with Blue Shirts, Geek Squad Agents, community teams, and, importantly, other customers. Customers interact with like-minded others, posing questions, rating answers, awarding "kudos," and judging the best replies as "accepted solutions." They may not have "bought" anything and may have even come with a beef, but the result is the Best Buy Community's opportunity to find a solution, and that solution raises the company's reputation and creates value, deepening the relationship on all sides.

Monitoring engagement as a leading driver requires you to mine data about consumers' interaction with your brand, online and off. A ready example of the importance of engagement as a leading driver comes from membership associations, where associations can stay relevant to those engaged members who Co-Create innovation over time. Engagement is a reliable indication that members perceive value, receive value, and experience value's impact in their lives. Engagement leads to the belief that "I am better off because I belong to this association."

Engagement is what you choose to invest in, volunteer for, buy, and buy into. Engagement reflects what individuals choose to prioritize. At the same time, if you, your products, your team, or your services are not among your key stakeholders' priorities, your future relevance is in question.

Sentiment, reputation, and engagement are leading drivers of what stakeholders are thinking, what they trust and care about, what they prioritize. A finger on that pulse is essential to your innovation and marketing functions, and thus to all the operational units that support those functions. This is why external-facing leading drivers belong on an evolutionary performance dashboard.

Internal Leading Drivers: Buying-Cycle Alignment and High Performers/High Potentials

Buying-cycle alignment and high performers and high potentials are internal-facing leading drivers rather than external, because they are about what fuels your organization's innovation engine, not just its go-to-market strategy.

Buying-Cycle Alignment: Whether they call it a sales process, a funnel, or a cycle, too many organizations monitor *how they sell*, not *how customers buy*. Your customers and other key stakeholders have their own processes, as I discussed in chapter 4. Aligning the buying cycle means increasing efficiency and effectiveness in meeting buyers where they are in their Customer Experience Journey. To recap, in a Co-Create enterprise we see purchasing (or any kind of uptake—of ideas, credibility, repute, or even something more transactional such as employment) as the medium in which transformative relationships take place. When we become so aligned that we perceive and fulfill the unmet need of another anywhere on the cycle, the recipient of the value often becomes an evangelist and goes on to influence others. This is how customer retention drives the upward spiral of growth.

One way of measuring buying-cycle alignment is by monitoring customer on- and off-ramps, where customers step into or out of some kind of interaction with us, at which point we should ask: What unmet need might we fill, what conversation might we elicit, what demonstration might we make to engage this customer in Co-Creation? Sometimes a solution is very simple: think McDonald's and all-day breakfast. If I can't get an Egg McMuffin at 10:00 p.m., I'm not going to McDonald's. That negative association may still linger the next time I want a fast-food meal, rendering me less likely to patronize the restaurant. Listening to years of customer requests (and complaints), the company did an about-face. After the spring launch of all-day breakfast in 2015, the earnings-challenged chain reported a 5 percent rise in sales by early 2016.[7]

High Performers and High Potentials: If you don't have rising talent stars within your organization, it doesn't much matter how well you are performing with external stakeholders. High performers and high potentials are leading driver metrics of your organization's ability to meet and exceed customer expectations going forward. You must identify those in your organization who consistently exceed even the highest expectations when it comes to engaging and influencing the thinking and calls to action of your customers. Similarly, which individuals show a stronger level of commitment and eagerness to learn and grow with your brand, and have a work ethic to match? In those functions most susceptible to employee turnover, are you adequately protected by the quality of high performers and high potentials on those teams?

One easy way to apply this metric is to look at the front and back doors. Applicants across all levels should come from a solid educational foundation where they were challenged with critical thinking (a badly missing developmental asset from many of our academic institutions), have experience at high-value competitors, and, if recruited, ideally have some experience of and history with your company through on-campus contacts and internships. In other words, you shouldn't be the first one to recognize their intellect and ambition. Who's applying for equivalent positions at your competitors? Examining who is moving on—and why—is also informative. Some birds are ready to leave the nest because they love challenging roles and are always learning—and your company may no longer provide that for them. Others might be stuck, complacent, or unwilling to take on new workplace challenges—or they might not be a good fit in terms of culture.

For that new hire, what your organization and that individual Co-Create is a job with all its various implied relationships; for the company, it's all the value that the individual's knowledge, experience, and personal passion brings to his or her role every single day.

While sentiment, reputation, and engagement analysis is becoming more widely used, you are unlikely to find buying-cycle alignment or high performer/high potential talent appearing on any list of leading drivers. But if you accept my premise that a company lives or dies by its strategic relationships, the importance of these leading drivers should be abundantly clear. The challenge is to collect, analyze, and display that information in simple visualizations on dashboards adapted to the needs of individuals and teams across functional areas.

EXISTING, IMPENDING, AND CREATED NEEDS

Remember that the ultimate goal of KPD metrics is to fuel your upward spiral of growth. I expect you to use these KPDs to anticipate emerging needs among existing customers (and therefore new prospects like them) and respond with frequent innovations that keep you an object of interest.

There is a range to your target market's types of need, and the premium to you increases the higher you ascend that scale. At the lower end are the customers' *existing* needs—whatever it is they know they need, whatever value they are actively looking for. If it's 8:00 a.m. and you're a coffee-drinker, caffeine is an existing need. *Impending* needs are those your potential customers have thought of but are not urgently seeking. At 8:00 p.m., tomorrow's cup of coffee is only an impending need. *Created* needs are those your market has never even imagined. If it's 8:00 a.m. and I invite you to an invigorating group cycling class, you might discover that you focus better and get more done thanks to the neurological effects of the competitive group cycling. Aha! I've created a need for you. Tomorrow, you'll call me and ask when are we going to the next class. Created needs come from strokes of insight that take ideas to a whole new level.

At the "existing" end of this scale, offerings are not unique. If a need is impending, however, there are fewer solutions offered. Thus, value increases. If you can create the need, you become a priority, an object of interest. Your target market becomes incredibly receptive to your value and loyal to you as its provider. The uniqueness of the group cycling class compels you to inquire about the very next opportunity. You begin to explore other forms of unique and challenging cycling experiences. You purchase a road bicycle and get involved with a local cycling club to train for an upcoming road race. You subscribe to cycling magazines and even attend a consumer show all about cycling for more education and opportunities to enhance your overall experience with cycling. Now I'm your go-to cycling guy.

The Co-Create economy demands a much deeper knowledge of your customers' experiences. Day by day, what are they struggling with? What do they need? If there is no need, you have a solution looking for a problem. If there is a need, but many other people can fill it just as well as you can, you have a commodity. Ultimately, the relationships that generate sustained results for both sides are the ones that are grounded in Co-Creation of new value. They arise from your ability to understand others' needs and demonstrate how you uniquely can address them.

This is where adaptive innovation (chapter 2) thrives, at the edge of business where the voices of the recipients of your value can be heard the loudest.

When a customer contacts you with an RFP for the solution you sell, that's an existing need. You may be proud of the reputation that made them seek you out. But don't be too pleased—you weren't invited into Co-Creation of the value they seek. You just lost an important differentiator. It doesn't take a leading driver to detect an existing need.

Impending needs give you some advance notice, some time to prepare to accommodate them, if you have been paying attention to leading drivers. Impending needs are when the customer is in the canyon but you're perched up high and can see around the curve ahead. How can you, with the known present, extrapolate the future, start anticipating what's coming next for your customers and key stakeholders?

Start having those conversations now. The impending need you bring to their attention—this sharing the advantage of future need—is a tremendous enhancer of loyalty, and an invitation to collaborative Co-Creation that may be transformative for both sides.

In a sense, filling an impending need can be an upsell, often an if/then equation. If you've hired me to do the software upgrade on your content management system (CMS), then this might be a great opportunity for us to offer new training/retraining. That ups your company's efficiency and hence performance, and raises our relationship in your eyes, making any further unique suggestions I make potentially that much more attractive.

But created needs are where legends are born. When you create a need, the recipients of that value have never even thought about it. Created needs are category makers. Consider recent tablet devices. Steve Jobs famously created a fantastically successful separate product category in tablets by recognizing that we needed something that bridged the gap between smartphone and laptop. In terms of fueling your growth spiral, creating a need has proven to deliver a significant premium. When you begin to truly understand created needs, you see them everywhere. Bottled water, increasingly capable smartphones, on-demand video and audio services, YouTube, Match.com, Spotify, the cronut, same-day delivery, Amazon Prime—these are just a few examples. Look at them all and realize that they aren't individual products; they are often categories that did not previously exist.

Looking Beyond the Buyer

Your understanding of existing, impending, and created needs is most relevant in the customer/vendor equation, but the same concept applies with employees. Creating a job for an employee instead of finding a warm body to fill a job description is one important way to exercise Co-Creation in the talent department.

Let's say that on a campus-recruiting visit, you meet an incredibly talented individual. Your first thoughts are probably, "How can I plug this person into an existing opening?" But then you realize talent of this caliber would be bored in that position after six months. The answer is to create a job. But you do it with them. Co-Create. Focus on the outcome: "Here's where we're trying to take the organization. Why don't you come spend the summer with us and let's figure out where you'll be most challenged."

As a leader, I need to realize how to take you—as you come—and craft a development program that gets you working with the smartest people. Because this is what the exceptional companies, the Googles and Intels and LEGOs of the world, are doing.

Investments work the same way. Before an investor considers a company, they ask for a use-of-funds statement. Typically, investors want to put that money into acquiring more customers to spur revenue growth.

The investor and the company put their heads together, based on the experience on both sides of the table, based on market dynamics, to discuss the best use of those funds to accomplish that goal. What's the best way to dramatically grow the customer base? Create a need.

It's rarefied air in that space. You're not competing with anyone else. You have elevated the perception of the impact, the outcome you create. You are no longer lost in the noise. Of course, it's easier said than done. It requires a greater investment in the ecosystem—understanding not just the buyers' experience journey but also the evolving industry dynamics, the company culture, the team strengths, and the individuals leading key initiatives.

The connection should now be increasingly clear between dashboards showing KPDs based on leading drivers and the process of adaptive innovation I described in chapter 2. All that listening louder, identifying faint signals, validating critical assumptions, and iterating pilots and prototypes is designed, as you'll recall, to keep the pace of innovation matched to, or even a step ahead of, the pace at which customers themselves evolve.

The fuel propelling your upward spiral of growth is essentially this: access to real-time, relevant leading drivers that help you identify or, better yet, create future needs that you then fill better than anyone else. Your reward will be customer evangelists who make you an object of interest with increasing Market Gravity.

Now it's time to talk about how, exactly, the individuals throughout your organization keep their eyes on that prize. The answer is evolutionary performance dashboards.

EVOLUTIONARY PERFORMANCE DASHBOARDS

The Co-Create economy challenges companies to become much more proactive through the use of evolutionary dashboards, customized to the needs of different roles, and fed by a river of data from leading drivers. This is the only way to achieve the kind of near-real-time business intelligence the new paradigm demands. Dashboards of the future must be geared to evolution and adaptive innovation, most significantly to a refocusing on the greatest off-balance-sheet asset of any company—strategic relationships. To bring about this sea change in the use of data visualization, companies are going to need a new role at the leadership level—the insight architect.

First, let's take a closer look at what's wrong with current practice, how that might be transformed, and who will be needed to make that transformation come about.

What Is Wrong with Today's Dashboards?

Unfortunately, the dashboards I've seen in use—when they are in use at all, which is another problem—are designed around lagging indicators. Thus, they are less functional than they should be, while also tending to be available only to a few people, with those few often quite far from the customer. In short, they are based on flawed premises concerning what the content should be, who should have it, and what they should do with that content. For example, the CTO might be able to tell that every device under his purview is functioning, but the tech in the van can't see that she's driving past an account with a recurring IT issue.

The Co-Create world demands much greater transparency. The sooner every individual whose efforts impact strategic goals has access to actionable insights, the better for the organization. If you want employees, customers, partners—any of your key stakeholders—to genuinely, authentically, join in the process of Co-Creation, you must give them the data that will help them think and act differently. Candor is more critical than ever. Numbers seldom lie. Dashboards tailored to role should be available to everyone from the front line to mahogany row—but sadly, this is almost never the case.

Sadly, too many of today's dashboards are designed to reflect the past, not give a view into the future. They draw their numbers from organizational structures and accounting mechanisms that produce data based on a point in time that is already history. They are not aligned with what's really happening.

How users consume dashboard information can also be problematic. We don't have a common language to share the insights. Take a simple question like, "How many employees do we have?" If the answer is, "It depends," that's a problem. Something that should be definitive, black or white, is instead variable. "Are you talking about full-time employees only, or do you want a count that includes part-time as well?" "Are we talking about independent contractors as well as staff?" "Are we including the international teams or just talking domestic?" When every driver on the dashboard requires a conversation to properly understand it, the visual display has flunked its assignment. Dashboards customized to specific roles address this flaw. In other words, perhaps a breakdown of all the different kinds of employees is only useful to HR managers of truly large companies, where they're tasked with tracking personnel for purposes of payroll, benefits, and headcount goals. On other department managers' dashboards, that number would be less fine grained. On the other hand, the HR manager's dashboard might show only top-level sales figures by product line, while the operation manager's dashboard might show cost of labor, materials, and shrinkage during transportation.

Content that is contextually relevant is critical. One of the most powerful capabilities of a forward-thinking dashboard is the ability to explore "what if?" scenarios. In almost every instance there are levers that could, in real time, be pulled to modify and influence outcomes. Here's what I'm talking about. If you're an IT customer-service manager of an international organization, you're going to want warnings of large-scale weather events as far in advance as possible. Because *if* your customers are hit with power outages and for some reason backup systems fail, you're going to need extra personnel on hand to weather the tech storm. Who has training in handling the complex infrastructure? Now you're not just prepared, you're ahead of the game, and your SLAs will be fulfilled. An evolutionary performance dashboard allows you to simulate different scenarios, without adding undue complexity. I have seen very few existing dashboards that allow this kind of drill-down for thoughtful interaction with the content and context, in real time.

TRANSFORMING OUR USE OF DASHBOARDS

If we are going to put the right content where it can be consumed by the right roles, we need to seriously consider the following questions:

1. **Who's the audience for this specific dashboard?** What data do these individuals need to make their decisions? This is why dashboards must be role specific.
2. **What does this role care about?** What decisions are individuals in this role responsible for, and what data and insights might they need?
3. **What information do we have?** Taking into account my earlier recommendations regarding external and internal leading drivers, what metrics can you produce? At what level of frequency and granularity?
4. **What information is missing?** You may not have a method to collect leading drivers yet. How will you close that gap? Note that the data you choose to include in any dashboard will almost certainly come from multiple sources. How will you combine

Figure 6.4: Dashboard Example

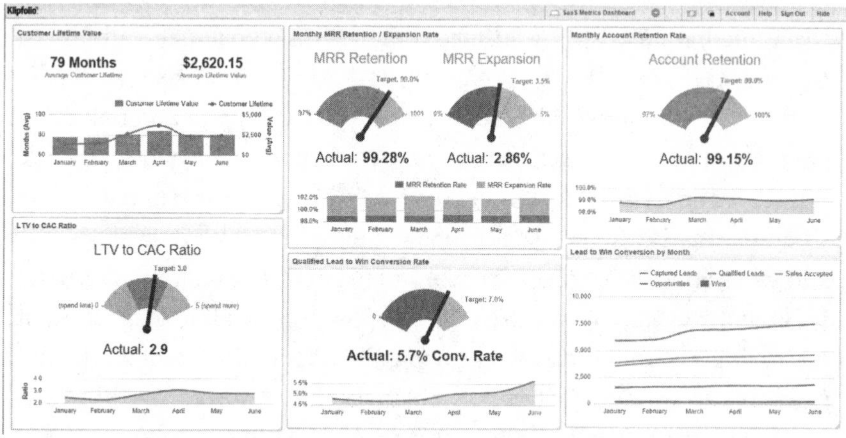

A sample Klipfolio social marketing dashboard.

that raw information into displays that easily yield actionable insights?

5. **How can we make it real time?** Prepare for an organizational mind-set shift, from just monitoring lagging indicators to anticipating real-time leading drivers.

6. **How can we make it mobile?** Most of us are not tethered to our desks, so our dashboards need to be mobile, and I don't just mean mobile access to a desktop application. Think about the real estate available on your smartphone: you can't easily draw insights from a spreadsheet with thirty-six rows and seventy-five columns. How can a dashboard display the information I need, at the time of my choosing, and on the device of my choice?

7. **What is the frame of reference?** Year over year, month over month, North America vs. Latin America? Data almost always raises the question, in comparison to what?

8. **What is the trend?** Likewise, dashboards should make it easy to connect the dots between leading drivers and current trends, between past indicators and anticipated future performance. I am baffled by how many clients tell me that "business is fantastic" but can't explain exactly why and how.

Figure 6.4 shows a social media marketing dashboard from a clever company called Klipfolio, with information that is very helpful to the social media manager, social media marketing personnel from top to bottom, and also strategic planning and sales overall. Social media staff has the budget to buy Google AdWords and run Facebook campaigns and boosts, as well as to engage customers across platforms like Pinterest and Twitter and to make short videos for YouTube. Because some of this is pay-per-click (PPC), they need to know what works and what doesn't in order to nimbly adjust and tune their marketing.

Of course, this is just the first screen, and behind it lies a world of increasingly granular information to guide everything from marketing segments to product design to website user experience. Within each venue, the user can determine what kind of device a customer is using; where they've come from and where they're going; their physical location; how much time is spent on a page or site; and can delve more deeply into engagement. They can track Google AdWords ROI, and its real-time version can help sales and marketing follow short-term trends, particularly around events like product introductions or service and product upgrades.

With a dashboard designed in response to these questions, whatever your role, you will have content and a mode to consume it that makes it far easier to understand *why* something is happening, not just *what* is happening. An evolutionary performance dashboard has the functionality to explore hypothetical scenarios, and to drill down into the data. So sales are trending up in California? I double-click to explore why and discover that municipalities are buying our software to track and control water use after a new round of statewide restrictions. Is there perhaps a way to adapt our software to craft an app for homeowners? Where else is there drought and can we access that market? I see we have a customer there who bought more from us in the current quarter than ever before. What drove that purchasing? What does that customer know that we need to know? That our other clients could benefit from knowing? By carrying out these sorts of analyses throughout the value chain—and this is the real power of Co-Creation—insights begin to emerge. You are not just learning more about your operation but also about the ripple effects your value proposition has through the value chain.

Mobile, real-time, contextually relevant, interactive—an evolutionary performance dashboard makes visible the impact on strategic outcomes of the activity of the entire ecosystem around a company, including its customers, internal teams, suppliers, and even the media.

FRAMING SMAC—SOCIAL, MOBILE, ANALYTICS, CLOUD

In 2005, tech writers Michael Copeland and Om Malik declared that the "epic technological transformation" of cheap, powerful computer hardware (especially handheld devices), broadband internet access from almost anywhere, and a general sense of "technological openness" had ushered in computing's "fifth wave."[8] Technological advances in the last decade have had far greater impact on the way we conduct business than the previous fifty years, they predicted—and I still agree. However, today's version is slightly more complex than even the future that Malik and Copeland sketched out in *Business 2.0*. This can be attributed to four fundamental drivers of change, which are referred to by the acronym SMAC:

1. Social
2. Mobile
3. Analytics
4. Cloud.

Each (separately and together) is disrupting business and revenue models. Big Data strategist Mark van Rijmenam breaks down the key components of SMAC into analytical categories, using the human body as a leading metaphor. Social, he says, is like the hands, constantly interacting and sharing; mobile uses the senses, connecting with the world to take in the external environment. As for analytics, they're the brain of the operation, and cloud is like the skeleton—intangible as the cloud is, it is still the structure that holds everything together.[9]

SMAC is not wishful thinking. "The convergence of Social, Mobility, Analytics and Cloud will lead business technology for the next decade," van Rijmenam assures us, and SMAC will act as "an enabler for the next generation of technological trends." As entire industries and business models are increasingly becoming digitized, "market leaders are information-based, implementing a SMAC stack; an integrated technology platform where the combined components are greater than the sum of their parts."[10] Deployment of SMAC technologies can be tied directly to business impact. That impact can be visualized on a KPD dashboard, and thus used to drive decision-making. SMAC can fuel an upward spiral of growth.

I frame the topic of SMAC technologies in terms of their impact on individuals, teams, and organizations. I will ask you to consider the application of these technologies in your business: What are you doing today, and what will become part of your strategy for the future? How will you think big but start small and find a way to scale?

By visualizing a matrix (as shown in figure 6.4), you can readily see how these questions apply.

Let's take a closer look at the four technologies that comprise SMAC, including their significance for the individual, the team, and the organization.

Social: Social media is about collaboration, collective learning, and the collective experience. Effective use of social media results in opt-in knowledge management at scale instead of the often ignored "Reply All." As an individual, you should be finding ways to leverage social media to learn, work out loud, and listen louder. Google alerts on relevant topics, for example, keep you on top of trends, and following industry thought leaders through their tweets, posts, and blogs always gives you something to think—and talk—about. As a team, put in place social environments that share the different team members' experiences and access to insights for greater team efficiency and effectiveness. A team might have, for example, a closed Facebook group dedicated to a single, confidential project but also a collaboration page where partners outside the company are invited to participate. That social environment should be infused throughout your organization and across its relationships to become part of your value proposition. Some CEOs have a "morning tweet," and many companies have monthly e-newsletters that offer global content that is relevant to all.

Mobile: As an individual, you should be familiar with common mobile apps, and you may already engage with some of them (Waze, Uber, Snapchat, WhatsApp) for several reasons. When you capture your own user behaviors—what works for you, why you use certain apps and not others—you are part of the conversation, the community, and can learn enormous amounts of leading-edge information. Do you understand that very important "front-page real estate," where the apps that most impact our daily lives reside?

At the team level, you should be using mobile apps to disseminate information and insights to all members and leveraging the apps for team collaboration in real time. For instance, apps simplify many of the routine frustrations of collaboration, like scheduling a meeting where participants span time zones. How many cycles have you wasted to clarify the meeting is at 8:00 a.m. in San Francisco, 11:00 a.m. in Atlanta, and 4:00 p.m. in London?

As an enterprise, making mobile apps a communication channel for actionable insights is a must. Start with internal stakeholders, and then move to external audiences. Do members of your value chain, from supply partners to distributors and field reps, use mobile effectively? Maybe there is value you can offer in changing behavior for an improved experience, even, or especially, when that means opening a platform directly to customers' use and input. If you're a vendor and share a common inventory app, you can reduce a customer's monthly order when you know they would otherwise be overstocked. Maybe that leads to a conversation about why an item isn't selling in certain locations, which then leads to smarter distribution and product innovation to address geographical and seasonal preferences. As an organization, do you offer mobile payments? This isn't just about B2C. Once consumers discover a unique personal utility, they often want to integrate it into their business at the office, making that mobile payment functionality very relevant to B2B users as well.

Are you using mobile effectively to communicate between customers, corporate, and a distributed workforce? Here is an example of a less-than-effective attempt to deploy mobile at the organizational level. A company gave an iPhone 6 with a trouble ticket app to all its field technicians, who quickly came to feel that the "half-baked" mobile app added very little value. Concerned about carrying so many devices, the technicians began to leave the company iPhones in their cars. Then a centralized dispatch tried to send a trouble ticket to one of those iPhones, which was in the car, and you can take it from there. By turning those smart devices into a dumb terminal thanks to a poorly designed mobile app, the company's initiative failed.

You should be thinking deeply about how you can use mobile to improve your business, make it much more real-time, and bring your workforce closer to your customers. If you need a place to start, look to companies who have learned how to effectively engage consumers on their mobile devices.

Analytics: The data available to businesses continues to grow rapidly in quantity and quality, leading to deployment of analytics to cluster, segment, score, and predict scenarios. Analytics guides strategic decision-making, as discussed earlier in this chapter. What use of information can you create for yourself in order to fundamentally improve your team's or your organization's ability to drive growth in the Co-Create economy? Analytics requires bringing together data from multiple sources into a repository or warehouse, and this leads to the fourth driver.

Cloud: Social, mobile, and analytics are no longer constrained by geography. You are not physically bound by software that has to be installed on a server, or those shiny discs we used to call CDs, which now make fantastic Christmas tree decorations and keep the birds off the fruit trees in the garden. The cloud gives us access to content across multiple devices and platforms. With cloud storage I can edit a file in Kuala Lumpur that I created in Atlanta. As an individual, you should be leveraging the cloud, increasing efficiency and productivity with the tools it offers. Bring your team into a public or private cloud environment—perhaps by collaborating with tools like Basecamp, Dropbox, or Atlassian. As an organization, focus on increasing access for internal and external constituents using cloud technology. Tools are out there; you just have to find the right ones. A common discovery is that, by moving to the cloud, you can gain cost efficiencies through reduced infrastructure.

Technology Must Become More Strategic

I'm working with two clients now where IT appears to care more about blocking people from watching YouTube videos than disrupting themselves with deployment of SMAC for strategic advantage. We're not talking about Bob's Bicycle Shop; I'm having this conversation with the CEO of a fifteen-thousand-employee, $8 billion company. There is a seat missing at the C-suite's table, and it's not IT as we've known it, but rather the insight architect. Every key initiative is being held back by a lack of insight from technology. Technology is critical to the success of Co-Creation, in many ways: security, business intelligence, mobile apps, data warehousing and analytics, digital marketing, infrastructure—the list goes on. These are the nutrients of the Co-Create economy organization, and we need them in place everywhere, at every level of the company, for it to live and thrive.

Put simply, technology has that much more impact when it works in real time. Walmart and Procter & Gamble collaborated to improve their supply chain management, with a goal of eliminating excess inventory and increasing sales. Through better sharing of information between the two organizations, they were able to collaboratively forecast when to replenish P&G products in Walmart's stores. The two firms were better able to understand their retailers and their consumers, and they made better decisions as a result.[11]

Think of the ripple effect of that kind of information exchange throughout the supply chain—how we get the right products into the right locations, how we merchandise those products with other products.

Co-Creation and SMAC: Travelport Labs Accelerator Case Study

Can SMAC really be relevant to the most mature companies in the most mature industries—companies that came of age long before computers leapt off our desktops and into our pockets, cars, and home appliances? The example of Travelport, introduced in chapter 5, suggests that the answer is yes. Let's apply the SMAC framework to the innovations coming out of the company's Co-Creation initiatives.

Two times per year, the Travelport Labs Accelerator enrolls a few start-ups into its program. Let's view six companies from the first cohort through the lens of SMAC, as shown in table 6.1. (Note, I have only credited these companies with cloud technology if it is part of the value proposition of their customer experience. Simply using the cloud for back-shop operations isn't enough—even your dog's

Table 6.1: How 6 of Travelport's Start-Up Companies Score on SMAC

Start-Ups	Social	Mobile	Analytics	Cloud
Unboundly: Flight search engine designed to ignore cozy airline partnerships and analyze routes to find flights for less. Social is the primary means by which Unboundly acquires customers.	•		•	•
Asemblr: Platform designed to make booking an event much faster and cheaper, with access to vetted local suppliers and live customer support. Cloud-based technology is critical to the link between Asemblr and its suppliers, the hotels.		•	•	•
Livingua: App that provides real-time, on-demand travel guidance from hand-picked locals and translation services via VOIP and geolocation, utilizing the sharing economy model.	•	•		
Neibbor: Empowers local businesses to work better together by making the process of exchanging referrals seamless and transparent.	•	•	•	
PicThrive: Helps tour operators and outfitters maximize photo sales, social sharing, and customer reviews, to drive new bookings. PicThrive will analyze sales across the market and recommend pricing to their customers.	•	•	•	•
Tagible: Digital marketing platform that uses hyper-local video content that encourages potential customers to take action and book trips, thereby increasing travel companies' bookings.	•	•	•	•

While not all Travelport-funded start-ups use all SMAC channels, note the heavy involvement in SMAC by these start-ups.

groomer is doing that by now. Using cloud for file storage is table stakes, not news.)

How You Respond Will Make or Break Your Upward Spiral

SMAC has tremendous potential to create competitive advantages for the companies that lead their industry. We can't depend on CIOs alone to drive this game-changer. Technology must become more strategic, which means we need technologists who understand business and CEOs who understand SMAC.

The topics in this chapter focus on various aspects of using insightful KPDs to fuel your organization's growth. Leading drivers, internal and external, need to be customized to specific roles and made easy to use through visual representation on dashboards. This creates the capacity for adaptive innovation, through sensing and filling existing, impending, and created needs. We need information architects on the board and at the executive table because SMAC technology is driving disruption for every enterprise, and your response will either set the course of your upward spiral or leave you on the sidelines.

TOOL 6: SMAC MATRIX

The Co-Create Toolkit PDF, available to you to download for free from CoCreateBook.com is intended to help you apply some of the key ideas you've just read in this chapter.

Co-created growth is transformational, because it yields net-new opportunities: previously untapped markets, customer segments, or audiences, or game-changing disruption to the value chain. The SMAC Matrix offers a lens through which to view any Co-Created market opportunity and potentially discover, facilitate, enable, or accelerate that next innovation in which the result is much greater than the sum of its parts.

This tool is designed to help you uncover the opportunities to Co-Create a market opportunity related to social, mobile, analytics, or cloud technology.

Chapter Six Takeaways

- Use leading drivers to give you sufficient advance notice to make strategic decisions and course corrections.
- Monitor key performance drivers (KPDs) using dashboards that display metrics for leading drivers of growth.
- Customize the dashboards for individuals in different roles, reflecting how their contributions drive business results.
- Use data from KPDs to anticipate new customer needs and respond with frequent innovations that help you remain an "object of interest."
- Demand strategic technology that leverages "SMAC"—social, mobile, analytics, and cloud—to drive competitive advantage.

SEVEN

CO-CREATE AWAY: CREATING EXCEPTIONAL
EXPERIENCES AND ORGANIZATIONS

 In this chapter you will learn:

- What ever-increasing customer expectations mean for organizations;
- How technology is disrupting organizations, but also giving organizations the tools to respond to that disruption;
- Why cognitive computing's incredible potential is the next major revolution, and how to harness it; and
- How cognitive computing elevates Co-Creation.

The Co-Create model requires constant vigilance, because every day new developments raise customers' already high expectations to even greater heights. These rising expectations are leading drivers of what we expect in all areas of our economic lives—at the workplace, in B2B dealings, and within professional communities. They're also likely to mirror those faint signals we discussed in chapter 2, the tiny blips that eventually drive adaptive innovation. In hindsight, they seem obvious, but in the daily whirlwind, they are easily missed—unless you're looking very carefully.

To get a sense of the kinds of new developments I am talking about, consider Catapult, a wearable technology for elite athletes. For several seasons, championship teams in the NFL, NBA, and NCAA have been using Catapult to monitor their athletes' health. The company has brought an evidence-based scientific approach to physical performance, creating the world's first analytics platform for athletes. The insight behind that development? We're all familiar with the image of the fantastically fit athlete on the treadmill, mouth and nose covered with a device to measure oxygen consumption, leads taped to chest and arms to monitor other functions. But performance on a treadmill may not be informative about performance in the actual sport—pole-vaulters, divers, sprinters, pro golfers, all must be monitored in unique ways most relevant to the physical demands of their sport. Catapult recognized that athletes must be monitored in their natural environment, exerting themselves as they would in competition if the resulting data is to be useful.

Catapult essentially took the lab to the athlete—and by doing so, raised expectations of what wearable fitness monitors could be and do. The company's devices measure things like an athlete's movement efficiency, range of motion, and power. This data stream can be analyzed to uncover whether an athlete might be about to develop an injury, or whether a certain workout is a poor fit for that individual's body and condition. The data stream "helps teams keep their players safe and game-ready," reports *Fast Company*, which included Catapult on its Most Innovative Companies list in early 2015.[1]

Catapult demonstrated spectacular application of the SMAC framework I discussed in the last chapter, combining social, mobile, analytics, and cloud technology to deliver functionality that lifts its clients to the height of competitive advantage on the playing field. Imagine what might happen if the geniuses behind Catapult find a way to marry this deeply disruptive technology with **cognitive computing**—the self-learning systems that use data mining, pattern recognition, and natural-language processing to solve problems and make recommendations. Imagine someone like LeBron James receiving coaching support in real time, mid-game, from his Catapult fitness tracker.

Nourcabulary

Cognitive computing refers to hardware and software that mimics the learning and analytical skills of the human brain. Cognitive computing (also referred to as artificial intelligence or deep learning) is often applied to improve human decision-making.

Now, take that "what-if" scenario one step further. Imagine that LeBron and his teammates, the NBA staff, a handful of knowledgeable fans from midcourt, team owners, and some heavy hitters from the sports media all contributed to the creation of whatever new innovation Catapult derives to disrupt itself before other fitness device makers get a chance. That might be a revolutionary fitness regime, or perhaps a coaching app that puts your favorite player's voice in your ear, or a device that heads off concussions in teen sports or helps veterans retrain their brains and bodies after traumatic brain injury. That is the promise of collaborative Co-Creation, and that type of disruption is the premise of this chapter.

The technology behind cognitive computing is facilitating collaborative Co-Creation that creates exceptional experiences for consumers, even as the "exceptional" bar becomes increasingly difficult to clear. Let's start—where else?—with the Consumer Experience Journey.

CONSTANTLY RISING EXPECTATIONS

Consumers' expectations of their experiences are constantly ratcheting up. It only takes a few extraordinary interactions to start us thinking—why aren't more of my experiences this great? For me, this epiphany came in a butcher shop in Iran on an ordinary day in 1994. I had gone back to see my parents for the first time since leaving home over two decades earlier. A couple days after I arrived, I accompanied my dad on his round of errands in the market. We walked into one particular butcher shop. We were served a glass of tea, and my father sat chatting with other customers while the butcher prepared his order. When we got home, my mother removed the paper wrapping. I was surprised to see that the meat, typically sold in bulk, had already been prepared in just the way my mother likes for her stew. The fat was trimmed away from the three different cuts of meat, which were tenderized and wrapped in high-quality wax paper that didn't stick to the contents. I asked my father how long he had been going to that butcher. "Since the butcher was his grandfather," he replied. Even though this grandson was new to the family business, he fundamentally understood the value of creating an exceptional customer experience.

That story is from thirty years ago, in what many would call a Third World country; this notion of exceptional customer experience is certainly not new. But making it part of the culture of a company, weaving it into the fabric that defines every aspect of that culture, is still more of an aspiration than a reality for far too many organizations. You may also think that the butcher shop is a small, local mom-and-pop business with a dozen customers. Not true! This particular fifth-generation butcher shop has hundreds if not thousands of customers, and yet the owners make a conscious effort to customize and personalize each and every interaction. You won't be surprised to know, there is no CRM system and their accounting infrastructure consists of a simple handwritten ledger and an abacus! What they do invest in is a consistent and intentional Customer Experience Journey.

In chapter 4 I discussed the Customer Experience Journey, consisting of six stages from evaluation through discovery and consideration, fol-

Figure 7.1: Improved Customer Technologies Are the Biggest Accelerator of Change

lowed by further evaluation, purchase, and use, which leads to—you saw it coming, didn't you?—more evaluation and, if the experience is consistently positive, an ever-deepening relationship. All along that journey, products and services compete with features and benefits, the bits and pieces we take into account as part of our logical need to evaluate options. But what determines our preference—even our insistence—for one individual, team, company, or brand over other logically acceptable options is the experience that teams, companies, or brands create, not "for us," but *with us.* Exceptional customer experiences derive from collaborative Co-Creation, not transactions, taking place consistently over time, just as my mother's stew recipe drove my father's shopping list and led the butcher to know just exactly what my father should carry home in that paper bundle.

Today, consumer expectations are rising faster than ever. One reason is that technological advances keep making our lives even more convenient. On my smartphone, one app allows me to call Uber to take me to my hotel; another app allows me to choose my bed type, what I want in the refrigerator, and the style of robe I find in the closet. We are becoming experience snobs, and, as such, our expectations are always creeping up.

Rising consumer expectations affect the world of work as well. Remember Ronnie West, chief people officer of Ipreo, from chapter 5? He's the one who advocates replacing résumés with brief self-made videos from applicants. His reasoning? If you don't know how to position yourself to add value for the firm in a three- to five-minute video, then his company is probably not the place for you. And yet, if the smartphones in our pockets couldn't record videos, I doubt he would have come to this conclusion. I'm not advocating that practice for every company, but I do admire how he leveraged the ubiquity of a consumer technology to create a useful business application. Technology elevates our experiences, and our expectations ride that updraft.

Consistently Invest in People, Processes, Tools, and Technologies

There is only one way your company can keep up: by consistently investing in the accelerated development of your people, dramatically optimizing your processes, and elevating the tools (and technologies) your organization uses to get ever closer to its customers. It is not your customer's job to buy from you. It is your job to find out what would make for an exceptional experience from their point of view, and invite them into it.

Another sign of the times is the rise of "curated" websites. In short, we now turn to trusted sites—sometimes connected to a highly respected individual or brand, sometimes crowdsourced—that pre-sort and recommend content so we don't have to sift through thousands of choices. In fashion that would be Gilt, in media Reddit, Lifehacker for productivity, and there's even one for marketing called CMO, and for social science research relevant to our lives, the Monkey Cage. In the Co-Creation economy, offering curation is one way to tailor the customer experience, and your curating reputation becomes the thing that drives others to want to work, share, play, and create with you. It is a short path to get you to anticipate customer needs, to think like them. If they don't value it, why should you?

Accelerating the Development of Your People: Start investing in people who have the experience, educational foundation, and intelligence to make the right decisions outside of a "command-and-control" organizational structure. Look around your industry, at those competitors you admire, and ask, where do they find their rock stars? Look outside your industry: What other kinds of businesses need the same skill set you do? Maybe there's a particular military performance profile that fits your bill. Can you partner with the appropriate department of a nearby college or university professor to grow candidates if necessary? What if you could shape the curriculum so new hires arrived with little need for specialized training? Perhaps a sponsored research program could establish a professional relationship dedicated to innovating your evolving solutions.

Dramatically Optimizing Your Processes: Put in place standard operating processes to capture the information that customers are willing to share with you. Institute processes that leverage the information for their benefit. The online designer clothing and accessories rental company Rent the Runway enlists its customers to give feedback on their needs and choices, which has directly guided a constant evolution of their business model. They mitigate the "did I order the right size?" question by letting customers choose a second size, offering free returns, and adding much-requested plus sizes. That business model has undergone huge change. It began in 2009 as "that site where you can rent prom dresses." After initial enormous success and some rocky roads while scaling up—and tens of thousands of social media responses—today many professional women are choosing their "Unlimited" option, where, for less than $139 per month, you can rent as much as you want and keep it as long as you want, thus avoiding late return fees. Insurance, dry cleaning, and shipping are all included in the cost. And with a new corporate partnership with publishing giant Condé Nast that subsidizes employee memberships in the subscription program, if Rent the Runway can successfully navigate exponential growth, they're poised to become the millennials' signing bonus of choice, the next generation's company car or free gym membership.[2] They've effectively "Netflixed" the clothing space.

Elevating Your Customer-Centric Tools: Do you have the tools and technologies to support your people and processes to scale? Richard Branson, head of the Virgin group of companies, told a *Forbes* writer that the success of his highly visible airlines comes from happy, proud employees. "Give them the tools"—new planes, leather seats, the best in-flight entertainment—"give them every little detail," he explained, and travelers will choose you every time.[3]

Technologies: This is where cognitive computing comes in. With the right tools, you can both interpret the data and extrapolate information from it to learn about your customers' aspirations at each interaction. What would dramatically enhance their experience? Companies must learn from every interaction with every customer, and reflect what they've learned back to that customer in each subsequent interaction.

Customers take enormous delight in customization and personalization, which invites an emotional connection. Better yet is an invitation into Co-Creation of value, so that experience becomes exceptional. (Keep in mind that I am equating "customers" with "stakeholders." We could be talking about employees, partners, investors, or media relationships.) Your people, processes, and tools must be aligned around customization and collaboration, which create opportunities to deeply understand your customer's experience journey.

To discover what would delight consumers, you have to get out of your comfort zone. Too many people still think their situation is so unique that only certain approaches (that they already know and have tried) will work.

Get out of your office! Not much happens in there. "In thirty years [*sic*] time, as technology moves forward even further," Branson proclaimed on Virgin's blog, "people are going to look back and wonder why offices ever existed."[4] Go to the Consumer Electronics Show. Go to South by Southwest. Attend the Fast Company Innovation Summit or a Milken Institute seminar. Visit other companies. Two senior executives of equal stature in noncompeting organizations could agree to let each other see how they do product development or compliance. Leave behind your preconceived notions and perceptions. I spoke with a managing partner at a law firm who attends five different roundtables with global counterparts in his role, all focused on how to run a law firm. Call me crazy, but I suggested he cut back to two such meetings a year, certainly sufficient to stay on top of managing his firm. And replace the other opportunities with trips outside his normal sphere.

Get outside not just your company but your industry. Get beyond the sacred cows, beyond defending the status quo, beyond chasing this quarter's numbers. To understand constantly rising customer expectations, first you must challenge your current assumptions.

Consistency Matters More than Ever Before

Beyond your efforts to customize an offering, and collaborate with others to make it memorable, the people, processes, and tools you invest in must contribute to creating consistent experiences. Can consistency really trump quality? Yes! Unpredictable quality is frankly frustrating, even if the high points are extremely high. Our expectations as consumers are based on consistency that, if shaken, returns us to the "evaluation" phase of the Customer Experience Journey and propels us to consider alternatives. Remember, your customer is creating a self-/brand narrative—with every purchase, he or she is mentally rewriting the story of the self-/brand relationship by mapping this new interaction onto memories of past experiences with your product, category, purchase, or with a particular individual or team. (Customers do this both as individual consumers and as business buyers.) The key component of that story, though, is that the customer is *always* the main character in the narrative. More than simply being satisfied with a product or service, your customers need to feel consistently connected to your brand by experiencing the role it plays in the story of their lives.[5]

These self-brand narratives can be simple or complex, short-lived or lifelong. You tried a new brand of tomato soup, but you didn't like it, so you went back to Campbell's. You remember that red-and-white can from your grandmother's kitchen, and, while it's not an important part of your life, you'll probably reach for Campbell's when you do want soup. Similarly, people associate certain makes and models of cars with life changes: first driver's license, first cross-country road trip, first move, first love. They imbue the experience of driving certain cars with rich emotional detail and history and, when that car retires, they mourn the passing as they would that of a beloved pet.

Every time my father visits that butcher shop in Hamedan, Iran, he is greeted with consistent service that makes him feel at home among friends. If he came back one day and wasn't offered a cup of tea, it might not be a deal breaker. But if on the next visit he found a strange face behind the counter and on the subsequent trip he got home to discover my mom's order hadn't been prepared in the customary way, he would be more than disappointed. He would be evaluating new options for buying his family's meat.

Consistency is crucial to loyalty. I've long believed that you cannot improve something you don't measure. If processes are clearly defined, if the people who execute those processes are thoroughly trained and developed, if there are metrics and compensation directly tied to individual performance but also to that of the whole team, and all of that is aligned around consistently driving exceptional experiences, it's amazing how consistent your consumer experience will be.

Take Your Customer's Journey Yourself

Everyone on the team, from the front line to the senior executives, needs to go through their customer's journey on a regular basis. Many companies have secret shopper programs. Why can't that shopper be the CEO of the company? I heard A. G. Laffley, chairman of Procter & Gamble, say that whenever he flies into a new city, he avoids being met at the airport by his entourage. Instead, the first thing he does is go shopping with a local mom. He wants his thinking to be at the edge of where his business creates value for its intended audience. These one-on-one experiences help him understand how real moms live, the decisions they make and why. It's not hard to see how insights from watching a mom struggle to get through her shopping with two children in tow led P&G to partner with Amazon to come up with the Dash Button—a simple Wi-Fi-enabled device that makes it one-click-easy for Amazon Prime customers to have consumable products drop-shipped to their doors. Where do ideas like that come from? Not from executives in leather chairs in their mahogany row offices. Go get dirty where business happens, where your customers and their customers are. Consider all the brands so many of us use; look at all the companies we buy from, or buy for. We need our teams to take our Customers' Experience Journeys for themselves, frequently enough that they develop an innate empathy for their customers' experience and an accurate appraisal of how well (or poorly) it meets ever-rising expectations.

Here's another helpful concept that can have eye-opening consequences. The corollary to "Eat your own dogfood" is "Eat your own dogfood's customer service." Do you know how many higher-ups have never used their company's website, live chat, e-mail, or phone customer service? Do you even know what your company's most frequent customer complaint is? Because turning a negative—the reason the customer is engaging with you directly—into a positive can have a significant impact on how they view you. Hey, they solved my problem—and fast!

To summarize, technology is elevating our expectations as consumers, and that has implications for everyone with a role to play in meeting and exceeding those expectations. And yet, you cannot abdicate your relationships to technology. Technology can become an enormous enabler of your efforts, and the rest of this chapter will explore how that can happen. But before we go there, let's pause to remember our place.

As Mark Hoplamazian, CEO of Hyatt Hotels said, you are a guest on your customer's journey! You are not entitled to a share of their minds. I have yet to find a single product or service, a single brand, that dominates a preponderance of anyone's thought or action. As the provider of a service or product, you have a place in your customer's journey, but it is just a sliver of their day or week or month or year.

Years ago, a mentor asked me, "David, what are you doing to create Kodak moments in your business?" His intent was to make me reflect on what I was doing to not only capture delightful moments with Co-Creators but to make them want to share them with others as well. I pose the same challenge to you (updated for present day): What are you doing to create Instagram moments that make others want to talk about you? The entire journey matters, but specific pivotal points along that journey can be identified and leveraged to create enterprise evangelism. What would happen if your employees proactively uncovered problems? What if they came out from behind the cold and distant counters not only to apologize but also to express real contrition, offer upgrades or other perks on the spot, and reimburse customers for their inconveniences? Add to that a call from the regional manager to offer her apologies as well and solicit the customer's ideas for improved overall experience. Your employees may just turn every disgruntled customer into a brand evangelist!

Here's a way to jump-start this process: pay customers to engage. A few consumer product companies like Proctor & Gamble and Goose Island Beer Company are working with a start-up called Pay Your Selfie to encourage consumers, mostly millennials, to do just that—take and post a selfie with their product and make a small sum, usually a dollar or less. Your product gets out there in a fun and authentic way—and the companies get to see how you actually use the product—when, and toward what impact, result, or outcome. One finding about P&G was that selfie-takers were brushing more between 4:00 p.m. and 6:00 p.m., thus suggesting changes in the timing of online ads.[6] Other insights included preferences about snack foods and where to locate new healthy fast-food outlets.[7]

We need to understand our customers' journeys well enough to create those capture-worthy moments. We need to fold that understanding into the innovations we create to meet our customers' rising expectations tomorrow.

DISRUPTIVE TECHNOLOGY TO ANTICIPATE AND ENGAGE

Thanks to innovative technologies, consumers increasingly expect their experiences to be customized to their tastes. (B2B leaders, don't think you're off the hook: even business buyers are consumers first.) What does this mean for brands that want to remain relevant well into the future? Wake up and smell the Keurig!

Just as pod coffeemakers have taken over kitchens worldwide by offering each coffee drinker personal choice, personalized products and services, digital devices, and apps continue to proliferate, reshaping the experiences we expect from brands. We want the ease of Uber and Open Table. We want the real-time analytics of Fitbit or the next generation of Apple Watch. I don't know what's next on the horizon. But the minute I experience it, I will expect it everywhere, on demand.

Consumers may not conceive of the technology in their lives as disruptive, but as business leaders, we need to view it through that lens. That is how we will find new ways to anticipate our customers' needs and engage them in Co-Creating solutions. After all, ten years ago, we weren't all walking around thinking, "I wish I had my computer in my pocket." But when a technology comes along that makes wonderful new things possible, we adopt it—and never look back.

Disruptive Technologies Are a Wake-Up Call

Companies need to leverage unique technologies to provide leading drivers of where customer expectations are headed. We need technology that is nonintrusive, that generates usable data as close to real time as possible, and that is scalable in a way that keeps the customer experience highly customized, even as it evolves into the next new thing.

You have to find ways to immerse yourself in a customer's experience, feel its ebb and flow, its heartbeat. Doctors can read an EKG and know which patient is very likely headed for a heart attack. What can you likewise do to discern what stakeholders want or need next in their journey?

In my consulting work, I advise individuals, teams, and companies to get closer to what their customers experience when they experience it. I'm not advocating for them to attach webcams to their customers' clothing; we must never be intrusive. But what would you learn if you could sit on a customer's shoulder, go through their daily journey with them, in real time, capturing what they experience? What if you could actually respond in real time to change that journey if it isn't the one you want them to experience with your brand? I believe that is the potential in cognitive computing: it can provide the insights that allow us to virtually follow our customers through their journey in a completely nonintrusive way, but it would allow us to intervene when they need us, thanks to what leading drivers tell us.

Looking at some of the companies partnering with IBM's Watson platform—a platform we'll analyze in greater detail later in this chapter—gives us an idea of what this might look like. (The massive computational power necessary for such efforts has limited products and services so far, but they are coming.) AlchemyAPI wants to develop deeper processes of what is called "Intent Mining." CEO Elliot Turner told leading natural-language-processing researcher Seth Grimes that, while we can use social media trends, likes, shares, and hashtag analysis to get some idea of where customers are in their journey, we're not quite there yet. "Success in this task," he said, "will combine other elements like a person's interests, relationships, geography—and ultimately their identity, purchase history, and privacy preferences—so that applications can plot where a person is in their journey and provide the best offers at the best times."[8]

FluidXPS is also using Watson to develop the world's smartest personal shopper to help activewear and outdoor sports retailer The North Face provide fast, appropriate, and intuitive choices for its customers. The FluidXPS program, while soliciting information and thus "learning" during every customer interaction to individualize and personalize every choice, can also process and, in a sense, internalize product catalogs, web pages, and social media reviews and interactions involving that product or product group to more sharply hone its advice.[9]

Two Best Practices for Navigating a Disruptive World

The winners amid disruption will harness technology to meet customers' desire for convenient, customized experiences. Disruptive technologies and innovation must be on the radar of CEOs. If not, firms will continue to suffer from incrementalism (doing the same things better) instead of experiencing real innovation, which is doing things dramatically differently. Innovation must be a priority at the highest level if not throughout the entire organization. Every company should have a chief innovation officer with a passion, if not an obsession, to reinvent the business. Taking direction from that chief innovation officer should be experts in execution with the agility of a SEAL Team Six, not a cumbersome and often outdated battalion.

Boards can also take greater responsibility for keeping disruption on the agenda at that highest strategic level of priority by using an innovation committee to engage the CEO and the management team.

I've seen firsthand how extremely difficult it is for large companies to innovate. For a bureaucratic behemoth, it is frequently easier to buy rather than build. A strategy of acquiring innovation and becoming adept at integrating it into an operation might be the most practical course for a big company. Kodak, Blockbuster, JC Penney—the list of businesses that have suffered disastrous declines due to a myopic view of their customer experience is long. No one—not the large company or the small, the B2B or the association or the governmental agency—gets a pass from the wake-up call of disruptive technology.

Understand the Long Tail of Implementation

The recipe for better understanding your customers includes using leading drivers to remove the friction in their experiences, anticipate their future needs, and embrace the long tail of implementation. If I know my customers' behavior patterns, I can more confidently anticipate what's going to happen next, including how I can be of service. This takes consultative selling and extends that relationship—and opportunity for customer insight—into the customer's experience of using the product.

Parenthetically, let's remember that we could be talking about talent or investor acquisition, not simply customers and purchasing. The Customer Experience Journey in question could be the way you interview, onboard, or stay in touch with new hires through their first year, assessing how well they assimilated and are performing in their job and measuring the impact they are creating for team members, the organization, or its customers.

It should be eminently possible to anticipate what's next around that journey. The challenge is scalability, as your company moves toward the visionary end of the spectrum and, correspondingly, growth opportunities increase.

In chapter 2, I mentioned Bruce Kasanoff's "SMART" model, in which he challenges us to transform customer touchpoints into data-gathering engines that allow us to learn from every interaction. Those touchpoints must be sensors that ascertain what's happening along the customer's journey—what job is she trying to accomplish? What is she experiencing? What is she struggling with? What does she need from us at this point? What is the trigger she needs to move her to the next stage of the journey?

If you don't have sensors to gauge what's going on throughout that figure eight, leading drivers that signal you to take notice, you will have no idea how to diagnose or do something about a customer who is struggling. If you can't anticipate what they need, you can't engage with them to their satisfaction on that journey. But so much depends on the coordination! A Customer Experience Journey is a complex mechanism in which the parts of the system have to work well together. The handoff from one stage to the next is just as important as the performance at each stage, because stages don't exist in isolation, but rather along a continuum. The Customer Experience Journey is an operating system within the industry ecosystem. It's not just B2C; B2B touchpoints can be even more poorly conceived and executed.

Consumers' increasing expectations are causing companies to turn to technology to provide leading drivers of where those rising expectations may go next. Cognitive computing has tremendous potential to make sense of that stream, so let us turn our attention to this rapidly growing field. But before we do, let me recap three key concepts about disruptive technology:

1. It must be a priority at your organization's highest level, including to your CEO and the board.
2. When you move your thinking, approach, and investments from the merely functional to the strategic, you will increase your growth opportunities—which will introduce the challenge of scalability.
3. In order to scale your enterprise, make use of smart touchpoints to gather data throughout the Customer Experience Journey (including the implementation and usage stage). These will produce leading drivers that allow you to anticipate customers' evolving expectations.

COGNITIVE COMPUTING

We are on the cusp of a revolution—the use of cognitive computing technology that can sense, learn from, and interact with people in natural, real-time ways. Cognitive computing has incredible potential to collaboratively Co-Create both with us and for us, in our personal and professional lives.

Improvements in speech recognition and natural-language processing (two separate but related technologies) are making it easier for deep machine learning. Meanwhile the SMAC technologies are generating vast amounts of data, especially the unstructured kind that has previously been so difficult to use. Machines that process natural language and images to provide decision support and data visualization will inevitably develop ultra-sophisticated recommendation engines that "listen" at every customer touchpoint. In the Co-Create economy, agile response to real-time insights is the only way to remain relevant to customers as their expectations change. The most disruptive technology of all is likely to be the one that is powered by cognitive computing. This technology greatly increases an organization's capacity to *listen louder* to its customers. This is how you transform customers into active participants in Co-Creating iterative improvements and, better yet, groundbreaking innovations.

As consumers, we are already seeing this shift in the proliferation of virtual agents designed to remove the friction of interacting with computers. Consumer technologies like Google Home, Amazon Echo, Microsoft's Cortana, and Apple's Siri apply cognitive computing based on voice recognition to accomplish daily tasks. The business applications of cognitive computing are also vast, and highly relevant to the Co-Create model, if not yet as visible as the consumer applications.

I started my career as a co-op at IBM supporting System 36 mainframes and green-screen PROFS back in the Neolithic era. I was at ComputerLand when they were selling 286 PCs and 486 servers and storage. I was with Silicon Graphics when they went to high-end, MIPs-based chips, the UNIX operating system, and graphic-intensive applications. The arc of my own career definitively points to the primacy of cognitive computing, as I've seen machines evolve from command lines to mouse clicks to gestures and voice control. Working with IBM Smarter Commerce as a client has shaped my belief that cognitive computing is the next truly transformative generation of computer technology.

Much of the daily grind of many, many businesses is getting through often mundane tasks, many well-suited to technological solutions involving crushing amounts of data. Think about it: we're often presented with large sets of comparative data from which we have to extract meaning and apply it to the next iteration, one that concludes with a decision, plan of action, or other guidance. There is a reason Mark Zuckerberg wants an "AI butler." (He announced a 2016 New Year's resolution to build an artificially intelligent personal assistant, which he likened to Jarvis, the AI companion in the *Iron Man* films.)[10] Jarvis, in real time, can solve mundane tasks that we waste human intellectual horsepower addressing.

We are at a historic juncture where the ability to store and access data in private and public clouds meets unparalleled ability to manipulate, process, and draw actionable insights from that data via cognitive computing. Forrester Research forecasts that revenue associated with cloud-based B2B will grow from $40 billion in 2012 to $160 billion in 2020.[11] In 2014 IBM announced the establishment of the Watson Group, a business unit dedicated to cloud-based cognitive computing innovations. The emphasis on artificial intelligence signified a strategic shift by IBM: instead of the usual licensing, it offered use of its tool to tech entrepreneurs under a conceptual umbrella called the Ecosystem. The only requirement was that their ideas conform to certain standards. Seventy-seven thousand developers showed up to play around with Watson and see how it could help their companies and organizations. Not only did they offer themselves as potential customers when the trial period was up but they delivered up a diverse market with niche segments IBM likely wouldn't have known about.

For example, IBM is applying Watson to a common healthcare problem: medication conflicts. Watson can search massive amounts of medical information to look for drug conflicts, then make recommendations. "Watson is already capable of storing far more medical information than doctors, and unlike humans, its decisions are all evidence-based and free of cognitive biases and overconfidence," reported *Business Insider* in April 2014.[12]

Further, cash-rich IBM made successful applicants strategic partners in the Ecosystem, giving them access not just to advisors and tech facilitators but also to the pool of $100 million that IBM will invest in Watson-associated firms.[13]

Manoj Saxena is the chairman of Cognitive Scale and a founding managing director of The Entrepreneurs' Fund IV, a $100 million seed fund focused exclusively on the cognitive computing space. He was previously the general manager overseeing the commercialization of IBM's Watson project. He is as bullish as it comes on both the promise and potential of the cognitive cloud.

"Watson's cognitive computing paradigm represents to me the fourth biggest knowledge innovation in history—alphabet, printing press, internet, cognitive computing," he told me in an interview. "It knows more than we know, gets smarter at each opportunity. It is the most meaningful and disruptive thing humanity has worked on! We're moving to a world where the internet is going away. Every business process will be cognitized, pervasive, and free learning."[14]

IBM's intent with Watson is to accelerate development and commercialization of a new class of software, services, and apps. How? Here's

Saxena again addressing the order-of-magnitude differences that Watson-like environments bring to the table.

"Computing for the past seventy-five years was structured data processing, essentially giant calculators. Eighty percent of data that is created," he explained, "is unstructured, like images, videos, tweets, dark data, opaque" and unreadable by ordinary computing devices. "Cognitive computing has three dimensions: it is able to process all available data—not just structured," he continued. "It is able to understand the data in the context of an industry domain model; it can create insights that are actionable and personalized," for retail, financial management, and telecommunications, for example. "Finally, it learns continuously on its own." He pointed out, too, that while Watson was able to marshal its computational and learning muscle to win Jeopardy, such systems are now embracing an entire industry domain model.

Think about the implications for Co-Creation. While your product may be what initially spikes the customer's interest, it is the ongoing, deep, Co-Creative relationships that you nurture around those hero customers that bring real growth opportunity. And, as with Watson, those hero customers might help you innovate a hundred other products based on your highly functional, interdependent relationship.

The Entrepreneurs' Fund

As customers' expectations change over time, cognitive computing is our technology solution to follow their evolution. It has incredible potential to fuel collaborative Co-Creation, as the following examples from Austin-based investment firm The Entrepreneurs' Fund (TEF) demonstrate. (Manoj Saxena is also the founding managing director of TEF and the chairman of CognitiveScale.)

TEF has staked out a position in the thick of the B2B cognitive computing growth industry by investing exclusively in cognitive computing start-ups, many associated with IBM's Watson. In TEF's portfolio are companies such as CognitiveScale, which powers a new class of data interpretation and learning systems; SparkCognition, which addresses both cybersecurity and physical security with predictive analytics on a cognitive platform; and WayBlazer, which uses cognitive cloud technologies to redefine the way consumers research, plan, personalize, and purchase travel. These cloud-based cognitive systems are designed to analyze structured and unstructured information in order to learn from their interactions with data and humans—they are essentially reprogramming themselves continuously.

SparkCognition, another of the TEF start-ups, harnessed the company's cognitive computing tool to build SparkSecure, a cybersecurity service that uses a variety of algorithms and pattern-recognition programs to detect anomalous activity on clients' systems, alert them, address the threat, and even predict attacks and propose possible solutions to prevent them. SparkSecure "learns" by securely interacting with systems, reconfiguring itself whenever it detects new information.

Cognitive Spark and National Retailer: Co-Creating Deeper Value

Saxena mentioned a project involving a large national retailer that wanted help with its online shopping platforms where, he told me, "80 percent of retail engagements are done anonymously. The retailer has no idea who the customers are or what they're looking for." The result? "Low conversion rates, and returns are massive, as much as 30 percent." The rules-based recommendation the stores had been using got customers' needs right about 10 percent of the time.

So, Cognitive Spark created "a cognitive commerce cloud with multiple digital brains—one engages the customer, another a store employee. Let's focus on the customer engagement. We plugged our brain" into their platform, and "we saw a jump of 380 percent in engagement and 40 percent in conversion." Say the customer is shopping for shoes. The machine looks at the images the customer is looking at. "It can read a zebra pattern, open-toe shoe, and understands *declared, observed,* and *inferred* behaviors and learns each time." At the end of the engagement, "we recommend a style DNA," built from deductions drawn from that customer's behavior. The customer learns, "Wow, I like red more than blue, this designer more than others, can I save my profile?—thus declaring themselves to the retailer." And stepping into an ever-deeper relationship.

Pangaea Takes Knowledge Management Further for J. Walter Thompson

Santa Barbara–based introNetworks was recently engaged by global advertising agency J. Walter Thompson (JWT) to develop a cognitive computing system that would transform customer engagement and scale employee expertise. They designed it to bring together what I call "seekers and solvers"—people who need information and people with the information they seek. JWT has licensed an artificial intelligence engine and retained introNetworks' principles to develop a presentation layer for that engine, a user interface called Pangaea. The system allows JWT employees to ask questions of, and connect with, other employees in the company all around the world. Like traditional knowledge-management databases, you ask questions and get highly relevant answers. But the engine also analyzes what questions are trending, in what categories, and who has key insights (a "know-how map"). The credibility of the answers provided is reflected in a rating system. If I work at JWT, I can ask Pangaea, "Who are the right people for my pharmaceutical pitch?" "Where can I find a wearable technology expert for my brainstorming session?" Imagine being able to reduce churn at your company simply by institutionalizing the knowledge, experience, and relationships that are walking its halls.

B2C Virtual Assistants

Well-established tech providers like Amazon, Google, and Apple are vying for leadership in the application of cognitive computing to consumers' lives. Some of these devices are taking a "do anything you ask" approach, like Microsoft's Cortana or Amazon's Echo. Others target specific tasks—take Ozlo, which combines multiple data sources like Yelp and Foursquare to help you find things to eat and drink, then guides you to their location. Or "Amy" from startup x.ai, which promises to end those incredibly inefficient e-mail back-and-forths simply to schedule upcoming events. You give Amy access to your e-mail and calendar, and "she" learns from every interaction. Amy studies your preferences, and then handles the legwork of correspondence to set dates and times. You copy Amy on the initial correspondence, and you don't think about it again until she places the meeting on your calendar. Imagine applying that very simple idea of scheduling an appointment to scheduling supply chain movements and other events that have an enormous amount of dependencies. When we see cognitive computing improve our daily experience as consumers, we will be quick to want those efficiencies in our professional lives. And there it goes again—consumer-facing technology ratcheting up customer expectations affecting B2B as well.

Do I Foresee a Backlash?

When I talk about cognitive computing, I am occasionally asked if I foresee any pushback. Concerns I've heard can be loosely grouped into three categories: privacy, effect on jobs, and trust.

Privacy: Cognitive computing apps need access to your data to learn from you—your habits, interests, opinions, and purchases. Data collection and storage of any kind raise concerns, particularly when children are involved. Yes: the security and privacy concerns are monumental—just as they have been for some time now. It is very easy to abuse access to data, as we learned when Edward Snowden leaked classified information from the US government. This is one reason I emphasize so strongly that the highest-level executives must make cognitive computing a priority. The security and privacy issues cannot be ignored.

Related to this issue is the data-for-service trade we make every day just by using Google or Amazon or Waze—or swiping our Starbucks card or making that Open Table reservation. We are giving access to our personal data and information to more and more companies, seldom pausing to consider that we have given away the right to control that data. (If you use AdBlocker, you know that certain companies will not allow you access unless you unblock them.) The most extreme expression of this is our right to be erased from the internet, "the right to be forgotten," which exists, after a long legal battle with Google, in the European Union and Argentina, but not in the United States.

Effect on Jobs: Yes, some jobs will become obsolete when machines can do them better and more cost effectively. There are two concerns here: the ability of small businesses to compete in this new paradigm and the automation of jobs previously performed by humans. Both arise from the fear that something we've relied on in the past will disappear in the future. I would argue that Co-Creation addresses both. So small companies can't afford Watson? This is a Co-Creation opportunity. They can partner to access the cognitive computing capabilities of larger, more resourceful companies. Watson has a free API so anyone can build tools leveraging its prowess. Will knowledge workers lose their jobs, like the laborers replaced by the assembly lines of the industrial revolution? Cognitive computing will change the way we work, mostly by automating the mundane. Dealing with the mundane has never been a good use of our resources. Humans have in the past proven to be very creative at finding new ways to employ their talents in meaningful work, and I expect that to continue.

Trust: Implicit in the promise of cognitive computing is our faith that once machines can learn for us, we can trust the solutions they provide. In 2016, Facebook was forced to respond to challenges that its "trending" newsfeed algorithm was inherently biased toward the liberal media. (On closer examination, it appeared that the human editors "adjusting" what was trending when the algorithm produced anomalies were the culprit.) We can assume that cognitive computing apps will reflect the inherent biases of their programmers as well. "By necessity they limit our choices—because their function is to make choices on our behalf," writes Will Oremus in *Slate*.[15] Again, I put my faith in Co-Creation. When we actively participate, we pull toward ourselves that which we sense is missing. We question received wisdom and the status quo. Just as we should manage our human capital with "trust, but verify," we should use due diligence with our artificially intelligent assistants.

Another concern is the kind of moral-hazard issues driven by these new technologies and the decisions we are going to have to make about them as a society. How do you write the algorithm that steers a speeding driverless car with a blown tire away from the crowded sidewalk and into that single oncoming car? Who is responsible when an AI-driven medical diagnosis is incorrect? Watson can't actually

Figure 7.2: Cloud-based cognitive computing

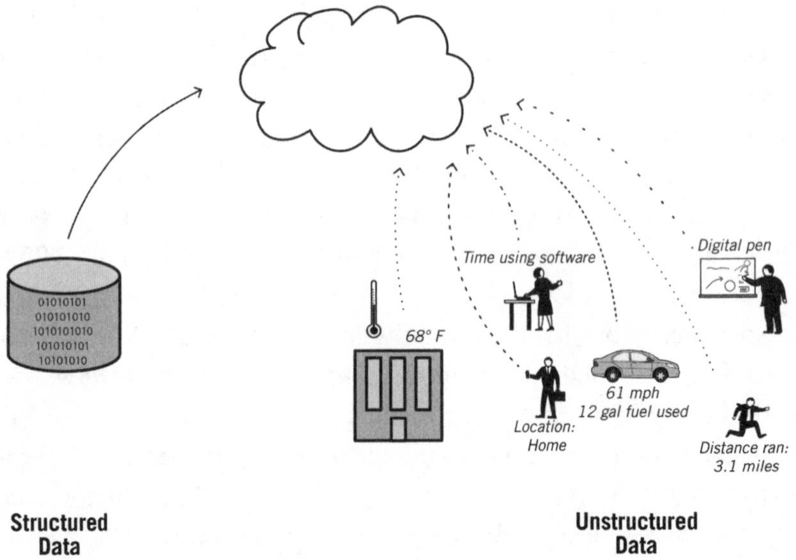

Time using software

Digital pen

68° F

61 mph
12 gal fuel used

Location:
Home

Distance ran:
3.1 miles

**Structured
Data**

**Unstructured
Data**

comprehend thought; it just manipulates symbols. It's not a brain; it's a processor. What elevates us as human beings is our ability to stimulate thoughts based on other thoughts. We can manage these risks if we don't limit ourselves by our own fear of the unknown.

As I've said, what is driving these very powerful applications is an unprecedented confluence of assets: big sets of unstructured data combined with natural-language-processing capability. Finally it is possible to parse that language, to understand its intent in order to apply that interpretation to anticipate and engage customers in all kinds of unique manners. Cognitive computing relies on building a corpus of knowledge, then learning to interpret it, then, through interaction and iteration, fine-tuning that ability to interpret just as humans have always learned, with the process continuing in an ongoing feedback loop. I have been imploring you to learn from every Customer Experience Journey; imagine the vastly greater learning that cognitive computing could bring to your pursuit of that goal.

Now that it is clear what cognitive computing is, how it is relevant to Co-Creation, and where the concerns lie, one more point must considered.

Give Cognitive Computing a Seat in the C-Suite

In Co-Creation, one approach is to gather the most intelligent people around a table to collaborate. No technology can ever replace that conversation. But what if that conversation was fueled by vast intelligence before, during, and after that collaboration process? What if Watson had a seat at that table? The real premise for collaborative Co-Creation is to bring machine learning to just such settings to automate mundane tasks in order to elevate the intellectual horsepower of the human capital seated there. If Watson *were* there, what would you ask it to do? How could a cognitive computing engine accelerate your ability to Co-Create unique solutions and, in the process, dramatically evolve the organization?

Unfortunately, we treat technology as an afterthought, a means to an end. A spreadsheet, a PowerPoint—these are just tools to present ideas. I believe cognitive computing will make the business impact of that technology much more visible. Think about the implications of being in a strategy discussion and turning to the computer to say, "Watson, given economic projections, what is the likelihood that this plan would increase our sales over the next two years, and by what percentage and under what market conditions?" If nothing else, I would welcome cognitive computing's ability to propose alternative options for consideration. I believe that this approach will not only accelerate our ability to get things done, but it will help uncover unintended consequences, including unanticipated "wow moments" that we wouldn't necessarily have discovered on our own.

When cognitive computing comes to the boardroom, the others around the table will soon understand the business impacts of Watson and other AI platforms to come. Business applications are making cognitive computing exciting. Hospital systems use Watson to search for conflicts and counter indications in prescribing drugs; banks are deploying Watson to improve customer experience as individuals move across devices of their choosing, at times of their choice, to inquire about financial products and services or complete online applications in multiple, independent sessions. Technology is removing friction from the Customer Experience Journey by gathering, analyzing, and constructing insights from massive amounts of data. Cognitive computing has incredible potential to enable our collaborative Co-Creation, as it starts to understand and to anticipate, to become more predictive and intuitive in making recommendations, to be more adept at making seamless the transitions from one stage of that journey to the next. To take a mundane example, just consider how much bother so many restaurant interactions seem to generate, from reserving through tipping. Think about the day when your dinner reservation is generated by your cell phone app, which also texts the restaurant in advance to specify your preferences as to water on the table, wines and their serving temperature, and table location, and can also alert the chef to any food allergies, convey any likes and dislikes, or adjust your reservation as parties join or fall out.

Collaborative Co-Creation Revisited

You are now rounding the final bend in the Customer Experience Journey. The concepts you were introduced to in early chapters—outcome-focused brand experiences, collaborative Co-Creation, contextual intelligence, listening louder, detecting faint market signals, needs-based segmentation, leading drivers—should now not only be finding their place in your vocabulary but also occupying prime real estate on your roadmap of what needs to happen next for your team, your organization, and your industry to thrive in the coming Co-Create economy. Chapter 8 presents the Co-Create Canvas, the visual schematic for your evolutionary strategy.

The key point of this chapter is that cognitive computing is dramatically elevating our ability to *listen louder* to our customers. This technology allows organizations to make customers into active participants rather than passive consumers by involving them in creating new offerings through the process of collaborative Co-Creation.

What are the key challenges and benefits of Co-Creation? What strategies, methods, and tools does it take for Co-Creation to succeed and to add value to organizations? I have challenged you to think about how well your organization is prepared to respond to disruption from technology while offering some ideas of what the answers to these questions might look like. Finally, we have explored how the principles of Co-Creation, when applied to the Customer Experience Journey, allow you to exploit the capabilities of advanced technologies so that exceptional customer experiences and exceptionally agile organizational structures evolve together.

TOOL 7: COGNITIVE COMPUTING READINESS ASSESSMENT

Don't forget about the Co-Create Toolkit PDF, available to you to download for free from CoCreateBook.com, intended to help you apply some of the key ideas you've just read in this chapter.

The next horizon of almost every business will reflect the development and application of cognitive computing now under way. Is your organization ready to participate in this sea change? As I said in this chapter, cognitive computing must have a seat at the table when your organization's strategic decisions are made. Use this tool to assess your organization's readiness to move into cognitive computing.

Chapter Seven Takeaways

- Improvements in consumer technology are the single biggest accelerator of customer expectations.
- Companies need to leverage technology to provide leading drivers of consumers' evolving needs.
- Cognitive computing facilitates the agile response to real-time insights required to stay relevant as customer expectations change.
- When you apply cognitive computing to customer relationships, you dramatically elevate your ability to invite them into collaborative Co-Creation.

EIGHT

THE CO-CREATE CANVAS

 In this chapter you will learn:

- How to use the Co-Create Canvas to map out strategic collaborative Co-Creation initiatives;
- What the essential aspects of the facilitated Co-Create Canvas Conversation are;
- What roles gamification, communities, and visual building blocks play in the Co-Create go-to-market strategy;
- What it takes to make the whole organization thrive in the Co-Create economy.

The Co-Create Canvas is an important strategic tool for shifting any organizational mindset, because it offers a roadmap to guide leaders in selecting the right opportunities for strategic Co-Creation initiatives. It provides a holistic snapshot of the necessary resources. It sketches out interdependencies and relationships that the initiatives might require as well as the financial implications of such opportunities for all stakeholders.

Far too many blog posts, articles, and even books share theoretical observations and then leave readers to figure out their application. Or worse, they leave you scratching your head, wondering what the author actually meant—and how you could even begin to internalize and apply their ideas. From the outset, I've set out to avoid these short-comings. The learning objectives at the beginning of each chapter, the downloadable PDF tool book from CoCreateBook.com, and the take-aways at the end of each chapter have been developed with one goal in mind: "the elevator ride." By that I mean the steady progression from theoretical foundations to case studies and examples that connect theo-ries to the next step: their application. But the elevator ride continues—how you will use the ideas, approaches, and techniques you've read about here to lead your organization to think, feel, and behave differently is up to you. Co-Creation of value is, I believe, the single most effective approach an enterprise can adopt to remain relevant to its biggest asset, its strategic relationships.

A fundamental insight of the Co-Create economy is the focus on retaining customer relationships rather than acquiring new ones. Your increased awareness of and attention to the six stages of the Customer Experience Journey should give you a new lens into how you can apply the elements of Co-Creation in your existing organization. Let's look at exactly how to go about that in such a way that you manage the pres-ent while inventing the future. But before we dive into the components of the Co-Create Canvas, let me ground the theory in an example.

In September 2015, Tesla launched its Model X, a sport utility ve-hicle that offers sustainable electric transport while remaining compet-itive with traditional SUVs on interior space, overall size, and other amenities—a remarkable package. But the design of its falcon-wing doors is where the Model X leaves mere iteration in the dust. Every facet of the design of this car takes into consideration all the complaints about today's minivans and SUVs. The falcon-wing doors solve several of these, and with amazing elegance.

For example, many SUV buyers have children. And yet, if you have car seats installed in the second row, it is often impossible to access the third row of seats—an incredible aggravation. Then there's the further hassle of tight parking spaces, when vehicles parked on either side are so close that you cannot open doors. The Model X's falcon-wing rear doors rise up and fold out of the way, requiring only a foot of clearance on either side. While Tesla obviously has bright engineers, I suspect that the company is actively Co-Creating its future with its customers, anticipating their needs and innovating radical, effective solutions.

Note, too, that Tesla founder Elon Musk has a vision: to accelerate the world's transition to sustainable transport. The Co-Create Canvas takes its direction from a common mission, vision, or enemy—which you should recognize by now as a central organizing principle of Co-Creation. The Tesla Model X challenges conventional automakers to rise to its level of elegance, simplicity, and attunement to customer experience. Companies like Mercedes and BMW have been excellent innovators in the past.

There is also *adaptive* innovation going on. The falcon-wing doors were found to have one annoying flaw: by opening at such a radical angle, they expose more of the interior to the elements. People were getting soaked while getting into or out of the vehicle in gusty rainstorms. With a mere *software* update, Tesla's designers changed how the doors behave, adding an "umbrella mode" in which the doors lift only part of the way. The space is still sufficient to enter or exit the car, but with more protection.[1]

Tesla's Model X demonstrates the true promise of Co-Creation and how the deep understanding of the Customer Experience Journey it exemplifies drives adaptive innovation. Here is a set of tools that brings together all the topics presented in this book to help you implement Co-Creation to drive transformation from the team to the business unit to the entire organization.

THE CO-CREATE CANVAS

To make this explanation of the Co-Create Canvas as relevant as possible, I will take you through the concept using examples from different functional roles. I will begin with a path through the canvas focusing on Co-Creation with customers, with the goal being revenue growth through customer retention. Then we will follow the path of Co-Creating value between an organization and a partner/supplier. With those examples, you should be equipped to replicate the same path for investors, media relationships, international opportunities, and more. The process is the same; the paths are parallel. What makes each unique

Figure 8.1: The Co-Create Canvas

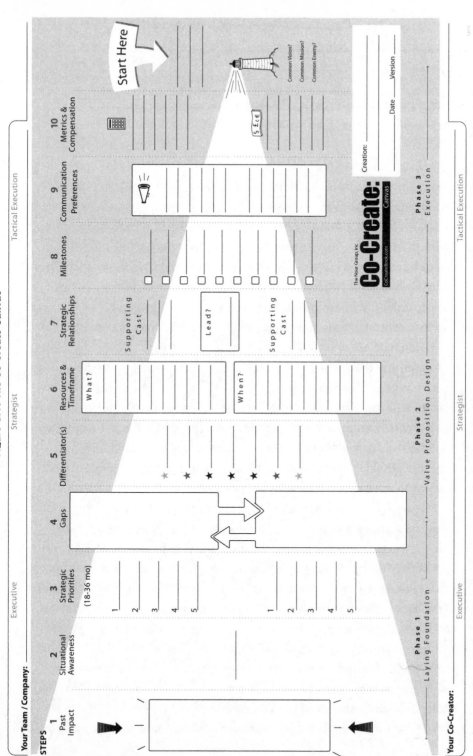

The Co-Create Canvas brings two strategic relationships together to address a common vision, mission, or enemy. Download a high-resolution PDF template at CoCreateBook.com.

Figure 8.2: Co-Create Canvas Critical Roles

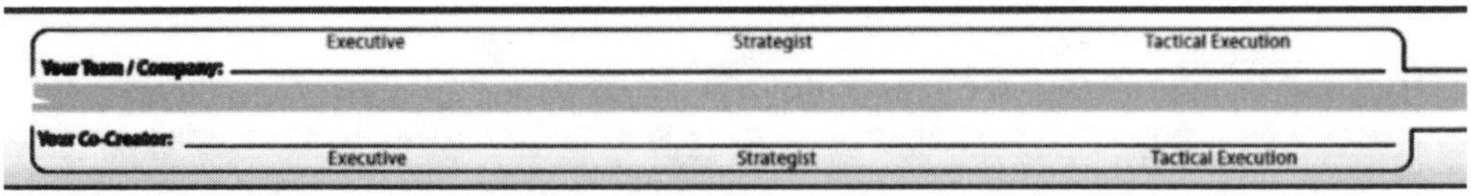

	Executive	Strategist	Tactical Execution
Your Team / Company:			

Your Co-Creator:			
	Executive	Strategist	Tactical Execution

Key individuals you invite to the Co-Create exercises will make or break it, so choose wisely!

are the individuals at the table and their common mission, vision, or enemy to address in the evolution.

Note how this diagram somewhat resembles a horizontal funnel, with the sides moving closer together as it progresses through the ten steps from left to right. In the upper left corner, step 1, label the diagram with the name of your firm at the top and the name(s) of the partnering customer or company at the bottom. Who might that be?

You cannot and should not move through this process with just any individual, team, or organization. Before you begin, give consideration to whom you will invite to join you. Since you are starting with that most traditional of business relationships—buyer and seller—think about customers you have developed real, meaningful, impactful relationships with, customers for whom you have created significant results or business outcomes. Which of your client/customer relationships are characterized by mutual respect, trust, and an authentic interest in each other's long-term success?

If you sell to organizations, identify no more than three to five of those customers and put them in the Co-Creator field. If you sell B2C, identify five to ten individual relationships that have endured for a number of years. (I suggest using the canvas to explore one strategic relationship—company or customer—at a time.) To use the language of Relationship Economics®, the relationships you choose should be strategic, companies or organizations that you are at the nurturing, sustaining, requesting, or capitalizing stage with. Also note that the customer here could be a defined buying segment—such as snowboarders ages eighteen through thirty—but those represented should have previously bought at least three to five of your products.

At the far right, all the steps lead to a common vision, mission, or

Figure 8.3: Co-Create Canvas Lighthouse

Without a guiding lighthouse (common mission, vision, or enemy), you'll lose sight of the Co-Creation purpose.

enemy. A common vision might be a plan to open up a new market. A common mission might be the creation of a new product or service category. A common enemy could be a piece of legislation affecting an entire industry, or a foreign competitor price-dumping in your market.

Think of the common element as a lighthouse illuminating the Co-Creation effort with a clearly visible, well-defined shared set of goals and objectives that provide the guiding principles for the collaboration outcome. This is your "why"!

One more consideration before we begin with an example: What will be the financial impact of this Co-Creation? While we will define this more deeply as we tackle each step, we need to keep the big picture in mind from the start. After all, you don't want to play "bet the company" on your first Co-Creation experience. As we go along, keep asking: What investment of resources (money, time, etc.) will be required; what rewards may be anticipated; and how will the "spoils of victory" be divided among the partners in the joint evolution?

Laying Foundation: Steps 1 through 4

1. **Past Impact.** With a few well-chosen words, capture the impact of where you've been and what you've accomplished together thus far. I don't mean what you did or how you did it, but the outcomes, because outcomes are critical at every stage of this process. An example might be something like, "With your new strategic marketing tool, our conversion rate increased 15 percent since start of FY." How are the two sides of this relationship better off because of each other? Your description goes in the box in step 1.

Figure 8.4: Co-Create Canvas Phase I—Steps 1-4 in Laying Foundation

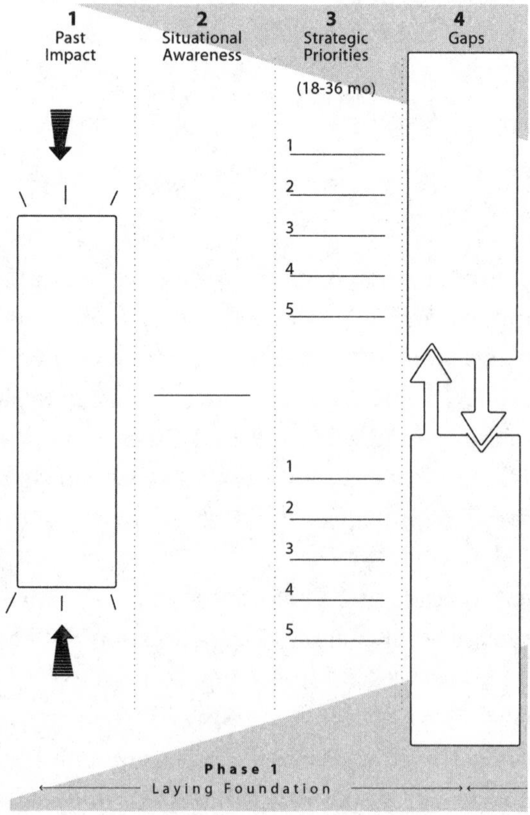

It's critical to really understand and capture a solid foundation that underlies where we've been together.

2. **Situational Awareness.** Your firm may be aware of industry trends. Your client may be aware of market trends. Technology, resource availability, learning, and development—note any trend occurring in your environment that could be relevant to your adaptive innovation. Put your contribution at the top of step 2 and your partner's at the bottom.

3. **Strategic Priorities (for an eighteen- to thirty-six-month time-frame).** Step 3 calls for transparency. This is a challenge; most of us are not accustomed to openly talking about our plans and priorities. But that reflects a last-century mindset that "in order for me to win, somebody else has to lose." For Co-Creation, we must shift that mindset to recognize that "this is truly about both of us winning because of each other." Put those priorities, from both sides, in step 3.

4. **Gaps.** What's missing from your efforts that the other side could provide? This transparency also takes fortitude. We are not typically comfortable saying to a client, "We don't know," or even more frightening, "We don't know what we don't know." Identify any relevant gaps, focusing on those the other side can actually do something about. Gaps, delineated in step 4, can be in expertise, infrastructure, capital, or even specific personnel.

Value Proposition Design: Steps 5 through 7

5. **Differentiator(s).** A Co-Creation opportunity is something you and your customer could do together that would create a unique differentiator for both of you. What outcome, process, or experience could set you apart? What unique benefit would create an unfair advantage for that strategic customer? How is that consumer better off using this product or service from your joint efforts? Keep in mind, customers often know what they want but seldom what they need; the difference will be your consultative approach in asking intelligent, engaging questions about their response to compelling market trends.

6. **Resources and Timeframe.** Given the value proposition identified in step 5, how will you collectively navigate toward your lighthouse? Take note of what has to happen, what resources will be needed, and what kind of timeframe is envisioned in step 6.

Figure 8.5: Co-Create Canvas Phase II—Steps 5-7 in Value Proposition Design

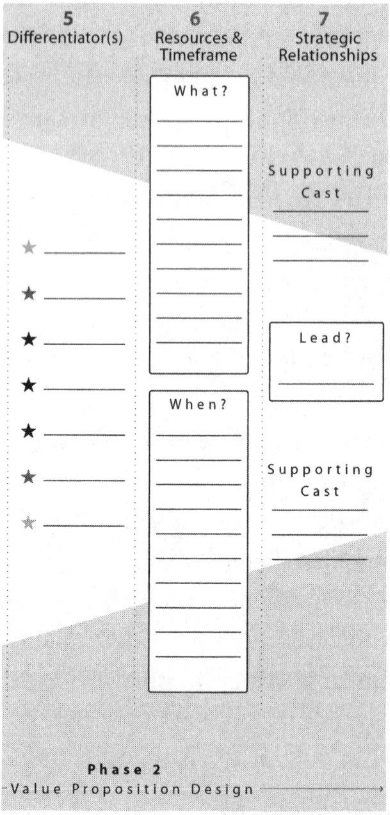

With a solid foundation, it's time to move forward with a unique, jointly crafted value-proposition where differentiators, resources, and strategic relationships will become critical to the success of your evolution.

7. **Strategic Relationships.** Now that you know what you are targeting and how you'll get there, "who" becomes critical. Co-Creation will require an equal investment of intellectual horsepower, creativity, and resources from both sides. The effort will require a champion, or lead, from each partner in the Co-Creation process, someone who will take extraordinary interest in it, someone who will face down forces of resistance, someone who will be an evangelist throughout the organization. That person will also need a "supporting cast," as none of us are scalable. Both sides should diligently consider and dis-

cuss their current internal and external portfolio of relationships, as well as others they'll need to uncover or add to the effort. You are going to need credible servant-leaders who have a sense of ownership and urgency of this joint effort as well as the authority and the responsibility to steward its progress. But they also have to understand they are part of a bigger picture, one interrelated component contributing to that lighthouse goal of common vision, mission, or enemy.

Executing Co-Creation: Steps 8 through 10

8. **Milestones**. There will undoubtedly be choice points in this process: identify the make-or-break milestones. If you are a manufacturer dependent on other suppliers who can't generally create new molds in less than six months, maybe you need to lengthen your trial roll-out to a year for testing and redesign or find a more agile supplier. In earlier chapters I've discussed creating pilots or prototypes whose successful execution represents milestones that, if missed, render the entire effort moot. Step 8 should define the critical elements that make or break this joint effort.

9. **Communication Preferences**. Individuals in any strategic relationship have their preferred communication styles. Analytical types prefer black or white spreadsheets; others inherently prefer a tech-enabled social approach using tools such as Slack or Chatter. Plan for a multimodal communication process and define it in step 9. Joint efforts require ways of communicating that meet the needs of their various members and that support peer level accountability for milestones.

10. **Metrics and Compensation.** For a client or customer, this is going to feel like an unnatural conversation. But if you see each other as having a vested interest in your respective success, it becomes clear that you need to understand how you are going to measure the progress of this joint effort and how the initiative will either make money, save money, or in some other way compensate the participants. Metrics and compensation drive behavior; effective execution requires both. Lay them out in step 10.

Figure 8.6: Co-Create Canvas Phase III—Steps 8–10 in Executing Co-Creation

All the due diligence and planning in the world won't matter if you can't get the joint idea off the ground. Here, you'll need to focus on a credible, prioritized plan to get a pilot/prototype out in the market with agility.

Laying the foundation stage is all about the due diligence, where you prove there is reason to hope for a mutually beneficial outcome. The value proposition design stage lays out three to five prioritized initiatives. And the execution stage puts a plan in place to go to market with a pilot or a prototype. I mentioned earlier that the financial impact of this joint effort should be part of the conversation at every step. As you proceed, keep the revenue model in view. If parties bring equal value to the table, I can't imagine why an equitable compensation can't be reached. The critical facet of step 10 is the *right* metrics focused on progress in the creation of net-new value!

Planning out these ten steps in detail will bring an identified value proposition to the point of readiness for go-to-market, which I will discuss later in this chapter. But first, let's consider the best approach to bringing parties together to have a successful conversation around the Co-Create Canvas, then go through the canvas again with examples to help you see its application with different stakeholder groups.

FACILITATING THE CO-CREATE CANVAS CONVERSATION

I have long believed that great relationships are derived from great conversations. The Co-Create Canvas is itself an invitation to have great conversations with customers, employees, suppliers, and others with whom you have strategic relationships, the intent being to create more impact in those relationships for mutual benefit. However, given that most of us are inexperienced at having the kind of candid, unguarded conversation the Co-Create Canvas invites, attention must be paid to every aspect, from who is in the room, to the venue, to mapping out objectives for what happens in the days and months after the initial canvas experience. Here are the essential attributes:

1. **The right setting.** The conversation must take place off-site—not just to put each party on equal footing but also to get away from working *in* the business so that all can work *on* the business (to paraphrase Michael Gerber in *The E-Myth*).[2] The venue should put people at ease and inspire the call to think and lead differently. Sitting on couches in an informal grouping beats sitting around a conference table. When we sit across the table from each other, our body postures unconsciously evoke feelings of confrontation. When we sit on couches, we feel more like we are with family and friends. I would go so far as to recommend taking the team to a locale that inspires, where shared activities outside the conversation itself can deepen bonds of empathy, understanding, and candor among all parties. I have seen firsthand the impact of taking an executive group to a ranch in Montana instead of hosting them in my home in Atlanta, a choice that encourages deep work while banishing the

ever-present minutiae of the business itself. Get away. Far away. Another possibility flows from the "doing good makes you feel good" idea. For a long-weekend retreat, spend Friday volunteering on a Habitat for Humanity work site or other social community project. In my experience, when people work together physically toward a worthwhile cause, it is often the route to other bonds as well.

2. **The right people**. You need SEAL Team Six, not a battalion. Invite those who can get in, get the job done, and then spread the enthusiasm that accelerates execution. Each firm should select its champions—its smartest thinkers, its most practical doers, its A-team of consistent execution. It is critical that the talent at the table from each side be equal in number and of recognizably equal business/organizational stature.

3. **The right facilitator.** The best facilitator will be independent, not an employee of either side, but not a stranger either. Ideally that person is building on a continuing or existing relationship with executives from both organizations. If that facilitator doesn't already have relationships with some of the individuals who will be in that room, he or she will need to map a relationship-development strategy with each individual—Skype, site visit, advance meeting on neutral ground—to connect with those individuals ahead of time, to relate with them in ways that uncover their needs, as well as their skills, and potential portfolio of relationships. The facilitator must be well versed in the nuances of the Co-Create Canvas.

4. **The right pre-work.** Requiring some pre-work from all parties before even a single meeting takes places makes the actual conversation richer, more intense, and more nuanced. The facilitator should encourage planning, thinking, and doing in advance of the event to get people in the right frame of mind to come, give their best, and apply their content later on. To build buy-in, a good facilitator will solicit detailed, goal-driven input from attendees on what they would like to learn, hear, or do within the Co-Create Canvas framework. As the date approaches, the facilitator should assign a case study to read, assign a self-assessment, or create a virtual "war room" where the work can begin. The role of the facilitator here is to prime the pump with contextually relevant material so that

participants begin to structure their thoughts and plans around the framework of the canvas. The point is getting people to think about the topic or issue so they arrive with their heads in the game.

5. **The right post-work.** Don't let a Co-Create Canvas Conversation be just a "one-and-done" event. Following the meeting, there will be a long tail of short-, medium-, and long-term prioritized pursuits. The conversation will have identified top strategic priorities the parties can accomplish together, as well as a champion to lead each side's respective efforts. Post-work should be framed around time-lines that are short term (six to twelve months); medium term (twelve to eighteen months), in which there are some choice points and if/then decisions; and long term, eighteen to thirty-six months. That is the realistic runway any team has to plan and execute a net-new differentiator, given the current market velocity and competitive veracity. Over each timeframe, the two sides will select champions and spell out dependencies, and priorities, with a genuine commitment to move with a purpose. At the longest timeframe, another aspect must be considered: How do we keep the momentum going? This leads to my next point.

6. **Long-tail accountability.** After the conversation comes to a close, the facilitator should become the accountability partner who assumes responsibility for holding the two parties to their respective commitments. He or she is in the unique position of not working for either side, but having the perspective of both, derived from accumulated experience in their presence. "Jim and Nancy, you two said you were going to produce a proposed budget through Phase One. How is that going?" The facilitator follows up one-to-one and in groups to learn what's worked and what hasn't. He or she never takes "I've been busy" as an answer. We all make time for what is important. Long-tail accountability increases the likelihood that the parties will deliver the intended Co-Creation of value.

We've all seen the euphoria, the sense of achievement that emerges when you get a group of people in a room and they achieve visionary thinking. That's fantastic, but then everybody goes back to their jobs and reverts to business as usual. To make time for seeing this endeavor through, participants have to have a vested interest in this organizational evolution—they need skin in the game. They need authority, the organizational capability to make what can be significant change happen. To maintain the momentum of those cascading changes, however, they also need a vested interest in seeing that the change is not static or momentary, but constantly evolving.

ThyssenKrupp Elevator's *elevate* initiative (discussed in chapter 3) was intended to improve internal processes through collaborative Co-Creation and indeed did introduce structural changes in process and communication that led to real efficiencies. The reason it has been so successful is that there is a vice president whose sole mission in life is overseeing and implementing it. Evidence of success: the program developed in the United States is being rolled out in Canada, Latin America, China, Africa, and Europe. What sprang up in 2014 in one country now has a global footprint. Why? Because it has an owner. It has the right team. Monthly meetings drive reliable momentum forward. *Elevate*, with its pilot programs, training and development curriculum, and personnel in key roles of responsibility, has driven real change in the organization. With all of these essential pieces in place, it has truly helped the organization to evolve.

Now that we have laid the groundwork regarding the Co-Create Canvas and the facilitated conversation it requires, let's apply that understanding via a hypothetical B2B example along product-development and launch lines.

A Co-Creation Approach in New Product Launch

For illustrative purposes, let's assume that a national organic-style grocery chain, Happy Planet Provisions, currently works with six different regional beverage brands in the organic, responsibly sourced market segment. Happy Planet wants to grow this market, but in a smart, sustainable way that avoids trucking beverages from one end of the country to the other. (This is a model developed by Nestlé, North America, which developed a portfolio of regional mineral water brands precisely to avoid high transport costs. Thus, the consumer finds the Ozarka brand of mineral water in the Midwest and Pacific Coast markets, while

Poland Spring dominates New England and Deer Park the New York tri-state region.) Happy Planet analyzes its business history with each producer and chooses three as Co-Creation candidates: Rocky River, Halo, and Crooked River Natural. Remember, the company is going to iterate through the canvas with each candidate separately. Happy Planet chooses Crooked River Natural to begin, noting past successes such as hitting significant delivery targets around a recent Fourth of July, during high summer and thus peak sales season. In several cities, the company also partners to tackle a common distribution problem, the empty-truck syndrome where trucks, after their last delivery, sometimes have to travel a hundred miles back to the plant with no cargo. Using Happy Planet's logistics expertise, Crooked River Natural trucks now shuttle returnable milk bottles in their crates from market to dairies on their return trips between cities. So both of these successes would fill step 1.

Step 2, situational awareness: Well, both sides have lots to contribute regarding industry and market trends here. Happy Planet knows what flavors are popular where, trends in various classes of beverage, while Crooked River Natural knows its large Texas and Southwest market and has used that knowledge to bring out seasonal offerings—prototypes that might join the lineup, much like craft brewers offer changing beers for changing weather. They also see a huge, untapped market in getting natural sodas into the fountain at fast casual restaurants like Chipotle, but they lack the capital or capacity to explore that.

What are the strategic priorities eighteen to thirty-six months out (step 3)? Here's where you'll find a mix of numbers and strategic goals. How much is each company willing to invest and with what expected gain? What are some concrete aspects of this partnership—to improve a process, introduce a product, use Happy Planet stores more consciously for effective prototyping?

For step 4, Happy Planet has developed a whole approach to supporting regional brands, even through direct financing and investment, and offers locations at which to experiment and test new products. Crooked River Natural has products that might be licensed to other bottlers to expand its brand without risking the core business—or needing to develop costly distribution infrastructure. That Cherry-Lime Rickey so popular with hipsters in Austin might be a hit with the SoCal lifestyle of LA, too.

Notice how iterating through each step narrows possibilities and begins to define the overall economics. With step 5, where we begin moving into defining the value proposition and picking three to five prioritized initiatives, things get even clearer. After some back and forth, both companies agree that their partnership is the biggest differentiator, the unique reputation, penetration, and range of offerings.

Suddenly, the lighthouse begins to shine, as they realize that co-branding might allow each to profit. They take their shared goals to be to use Happy Planet's leverage and superior marketing:

1. To propel Crooked River Natural's innovative, superregional beverages nationally;
2. To use some direct investment from Happy Planet to finance prototyping of five new flavors rolled out in markets with similar tastes, like Austin and Los Angeles; and
3. To reduce their carbon footprint while bringing in expertise from other regions by using local production licensing deals. What's produced in Vegas stays, if not in Vegas, then at least within the West.

Step 6 gets interesting, for here the two companies need to monetize the goals. What do various aspects of the budget look like to allow rollout of new flavors and over what timeframe? How much money is Happy Planet going to invest and under what terms while helping Crooked River Natural ramp up its product development?

Step 7 calls for identifying, at the outset, the human resources and relationships necessary to accomplish each goal. This is a place where some creative things can happen on the HR front. Maybe it makes sense for some employees from each side to go work on-site at the other's location. Or the companies can put the teams together, but in an independent venue like WeWork where they can tap local entrepreneurial and tech expertise by walking down the hall.

Before execution and the final three stages is a good time to make sure that your lighthouse is still blazing true and unwavering, that every step you're taking is toward that goal. Here, there have already been some changes, as both sides have decided to use a single existing

**Figure 8.7: Happy Planet Provisions/Crooked River
Natural Co-Create Canvas**

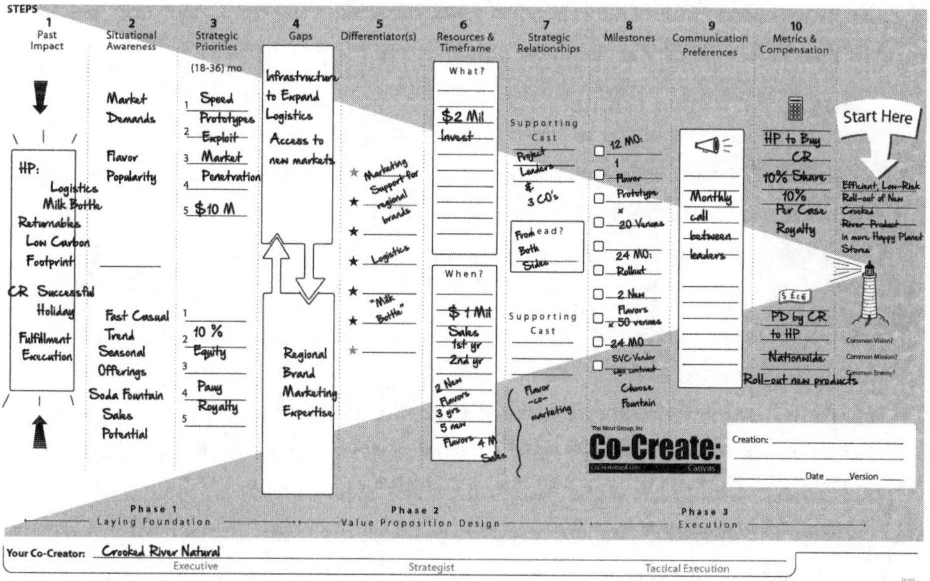

Crooked River Natural product not yet on the market to develop a marketing and implementation model. Happy Planet has long been aware that carbonated beverage sales dip dramatically in the fall. Crooked River has had a pumpkin-spice-flavored soda in the wings for a year, not quite knowing what to do with it.

Step 8 needs defined milestones for each side and the team, milestones made clearer by the earlier refocus. While they've set budget and production goals, the companies have also better defined responsibilities around the local producer, which neither side had really taken on board.

By this point, natural communications preferences (step 9) have become clear and decisions have been made about technologies. As well, the companies have created shared internal and external collaboration platforms.

The metrics and compensation of step 10 have also evolved naturally as budgets developed, the initial projects were defined and redefined, and projections became realities. Happy Planet will purchase 10 percent of Crooked River's shares, with that cash earmarked for specific

Co-Creation projects, and reap a per-case royalty for its contributions in process and personnel.

A Co-Creation Approach between a Consulting Firm and a Global Client

I recently facilitated a Co-Creation session between senior partners of a professional-service firm and executives of a multinational medical devices, pharmaceuticals, and consumer-packaged goods manufacturer. Both firms have been around for nearly a century, so we're talking very mature companies in mature industries. In this example, I've fictionalized aspects of that meeting to protect my clients' confidentiality but preserved the aspects of that engagement that are relevant to the Co-Create Canvas. For our purposes, the consulting firm is named GloBoCo and the healthcare firm Pills & More, or P&M.

At the outset, the two companies were reluctant. First, they were used to doing "account planning" with their internal teams only, and that is the lens through which they saw what I was talking about when I urged them to consider coming together around a Co-Creation approach. Second, inviting a third party in (the facilitator essential to Co-Creation conversations) went against both company's cultures. They initially believed there could be little value in asking someone who wasn't privy to their background information to take a key role. Finally, they found it difficult to decide who should be included in such a conversation. I continued to share my council that we include the fewest possible people to achieve a good balance of strategic thinking and tactical execution, and that those people should have the clout to influence the future. We finally agreed on three participants from each side: an executive champion, a strategist, and a leader of tactical execution. It was most important that the participants would bring equal business stature (regardless of titles) with relevant areas of responsibility. (All the pre-work that went into our Co-Creation conversation doesn't show up on the canvas. The logistics of scheduling when these six executives could be in the same place at the same time practically required an Act of Congress.) I interviewed each in advance, getting a preliminary view of what they brought to the topics that the canvas covers—their past impacts, what they were seeing in the market, their strategic priorities, and so on. These conversations intrigued them, and built their interest in coming to the Co-Creation session.

The big day arrived. The night before, we had dinner together, which served as an opportunity to develop the much-needed rapport. The next morning, I ushered them into a comfortable room where several enlarged versions of the Co-Create Canvas awaited them, and I facilitated the conversation.

At the top of the canvas I had written GloBoCo; at the bottom Pills & More (P&M). We gazed toward the lighthouse, the common mission, vision, or enemy. It could be a vision of partnering to sell more products in the developed markets where they were already fully established. It could be a mission to open up new market potential in developing countries where supply chains were less established. It could be a common enemy: Walmart putting mom-and-pop pharmacies—where P&M sells lots of higher-margin household goods—out of business. With no more clarity than that at the start, they had me write "safeguard our success" at the right of the canvas.

Then we launched into our work with step 1.

Laying Foundation: I was careful to explain that past impacts must be described by their outcomes, not their inputs. The parties quickly summarized the past impact they had created together, which reinforced the reciprocal value of the relationship. They shared their situational awareness (which is an early test of how transparent the parties in the room are willing to be). GloBoCo spoke to the difficulties of managing the multiple regulatory climates across a multitude of global markets that their work with other clients had made them aware of, and P&M described trends happening in their healthcare sphere brought on by the Affordable Care Act. Both sides discussed their strategic priorities for the next eighteen to thirty-six months—the need to overhaul all compliance guidelines. They discussed elements missing from their efforts that the other party might help obtain. Oddly enough, the gap both identified was the talent agenda. Because both sides operate with a global footprint, both needed to find, recruit, and develop multilingual employees. Both also identified real-time insights from technology as another gap—specifically, massive amounts of unusable, siloed data.

Value Proposition Design: Now GloBoCo and P&M looked for what they could do together. The conversation moved toward developing a global playbook. With the FDA's technically demanding Drug Supply Chain Security Act looming, many independent pharmacies and mid-size chains were scrambling to prepare to meet the government's new stringent demands to track and trace many drugs in their supply chain for up to six years. GloBoCo could help P&M package a compliance-ready model that P&M could offer to a modular playbook. You could plug in the modules that were relevant for each market. We agreed on a 60/40 balance for that playbook: 60 percent of strategy would be consistent across the globe, while 40 percent would be modules designed to be tailored to each country's local market conditions. In that way the global brand would be consistent across the globe but flexible to address the fundamental challenges and nuances in different parts of their businesses. P&M's is such a complex business; a one-size-fits-all approach will not work when the way Guatemala handles an issue like drug counterfeiting is very different from the way South Korea handles it. Yet, both sides knew, brand consistency as P&M grew would be the differentiator that could drive future success. Now the lighthouse became clearer—I wrote "consistency" above the statement about "future-proofing" by the lighthouse at the right and "global consistency" in step 5 for their differentiator.

We moved on to working out the resources and timeframe (step 6). Once we came up with the playbook idea, we had to break it into bite-sized pieces: What needed to happen for us to get there? In a highly regulated space, everything must be documented. We created a private cloud to share planning documents. Both firms had a project management office (PMO), which we noted in step 7. We outlined who would own this initiative and who would support it.

Executing Co-Creation: The leaders from GloBoCo and P&M now moved forward on plans to execute the global playbook initiative by identifying milestones for step 8. They discussed communication preferences (step 9) and decided on a monthly phone call, at 7:00 a.m., to seize the opportunity before the minutiae of the day intruded. They agreed to record the call so those who were unable to attend could catch up, and each executive named a strong "number 2" to delegate—not

Figure 8.8: Sample GloBoCo-P&M Co-Creation Canvas

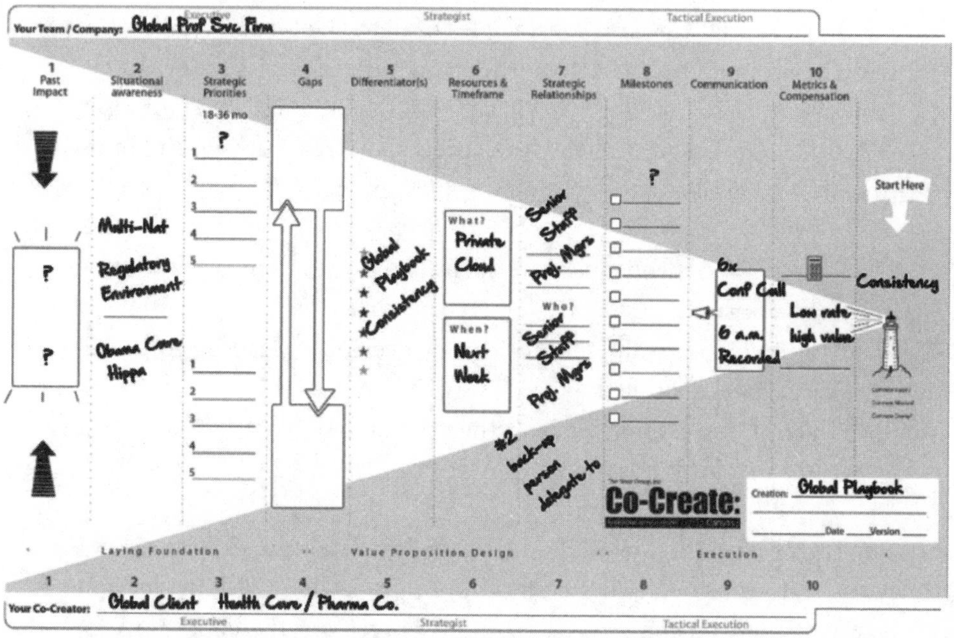

to abdicate. For step 10 they discussed metrics and compensation. Interesting to me, the compensation placed less value on the transaction and more on the transformative results they expected. A professional service firm like GloBoCo would typically bill by the hour, but for this initiative they agreed to a lower rate on a higher volume of business.

At this point, the GloBoCo-P&M joint venture was ready to put their plan in motion. Over the next two years, the radical idea to "bring the client into account planning" has led GloBoCo from $2 million in revenue with P&M to $25 million. Executives have told me the process was very well received, and we're scheduled to repeat it with two other common visions in 2017.

GO-TO-MARKET

When an organization's strategic priorities have been identified and the champions and their teams have been selected and aligned to address those priorities, the work of the Co-Create Canvas Conversation is complete. Now the next task begins: taking the value proposition to market.

The essential Co-Create principles of outcome focus, collaborative Co-Creation, and provocative leadership will require support to encourage and provoke necessary change in the organizational mindset. With the Co-Create Canvas, the whole Co-Create approach comes together in a vision of the desired business model:

1. Functional dependencies are identified in relation to a common vision, mission, or enemy.
2. A unique, joint value proposition is developed, leading to prioritized strategic initiatives.
3. A plan for execution clarifies the critical and prioritized steps the teams involved must take.

The organization should now be ready to evolve from a push to a Co-Create approach and thereby attain significant growth in a unique piece of their business. What remains is creating the conditions for people to start that work and keeping the momentum going. A number of tools help achieve this culture shift; among them are gamification, communities, and visual building blocks.

The Power and Promise of Gamification

Boy Scouts have their badges. Airlines have their Frequent Flyer programs. Dieters use the Weight Watchers points system to transform the drudgery of counting calories into something more like a friendly game. Using competition to motivate individuals is nothing new, but in the era of SMAC, it has risen to a new level: *gamification*. We are leveraging social and mobile technology, analytics, and the cloud to engage and motivate. This is proving to be powerful in achieving organizational goals. Gamification uses elements we recognize from group games and team sports: leader boards, badges for achievement of specific criteria, reward systems, and other elements that feed our human propensity for competition and desire to win. Gamification apps motivate users by promoting the self-esteem that comes from completing solo challenges and by valuing the peer recognition that comes from completing challenges in a social environment where progress is noted almost instantly and is constantly reinforced by the group.

One particular gamification expert is Gabe Zichermann, who has been helping industries as diverse as reality show weight-loss competitions and the Swedish Department of Transportation (the latter of which recently transformed traffic control by eliminating speeding fines altogether, moving instead toward a system of safe driving badges that also make law-abiding citizens eligible for the national lottery). But, against conventional wisdom, Zichermann warns, cash alone is a poor incentive.[3] He relies on a data-driven SAPS model pulled from behavioral economics that moves beyond positive reinforcement and financial rewards to get at what people really want out of interaction with apps and co-workers—namely status, access, power, and stuff.[4]

Gaming is profoundly social, and even when the stakes are low, people will invest a considerable amount of time to earn badges, trophies, and designations that help them stand out in a crowd, as evidenced by the success of social apps like Foursquare, which used to award users honorary titles such as "mayor" just for "checking in" at their favorite businesses, a feature that led to fierce competitions among friends to be the top patrons at local businesses until the feature was discontinued in 2014. Now, with mayorships returning to the company's larger social platform, Swarm, there is excitement about the notion of competing against the larger public.[5] What would it mean for your business to have millennials competing to be your most loyal customer?

Nourcabulary

Gamification applies typical elements of game-playing, such as scoring points and competing against others, to engage and motivate business relationships to achieve specified goals. Gamification works by tapping our basic human needs and desires, such as achievement and status. Apps that "gamify" various aspects of workplace behavior are based in game mechanics and game design.

If you build small teams that compete in a friendly way to complete their milestones, you create an incubator for the joint effort of Co-Creation. Gamification creates a sense of urgency, of drive, in the people who are "playing the game." It turns the old-style managerial strategy of trying to light a fire under people into a much more effective strategy that lights a fire *within* people.

Consider the example of Jubi, a learning platform that uses gamification to drive behavior change that leads to increased organizational productivity. Jubi (short for "jubilant") was founded by Larry Mohl, who had served as chief learning officer at Motorola, American Express, and Children's Healthcare of Atlanta. Mohl became so frustrated at the disconnect between traditional instructor-led training and any kind of lasting impact in the workplace that he left the world of corporate learning to create a better alternative.

Why gamification? "Gamification," Mohl told me, "can be applied to the learning process to make it more engaging and fun. It can add a sense of achievement, provide feedback on progress, and motivate people to follow through with their learning." Here's how he explains the Jubi value proposition:

> Jubi has an underlying behavior change model we call "Learn-Do-Inspire" that drives the adoption of new behaviors and skills on-the-job. Current platforms only push content with no way to bridge the gap between what I "learn" and what I "apply on my job." Jubi bridges this gap. The Learn component is where we deliver content in short quests. These quests can include any media element (such as videos) paired with interesting questions that unlock our brains and help us retain what we are learning. The Do component enables the assignment of on-the-job application activities that can be validated by a "buddy" in the system. The Inspire component includes a robust discussion form and "Inspiration Station" that rewards individuals for creating a collaborative culture.[6]

Observe what is happening with gamification like Jubi. We're taking training and motivation out of the classroom or seminar, out to the edge of where business happens. We're delivering it in bite-sized chunks that can fill spare moments that might have gone to checking a

Facebook feed. It's practical, it's effective, and the learning can be applied at the very next opportunity. Who uses Jubi? While Jubi does indeed lend itself to training call-center employees and retail workers, the company also helps develop next-generation leaders for pharmaceutical companies like Sunovion and Gilead and home-improvement retailer Home Depot.

Co-Create Communities

Related to gamification is the peer community—the individuals competing in the game, so to speak. In collaborative Co-Creation, we build an internal community of innovators—the innovation lab—but we also tap into communities of our target audiences. We invite key customers to serve on customer-advisory boards. We convene industry partners. Or we step outside our industry to create a roundtable or mastermind group where we cross-pollinate ideas and knowledge. By creating communities we become purveyors of relationships, not just products and services. Earlier I suggested that you bring a group of like-minded people together who are focused on a common mission, vision, or enemy. Leverage the collective insights of that community; make them part of the strategic relationships on the team. Combine gamification and communities to accelerate your pilots and prototypes, to accelerate commercialization of those faint signals in adaptive innovation.

Visual Building Blocks

Few things will better help you go to market with a product, service, or idea than visual building blocks, which create a vocabulary for conversations through a library of images. The fundamental premise behind visual building blocks is to avoid a "one-size-fits-all" approach to message delivery. A brochure is "one size fits all." A website is "one size fits all." The only way we customize or personalize our offerings is through dialogue. Therefore a crucial goal of your go-to-market strategy is to draw the recipients of your value into conversation with you. Visual building blocks are my preferred tool because we have become such a visual society.

My website includes a list of speaking topics I offer. Its sole purpose is to pique interest. Hopefully, in combination with the other ways I invite conversation through my blog, video blogs, position papers, and so on, the result will be that people pick up the phone and call me. The conversation will be about their events, their audience, and how they want me to customize my content to fit their audience. I immediately ask, "Are you online? Great, let's jump on GoToMeeting and let me show you." If I share examples of my work with you, something resonates with you about how it can be relevant to your audience.

Visual building blocks help me tell a story, and help the other side—clients, partners, employees, investors—frame the right challenge or opportunity and our solution to that. Visuals literally provide the construct to ask what-if questions and explore multiple scenarios. That frame helps us have an open-ended conversation. "If we did this, this is what I think would happen, and this is how we might address that." "What are other potential risks?" "What might be the unintended consequences of us doing this?" Visual building blocks help us define, frame, and discuss challenges, opportunities, and responses. They encourage us to see farther around the curves ahead.

There is a reason NASA Mission Control puts the same visual display in front of its team members in Houston and Cape Canaveral. Everyone is taking in the same trajectory, the same metrics, visually. If NASA changes the trajectory of a satellite, where will it be in three days, and in three months? Executive dashboards similarly provide a quick visualization of performance and an ability to easily explore what-if scenarios. If we tackle these initiatives, where will we be in three months, and in three years?

In strategy sessions, visual building allows individuals to come together with a degree of focus that:

- improves conversation, by reducing distractions;
- creates a roadmap, by aligning individuals on a shared view; and
- makes execution easier, by clarifying priorities.

But visual building blocks support more than just strategic planning. They help people comprehend the plan and spread the plan once a direction has been selected. Like the example of KPMG-ABC described in chapter 3, you can train individuals to use visual building blocks in storytelling. Like building with LEGO pieces, you can show your team how to build that structure with prospective clients, employees, and others using the visual building blocks. Visual storytelling heavily depends on having the right blocks and a process for effectively training the communicators on your team.

With gamification, communities, and visual building blocks, you create an ecosystem in which the culture reflects an ethos of Co-Creation, and everyone in that system is supported in taking products, services, and solutions to market.

WHAT IT TAKES: AGILITY AND RAPID RESPONSE

Remember, Co-Creation is a joint effort—not a merger. You will continue running your existing business while you make this investment in evolving your future. That is one reason for selecting no more than three to five prioritized initiatives; moving toward an organization-wide approach of Co-Creation will itself need to begin with pilots and prototypes in order to earn the buy-in of the entire team.

Because adaptive innovation is a core tenet of the Co-Create approach, the go-to-market strategy has to be incredibly nimble. No sixty-page documents allowed. We are going to build a prototype of the new concept, take it to market, learn from its customer uptake (or the lack of it), and rapidly apply what we learn to make course corrections.

An aptitude for course correction is rarely found in most traditional organizations' DNA—which is why they're not start-ups. Agility and rapid responses—both of which are critical to delivering value in the Co-Create economy—are also critical in leading the internal organizational shift from push to Co-Create. Organizational leaders must take steps to ensure that Co-Create evangelists are not isolated from each other or buried within their respective departmental silos. These evangelists will need ample opportunities to connect with each other and lend mutual support within the organization because they are bound to face pushback from individuals (and even entire business units) who feel more comfortable with the status quo.

The Co-Create economy is fueled by strategic relationships. It takes a connected community of Co-Create evangelists within an organization to carry out a successful transition from push to Co-Create.

Chapter Eight Takeaways

- To begin using the Co-Create Canvas, identify the partners in this joint venture and the common vision, mission, or enemy they intend to address.
- Laying the foundation is the concern of steps one through four: past impact, situational awareness, strategic priorities for an eighteen- to thirty-six-month timeframe, and gaps.
- Value proposition design takes place in steps five through seven: differentiators, resources and timeframe, and strategic relationships.
- Executive Co-Creation is planned via steps eight through ten: milestones, communication, and metrics and compensation.
- Working through the Co-Create Conversation requires the right setting, people, and facilitator.
- Create the conditions for executing the go-to-market strategy with gamification, communities, and visual building blocks.
- Agility and rapid response are critical to leading the internal organizational shift toward a Co-Create approach, especially when you encounter resistance to change.

AFTERWORD

Thank you for investing your time, effort, and resources to read through this book. Over the past two decades, I've learned that after you've read enough, thought about enough, spoken enough, or otherwise advised clients enough about a topic, you feel as though you have something to say. I've been thinking about Co-Create for the past four years, and in these pages I hope to have given you the tools in constructs, examples, interviews, and case studies to help you think and lead differently.

That aspiration doesn't often come easily, and it's seldom handed to you. At times, you'll be the dissenting voice, feeling like the lone survivor, or you will be looked at with incredibly perplexed expressions; you'll be talked about behind closed doors with concerns that you've lost your mind—#CrazyTalk; you'll be challenged publically and privately for taking on the status quo, and no doubt will hear comments such as, "That'll never work," and, "We tried that twenty years ago and it didn't work then!"

But that's what iteration, innovation, and disruption is all about: steadfast belief that there are always better ways. This conviction underscores that unless your personal brand; your team's performance, execution, and results; and your organization's DNA evolves, you'll struggle to remain relevant in your market and to your biggest asset: your portfolio of relationships. My hope for you from this book is that you'll take one or two of these ideas and put them to work sooner rather than later.

I'm grateful for amazing clients over the past two decades such as Phil Ostwalt at KPMG, Rod Moses at Hilton, Stefano Bertuzzi at ASM, Randy Seidl at HP, John Murnane at tke, Kathy Bedell at BCD Travel, Erin Meszaros at Sutherland, and Duffy Wilbert at InfoComm; incredibly talented colleagues and partners such as Lin Wilson, Jennifer Bridges, Jim Rodgers, Bruce Kasanoff, Matt Jones, and Mark Sylvester; and my family for their unconditional love and support to allow me to work with global clients in the evolution of their organizations.

This book would not have been possible without the support of dedicated professionals such as Sarah White, Michael Sanders, Sara Taylor, Tom Miller, Emily Carleton, George Witte, and the entire team at St. Martin's Press.

Let me close with three reminders from my own mentors over the years, which I've found particularly valuable:

1. It's never as good or as bad as you think; learn to pause!
2. Progress trumps perfection every time; version one is always better than version none!
3. Improve by 1 percent a day and in seventy days you're twice as good!

What will be your 1 percent after reading this book?

BE WELL AND STAY IN TOUCH,
DAVID

NOTES

Introduction

1 "Outreach's 100 Largest Churches 2015," ed. Ed Stetzer, The Outreach 100, special issue, *Outreach*, March 26, 2015, http://www.outreachmagazine.com/outreach-100 -largest-churches-2015.html (accessed March 26, 2015).

2 See W. Chan Kim and Renée Mauborgne, *Blue Ocean Strategy: How to Create Uncontested Market Space and Make the Competition Irrelevant* (Cambridge, MA: Harvard Business Review Press, 2013).

3 George Barna and David Kinnaman, eds., *Churchless: Understanding Today's Unchurched and How to Connect with Them* (Carol Stream, IL: Tyndale House, 2014).

4 Don Tapscott and Anthony D. Williams, *Wikinomics: How Mass Collaboration Changes Everything*, exp. ed. (New York: Portfolio, 2008), 36–37.

5 For an in-depth discussion of Alan Weiss's concept of Market Gravity and his trademarked Market Gravity Wheel tool, see chapter four of *The Consulting Bible: Everything You Need to Know to Create and Expand a Seven-Figure Consulting Practice* (New York: John Wiley & Sons, 2011).

6 Martin Blanc, "GoPro Dominates with 72.5% of US Camera Market: IDC," Bidness Etc, January 22, 2015, http://www.bidnessetc.com/33076-gopro-inc-dominates -with-725-of-us-camera-market-idc/ (accessed April 20, 2016).

7 Andy Stanley and Ed Young, *Can We Do That? Innovative Practices That Will Change the Way You Do Church* (New York: Howard Books, 2010), 2.

8 Ibid., 1.

9 Andy Stanley, "Invitation of a Lifetime," video, 43:07, North Point Community Church, November 29, 2015, http://northpoint.org/messages/invitation-of-lifetime/ (accessed April 20, 2016).

10 "100 Best Companies to Work for 2016," *Fortune*, http://fortune.com/best-companies /usaa-36/ (accessed March 30, 2016).

11 "Forrester's CX Index Ranks the Brands That Deliver the Best Customer Experience," The Media Center, April 20, 2015, https://www.forrester.com/Forresters+C

X+Index+Ranks+The+Brands+That+Deliver+The+Best+Customer+Experience/-/E-PRE7806 (accessed April 10, 2016).

12 Alejandro Alba, "See It: LEGO Launches New Online Game, 'Minecraft's' Competitor," *New York Daily News*, June 1, 2015, http://www.nydailynews.com/news/national/lego-launches-new-online-game-article-1.2242696 (accessed June 12, 2016).

13 Jonathan Ringen, "How LEGO Became the Apple of Toys," *Fast Company*, 192 January 8, 2015, http://www.fastcompany.com/3040223/when-it-clicks-it-clicks (accessed March 30, 2016).

One

1 Quentin Hardy, "AT&T's Strategy Is One Part Innovation, One Part Inspiration," *New York Times*, February 13, 2016, http://nyti.ms/1KNpMSE (accessed April 19, 2016).

2 "Gearing up for the Cloud, AT&T Tells Its Workers: Adapt, or Else," *New York Times*, February 13, 2016, http://nyti.ms/1KMzXqF (accessed April 19, 2016).

3 See Mary J. Cronin, *Smart Products, Smarter Services: Strategies for Embedded Control* (Cambridge: Cambridge University Press, 2010).

4 See Jayavardhana Gubbi et al., "Internet of Things (Iot): A Vision, Architectural Elements, and Future Directions," *Future Generation Computer Systems* 29, no. 7 (2013).

5 Allen Pierleoni and Malcom Gladwell, "Between the Lines: Malcolm Gladwell Shines a Light on Hidden Stories," interview, *Sacramento Bee*, February 12, 2016, http://www.sacbee.com/entertainment/books/article60136741.html (accessed April 19, 2016).

6 Max Chafkin, "Warby Parker Sees the Future of Retail," *Fast Company*, February 17, 2015, http://www.fastcompany.com/3041334/most-innovative-companies-2015/warby-parker-sees-the-future-of-retail (accessed August 22, 2016).

7 Richard Feloni, "The One Statistic That Matters Most to Warby Parker's Founders," *Business Insider*, March 5, 2014. http://www.businessinsider.com/dave-gilboa-on-warby-parkers-success-2014-2 (accessed January 30, 2016).

8 Keiningham et al. have expressed extreme concern over the promotion of the NPS system at the managerial level, saying, "The clear implication is that managers have adopted the Net Promoter metric for tracking growth on the basis of the belief that solid science underpins the findings and that it is superior to other metrics. However, our research suggests that such presumptions are erroneous. The consequences are the potential misallocation of resources as a function of erroneous strategies guided by Net Promoter on firm performance company value and shareholder wealth." For a detailed discussion of the questionable scientific basis of the NPS metrics, see Timothy L. Keiningham et al., "A Longitudinal Examination of Net Promoter and Firm Revenue Growth," *Journal of Marketing* 71, no. 3 (2007).

9 "About HubSpot—Internet Marketing Company," HubSpot, Inc., http://www.hubspot.com/internet-marketing-company (accessed April 23, 2016).

10 Personal interview via e-mail correspondence, June 15, 2016.

11 Matt Weinberger, "Why Coca-Cola Wants to Fund the Next Billion-Dollar Startup," Business Insider, May 14, 2015, http://www.businessinsider.com/coca-cola-is-in-the-business-of-bottling-billion-dollar-startups-2015-5 (accessed April 21, 2016).

12 Jay Moye, "Creating a Win-Win: Inside Coke's New Startup Model," Coca-Cola

Journey, October 16, 2014, http://www.coca-colacompany.com/stories/creating-a
-win-win-inside-cokes-new-startup-model/ (accessed April 21, 2016).

13 Larry Loeb, "IBM Watson Ecosystem Expands with 6 New Partners," *Information-
Week*, October 27, 2015, http://www.informationweek.com/big-data/ibm-watson
-ecosystem-expands-with-6-new-partners-/a/d-id/1322851 (accessed June 12, 2016).

14 Jordan Novet, "IBM Unveils 4 New Watson Partners: Under Armour, Softbank,
Whirlpool, Medtronic," *VentureBeat*, January 6, 2016, http://venturebeat.com/2016
/01/06/ibm-unveils-4-new-watson-partners-under-armour-softbank-whirlpool
-medtronic/ (accessed June 12, 2016).

15 Kevin Plank, "How to Build a Billion Dollar Business from Sweat, Technology and
Transparency," lecture, iCONIC:DC, The Warner Theatre, Washington, D.C., November 11, 2015.

16 "CNBC Partial Transcript: Under Armour CEO Kevin Plank Speaks with CNBC's
Scott Wapner Live from CNBC and Inc. Magazine's iCONIC Conference," November 12, 2015, http://www.cnbc.com/2015/11/12/cnbc-partial-transcript-under
-armour-ceo-kevin-plank-speaks-with-cnbcs-scott-wapner-live-from-cnbc-and
-inc-magazines-iconic-conference.html (accessed April 20, 2016).

17 Tom Foster, "Kevin Plank Is Betting Almost $1 Billion That Under Armour Can
Beat Nike," *Inc.*, January 6, 2016, http://www.inc.com/magazine/201602/tom
-foster/kevin-plank-under-armour-spending-1-billion-to-beat-nike.html (accessed
April 22, 2016).

18 Robert J. Sternberg, *Beyond IQ: A Triarchic Theory of Human Intelligence* (Cambridge: Cambridge University Press, 1985).

Two

1 Walter Isaacson, *Steve Jobs* (New York: Simon & Schuster, 2011), 408.

2 Clarence Polke, "FCC Approves Proposal to Boost TV Set-Top Box Competition,"
Reuters, February 18, 2016, http://www.reuters.com/article/us-fcc-tv-regulations
-idUSKCN0VR0GU (accessed April 30, 2016).

3 Although Apple TV is certainly the sexiest streaming device available on the market today, it has actually only captured 20 percent of the market share, tied with
another fierce up-and-comer, Roku (founded by Silicon Valley whiz kid Anthony
Wood). The Amazon Fire TV Stick comes in at 16 percent market share ahead of a
handful of other independent makers, but the real winner is the cheap and more
compact Google Chromecast, which has rocketed ahead in recent quarters. As of
January 2016, Chromecast has about 35 percent of streaming peripheral market.
This has other makers running scared, to the point that Roku's Wood is even lobby-
ing alongside Comcast to prevent the FCC from cracking set-top boxes in the hopes
that Google's superior software bring-to-market won't shut out hardware stand-
alones like the Roku and Apple TV completely. See Nicole Arce, "Chromecast Tops
Apple TV, Fire TV and Roku as Bestselling Media Streaming Device," *Tech Times*,
December 1, 2015, http://www.techtimes.com/articles/112147/20151201/chromecast
-tops-apple-tv-fire-tv-and-roku-as-bestselling-media-streaming-device.htm (accessed April 30, 2016); cf. Anthony Wood, "How the FCC's 'Set-Top Box' Rule Hurts
Consumers: Cable Already Has Steady Competition. Opening the Box Will Only
Raise Costs and Reduce Innovation," editorial, *Wall Street Journal*, April 21, 2016,
http://www.wsj.com/articles/how-the-fccs-set-top-box-rule-hurts-consumers
-1461279906 (accessed April 30, 2016).

4   Jon Fingas, "Apple's OS X Beta Testing Is Now Open to the Public," *Endgadget*, April 22, 2014, http://www.engadget.com/2014/04/22/os-x-beta-seed-program /(accessed April 29, 2016).

5   Apple's Beta Seed program continues to this day. To get in on the action, register your iDevice at https://beta.apple.com/sp/betaprogram/.

6   "iTunes Store Sets New Record with 25 Billion Songs Sold," Apple Press Info, February 6, 2013, https://www.apple.com/pr/library/2013/02/06iTunes-Store-Sets -New-Record-with-25-Billion-Songs-Sold.html (accessed April 28, 2016).

7   Conor Dougherty, "Cities to Untangle Traffic Snarls, with Help from Alphabet Unit," *New York Times*, March 17, 2016, http://nyti.ms/22pxs2d (accessed April 28, 2016).

8   US Department of Transportation, "US DOT Announces Seven Finalist Cities for Smart City Challenge," https://www.transportation.gov/smartcity (accessed April 28, 2016).

9   Steve Lohr, "Can Apple Find More Hits without Its Tastemaker?" *New York Times*, January 18, 2011, http://www.nytimes.com/2011/01/19/technology/companies /19innovate.html?_r=0 (accessed April 30, 2016).

10   Matt Ballantine, https://www.linkedin.com/today/author/0_0FR96GIeFrgLSVm- 8Jsjfb9 (accessed November 18, 2015).

11   See Joseph L. Bower and Clayton Christensen, "Disruptive Technologies: Catch- ing the Wave," *Harvard Business Review 73, no. 1* (January–February 1995); cf. Clayton Christensen, *The Innovator's Dilemma: When New Technologies Cause Great Firms to Fail* (Cambridge, MA: Harvard Business Review Press, 2013).

12   Clayton Christensen, Michael E. Raynor, and Rory McDonald, "What Is Disrup- tive Innovation?" *Harvard Business Review*, December 2015, https://hbr.org/2015 /12/what-is-disruptive-innovation (accessed April 30, 2016).

13   Karen Blumenthal, *Steve Jobs: The Man Who Thought Different* (New York: Bloomsbury, 2012), 236.

14   Kevin C. Tofel, "BYOD Didn't Kill Cisco's Tablet; It Was a Doomed Idea," Gigaom, May 25, 2012, https://gigaom.com/2012/05/25/byod-didnt-kill-cicsos-tablet-it-was -a-doomed-idea/ (accessed April 30, 2016).

15   Eric Wesoff, "Flextronics Buys Nextracker for $330 Million," *Greentech Media*, September 8, 2015, http://www.greentechmedia.com/articles/read/Flextronics-Buys -NEXTracker-For-330-Million (accessed May 5, 2016).

16   Rachel Brown, "Nordstrom Touts Merch with Pinterest," *Women's Wear Daily*, July 2, 2013, https://pmcwwd.files.wordpress.com/2013/07/wwd0702web.pdf

17   Arvind Gupta, "Adaptive Innovation: Create, Learn, Repeat," *Rotman Magazine*, University of Toronto's Rotman School of Management (Jan 23, 2013). https:// designthinking.ideo.com/?p=917

18   "G'Five Launches 'Made in Pakistan' Phones; G'Five Starts Assembling Line for Mobile Phones in Pakistan," *NetMag Pakistan*, March 15, 2016, http://netmag .com.pk/2016/03/15/made-in-pakistan-phones-by-gfive/ (accessed May 1, 2016).

19   Bruce Hoffmeister, interview by Steven Norton, May 27, 2016. http://www.wsj.com /articles/marriotts-cio-says-mobile-apps-are-changing-the-guest-experience -1464660061

20   Stan Phelps, "Adidas Reinforces a New Culture of Innovation with the Introduc- tion of Avenue A," *Forbes*, February 10, 2016, http://www.forbes.com/sites /stanphelps/2016/02/10/adidas-reinforces-a-new-culture-of-innovation-with-the -introduction-of-avenue-a/#c784e117b43b (accessed April 28, 2016).

21 Ibid.

22 For tips on nailing your next VC pitch and possibly avoiding PowerPoint–induced Ménière's disease, see "The 10/20/30 Rule of Powerpoint," guykawasaki.com, December 30, 2005, http://guykawasaki.com/the_102030_rule/ (accessed May 5, 2016).

23 Jeremy Jackson, "Rapid Prototyping: The Wright Way to Fail," Method 10x10, May 2011, http://method.com/ideas/10x10/rapid-prototyping-the-wright-way-to -fail (accessed May 5, 2016).

24 Peter F. Drucker, *Management: Tasks, Responsibilities, Practices* (New York: Harper & Row, 1974), 61.

25 Michael Hinshaw and Bruce Kasanoff, *Smart Customers, Stupid Companies: Why Only Intelligent Companies Will Thrive, and How to Be One of Them* (New York: Business Strategy Press, 2012).

Three

1 Emma Whitford, "Most Innovative Companies 2015: Instagram for Its Beautiful Relationship with the Fashion Industry," *Fast Company*, February 9, 2015, http:// www.fastcompany.com/3039584/most-innovative-companies-2015/instagram (accessed May 7, 2016).

2 Ellen McCarthy, " 'Green Burials' Are on the Rise as Baby Boomers Plan for Their Future, and Funerals," *Washington Post*, October 6, 2014, https://www .washingtonpost.com/lifestyle/style/green-burials-are-on-the-rise-as-baby -boomers-plan-for-their-future-and-funerals/2014/10/06/d269cfbc-3eae-11e4 -b03f-de718edeb92f_story.html (accessed May 7, 2016).

3 Amy S. Choi, "Entrepreneurs Reinvent the Funeral Industry," *Bloomberg Busi-nessweek*, June 20, 2008, http://www.bloomberg.com/news/articles/2008-06-19 /entrepreneurs-reinvent-the-funeral-industry (accessed May 8, 2008).

4 Danielle Rumore and Keenan Hughes, "Marketers Must Change How They Appeal to Consumers if They Want to Capitalize on Promise of New Media, According to Study; Yankelovich Unveils New Marketing Receptivity Study at Arf Confer-ence," *Business Wire*, April 18, 2005, http://www.businesswire.com/news/home /20050418005304/en/Marketers-Change-Appeal-Consumers-Capitalize-Promise -Media (accessed June 3, 2016).

5 Sarah Buhr, "We Took a Trip to the eSalon Professional at Home Hair Color Factory," *TechCrunch*, September 14, 2015, http://techcrunch.com/2015/09/14/we -took-a-trip-to-the-esalon-professional-at-home-hair-color-factory/ (accessed June 3, 2016).

6 Faye Brookman, "Esalon's Birthday Present: $30 Million," *Women's Wear Daily*, October 2, 2015, http://wwd.com/beauty-industry-news/hair/esalons-birthday -present-30-million-10251338/ (accessed June 3, 2016).

7 Marketing Leadership Council and Google, "The Digital Evolution in B2B Marketing," Corporate Executive Board Company, https://www.cebglobal.com /content/dam/cebglobal/us/EN/best-practices-decision-support/marketing -communications/pdfs/CEB-Mktg-B2B-Digital-Evolution.pdf (accessed June 3, 2016).

8 Lori Wizdo, "Myth Busting 101: Insights into the B2B Buyer Journey," Forrester Blogs, May 25, 2015, http://blogs.forrester.com/lori_wizdo/15-05-25-myth_busting _101_insights_intothe_b2b_buyer_journey (accessed June 3, 2016).

9 Kit Yarrow and Jayne O'Donnell, *Gen Buy: How Tweens, Teens and Twenty-Somethings Are Revolutionizing Retail* (New York: John Wiley and Sons, 2009).

10 Darrell Rigby and Barbara Bilodeau, "Management Tools & Trends 2015," in Bain & Company *Insights* (London, 2015), 9–12. http://www.bain.com/publications/articles/management-tools-and-trends-2015.aspx

11 Alexander Osterwalder and Yves Pigneur, *Business Model Generation: A Handbook for Visionaries, Game Changers, and Challengers* (Hoboken: John Wiley & Sons, 2013).

12 Adam Davidson, "Managed by Q's 'Good Jobs' Gamble," *New York Times*, February 25, 2016, http://www.nytimes.com/2016/02/28/magazine/managed-by-qs-good-jobs-gamble.html?smid=nytcore-ipad-share&smprod=nytcore-ipad.[AU: Date of access?]

13 Tim Leberecht, "3 Ways to (Usefully) Lose Control of Your Brand," video, 6:30, posted by TEDGlobal, https://www.ted.com/talks/tim_leberecht_3_ways_to_usefully_lose_control_of_your_reputation?language=en (accessed June 6, 2016); see also Tim Leberecht, *The Business Romantic: Give Everything, Quantify Nothing, and Create Something Greater than Yourself* (New York: Little Brown, 2015).

14 Jackie Wills, "Patagonia Urges Customers 'Don't Buy New, Search Ebay,'" *Guardian*, May 15, 2014, http://www.theguardian.com/sustainable-business/sustainability-case-studies-ebay-patagonia-recycle (accessed June 3, 2016).

15 Sarah Perez, "Instacart and Whole Foods Confirm Expanded Relationship, Plans for Expansion," *TechCrunch*, March 10, 2016, http://techcrunch.com/2016/03/10/instacart-and-whole-foods-confirm-expanded-relationship-plans-for-expansion/ (accessed May 12, 2016).

16 Jason Del Rey, "Whole Foods to Invest in Instacart, Signs New Multi-Year Delivery Deal," *Re/code*, February 23, 2016, http://www.recode.net/2016/2/23/11588138/whole-foods-to-invest-in-instacart-signs-new-multi-year-delivery-deal (accessed May 8, 2016).

17 Personal interview. June 14, 2016.

18 "About Us—ThyssenKrupp Elevator Americas," ThyssenKrupp Elevator Americas, https://www.thyssenkruppelevator.com/about-us (accessed May 12, 2016).

19 David Holcomb, conversation with author, June 21, 2016. Subsequent Holcomb quotations in this chapter are from this conversation.

20 Ibid.

21 Ibid.

22 Ibid.

23 "A Big Change Is Coming to Elevators, and It Matters More than You Think," *Time*, October 27, 2015, http://time.com/4088793/elevator-max-cloud-thyssenkrupp/ (accessed May 19, 2016).

24 Holcomb, conversation with author, June 21, 2016.

25 See Sherry Turkle, *Reclaiming Conversation: The Power of Talk in a Digital Age* (New York: Penguin, 2015).

Four

1 Dave Elzinga, Susan Mulder, and Ole Jorgen Vetvik, "The Consumer Decision Journey," *McKinsey Quarterly* 3 (2009): 96–97.

2 Jason Clampet, "Skift State of Travel 2016: Hyatt Hotels' CEO on a New Perspective on the Hospitality Industry," video, 15:14, posted by Skift, https://skift.com/2015/11/10/video-hyatt-hotels-ceo-on-a-new-perspective-on-the-hospitality

-industry/ (accessed May 19, 2016). Subsequent Hoplamazian quotations in this chapter are from this conversation.

3   Ibid.

4   Ibid.

5   Francis T. (Fay) Vincent, "Between the Notes," *America: The National Catholic Review*, November 5, 2001, http://americamagazine.org/issue/349/other-things /between-notes (accessed May 19, 2016).

6   Sarah White, *Principles of Marketing* (San Diego, CA: Bridgepoint Education, 2012).

7   Marketing Leadership Council and Google, "From Promotion to Emotion: Connecting B2B Customers to Brands," Corporate Executive Board Company, https:// www.cebglobal.com/content/dam/cebglobal/us/EN/best-practices-decision -support/marketing-communications/pdfs/promotion-emotion-whitepaper-full .pdf (accessed June 8, 2016).

8   Antonio Damasio, *Descartes' Error: Emotion, Reason, and the Human Brain* (New York: Penguin, 2005).

9   Sam Nathan and Karl Schmidt, *Think with Google*, "From Promotion to Emotion: Connecting B2B Customers to Brands," https://www.thinkwithgoogle.com /articles/promotion-emotion-b2b.html (accessed October 2013).

10   Elizabeth Dunn and Michael Norton, *Happy Money: The Science of Happier Spending* (New York: Simon & Schuster, 2013), 83.

11   Jennifer Edson Escalas, "Narrative Processing: Building Consumer Connections to Brands," *Journal of Consumer Psychology* 14, no. 1 (2004): 168–70.

12   Nicole Laporte, "Most Innovative Companies 2015: HBO for Making Itself the Belle of the Streaming-TV Ball," *Fast Company*, February 9, 2015, http://www.fastcompany .com/3039575/most-innovative-companies-2015/hbo (accessed May 19, 2015).

13   Janko Roettgers, "HBO Officially Announces April Launch of HBO Now at Apple Event," Gigaom, March 9, 2015, https://gigaom.com/2015/03/09/hbo-officially -announces-launch-of-hbo-now-at-apple-event/ (accessed May 19, 2016).

14   *Jerry Maguire*, directed by Cameron Crowe, TriStar Pictures, 1996.

Five

1   See Tom Peters, "The Brand of You," *Fast Company*, August 31, 2016, http://www .fastcompany.com/28905/brand-called-you (accessed June 12, 2016), one of the precursors to Daniel Pink's landmark monograph, *Free Agent Nation: How America's New Independent Workers Are Transforming the Way We Live* (New York: Grand Central Publishing, 2001).

2   Stephane Kasriel, "Why the Future of Work Will Look a Lot Like Hollywood," *Fast Company*, February 29, 2016, http://www.fastcompany.com/3057210/the -future-of-work/why-the-future-of-work-will-look-a-lot-like-hollywood (accessed June 8, 2016).

3   Sara Horowitz, "Freelancers Union and Upwork Release New Study Revealing Insights into the Almost 54 Million People Freelancing in America," Upwork, press release, 2015, https://www.upwork.com/press/2015/10/01/freelancers-union-and -upwork-release-new-study-revealing-insights-into-the-almost-54-million -people-freelancing-in-america/ (accessed June 12, 2016).

4   Dan Breznitz, "Unglamorous Freelance Manufacturers Could Boost U.S. Competitiveness," *Harvard Business Review*, March 1, 2012, https://hbr.org/2012/03 /unglamorous-freelance-manufact (accessed September 21, 2016).

5 Peter F. Drucker, *Management Challenges for the 21st Century* (New York: Rout-ledge, rev. ed. 2012), 116. Emphasis mine.

6 Tim Mullaney, "Big Senior Living Players, Tech Whizzes Unite at MATTER," *Senior Housing News*, June 2, 2015, http://seniorhousingnews.com/2015/06/02/big-senior-living-players-tech-whizzes-unite-at-matter/ (accessed September 29, 2016).

7 Michael A. Stanko, Jonathan D. Bohlmann, and Roger J. Calantone, "Outsourcing Innovation: With Budgets Tight, More Companies Are Hiring Third Parties to Come Up with New Ideas," *Wall Street Journal*, November 30, 2009, http://www.wsj.com/articles/SB10001424052970204488304574426521384198990 (accessed June 8, 2016).

8 Jeff Cole, Andy Pasztor, and Thomas E. Ricks, "Lockheed, Boeing to Design, Build a Joint Strike Fighter," *Wall Street Journal*, November 18, 1996, http://www.wsj.com/articles/SB848268889417149500 (accessed June 8, 2016); David Axe, "The Secret History of Boeing's Killer Drone," *Wired*, June 6, 2011, https://www.wired.com/2011/06/killer-drone-secret-history/ (accessed June 8, 2016).

9 You can "apply" at http://goplaces.theheinekencompany.com/en

10 Angela Natividad, "Heineken Just Made an HR Campaign That's as Cool as Any Consumer Ads It's Done," *Adweek*, September 15, 2016, http://www.adweek.com/adfreak/heineken-just-made-hr-campaign-thats-cool-any-consumer-ads-its-done-173289 (accessed September 28, 2016). (You can "apply" at http://goplaces.theheinekencompany.com/en.)

11 Ali Suliman, "Preview Nike's ACG Collection at Their Pop-up Shop in NYC: Nike Hike Is on Exhibit at 135 Bowery until November 29," *Fader*, November 9, 2015, http://www.thefader.com/2015/11/09/nike-opens-hike-pop-up-shop (accessed June 16, 20167); Erin Zimmer, "First Look: Chobani Soho," *Serious Eats*, July 31, 2012, http://newyork.seriouseats.com/2012/07/first-look-chobani-soho-greek-yogurt-bar.html (accessed June 16, 2016).

12 Sydney Ember, "Pepsi Turns Restaurateur, to Serve up Some Buzz," *New York Times*, January 28, 2016, http://www.nytimes.com/2016/01/29/business/media/pepsi-turns-restaurateur-to-serve-up-some-buzz.html?_r=0 (accessed June 8, 2016).

13 Andrew Sheivachman, "Millennials Are More Likely to Use Travel Agents than Any Other U.S. Demographic," *Skift*, June 13, 2016, https://skift.com/2016/06/13/millennials-are-more-likely-to-use-travel-agent-than-any-other-u-s-demographic/ (accessed June 30, 2016).

14 Personal Interview. Travelport Americas Customer Conference. June 8, 2016, Ritz-Carlton Biscayne Bay, Florida.

15 Örjan De Manzano, *Biological Mechanisms in Creativity and Flow* (Stockholm: Karolinska Institute Department of Women's and Children's Health, 2010).

16 Joe Gebbia, "How Airbnb Designs for Trust," video, 15:51, posted by TED2016, http://www.ted.com/talks/joe_gebbia_how_airbnb_designs_for_trust?language=en (accessed June 8, 2016).

17 Ronnie West, conversation with author, June 8, 2016. Subsequent West quotations in this chapter are from this conversation.

18 Ibid.

19 Ibid.

20 Ibid.

21 Ibid.

22 It is well worth your time to read Mihaly Csikszentmihalyi's *Creativity: Flow and*

the Psychology of Discovery and Invention (New York: HarperCollins, 1996). And to learn to pronounce his name so that you can recommend it to others at cocktail parties, but if you've only got twenty minutes to change your life, maximize the return on your investment by watching his TED talk about mental states: "Flow, the Secret to Happiness," video, 18:55, posted by TED2004, https://www.ted.com /talks/mihaly_csikszentmihalyi_on_flow?language=en (accessed June 15, 2016).

Six

1 Daniel Roberts, "Rent the Runway Exclusive: What's Behind the Exodus from Rent the Runway?" *Fortune*, November 17, 2015, http://fortune.com/2015/11/17/rent-the -runway-exodus/ (accessed January 12, 2016).
2 Heather Wood Rudulph, "How Jennifer Hyman Completely Changed the Way Women Shop," *Cosmopolitan*, April 28, 2016, http://www.cosmopolitan.com /career/a57537/jennifer-hyman-rent-the-runway/ (accessed June 12, 2016).
3 Roberts, "What's Behind the Exodus?"
4 Rudulph, "Jennifer Hyman."
5 Jeremy Taylor, "How to Use Social Media Monitoring for a Product Launch," *Our Social Times*, November 1, 2015, http://oursocialtimes.com/how-to-use-social -media-monitoring-for-a-product-launch/ (accessed June 12, 2016).
6 J. P. Mangalindan, "Klout Acquired for $200 Million by Lithium Technologies," *Fortune*, March 26, 2014, http://fortune.com/2014/03/26/klout-acquired-for-200 -million-by-lithium-technologies/ (accessed June 12, 2016).
7 Leslie Patton, "McDonald's Growth Surges after All-Day Breakfast Boosts Sales," *Bloomberg*, January 25, 2016, http://www.bloomberg.com/news/articles/2016-01 -25/mcdonald-s-growth-surges-after-all-day-breakfast-boosts-sales (accessed June 29, 2016).
8 Michael Copeland and Om Malik, "How to Ride the Fifth Wave," Gigaom June 15, 2005, https://gigaom.com/2005/06/15/how-to-ride-the-fifth-wave/ (accessed June 12, 2016).
9 Mark van Rijmenam, "What Is SMAC, and How Is It Reshaping the Enterprise?" *Datafloq*, October 24, 2015, https://datafloq.com/read/smac-is-reshaping-the -enterprise/17 (accessed June 12, 2016).
10 van Rijmenam, "What Is SMAC?"
11 Matt Waller, "How Sharing Data Drives Supply Chain Innovation: A Look Back at When Walmart Was Little and Big Data Was Small," *Industry Week*, August 12, 2013, http://www.industryweek.com/supplier-relationships/how-sharing-data -drives-supply-chain-innovation (accessed June 12, 2016).

Seven

1 "The World's Top 10 Most Innovative Companies of 2015 in Big Data," *Fast Company*, February 9, 2015, http://www.fastcompany.com/3041638/most-innovative -companies-2015/the-worlds-top-10-most-innovative-companies-in-big-data (accessed June 11, 2016).
2 Tyler McCall, "At Condé Nast, Clothing Rental Is Now an Employee Benefit Thanks to a New Partnership with Rent the Runway," *Fashionista*, May 24, 2016, http://fashionista.com/2016/05/conde-nast-rent-the-runway (accessed June 12, 2016).
3 Richard Branson, interview by Carmine Gallo, May 8, 2013, YouTube video.

https://www.youtube.com/watch?v=Fy4lYDN1gz4. See also Carmine Gallo, "The Little Black Book of Billionaire Secrets: Seven Ways to Inspire Employees to Love Their Jobs," *Forbes*, June 21, 2013, http://www.forbes.com/sites/carminegallo/2013/06/21/seven-ways-to-inspire-employees-to-love-their-jobs/#7af3a13c1e4c (accessed June 11, 2016).

4   Richard Branson, "One Day Offices Will Be a Thing of the Past," Virgin.com, March 4, 2013, https://www.virgin.com/richard-branson/one-day-offices-will-be-a-thing-of-the-past (accessed June 11, 2016).

5   Lin Guo, Jing Jian Xiao, and Chuanyi Tang, "Understanding the Psychological Process Underlying Customer Satisfaction and Retention in a Relational Service," *Journal of Business Research* 62, no. 11 (2009).

6   Christopher Heine, "This Mobile App Pays You for Your Selfies while Giving Custom Data to Brands: Narcissism, Monetized for All," *Adweek*, May 18, 2016, http://www.adweek.com/news/technology/mobile-app-pays-you-your-selfies-while-giving-custom-data-brands-171548 (accessed June 11, 2016).

7   Courtney Rubin, "What Do Consumers Want? Look at Their Selfies," *New York Times*, May 7, 2016, http://nyti.ms/1O6bfmL (accessed June 11, 2016).

8   Elliot Turner, interview by Seth Grimes, April 25, 2014. https://breakthroughanalysis.com/2014/04/25/analytics-semantics-sense-qa-with-elliot-turner-alchemyapi/

9   Doug Henschen, "IBM Watson: 10 New Jobs for Cognitive Computing," *InformationWeek*, March 12, 2015, http://www.informationweek.com/big-data/big-data-analytics/ibm-watson-10-new-jobs-for-cognitive-computing/d/d-id/1319427?image_number=2 (accessed June 11, 2016).

10 Salvador Rodriguez, "Mark Zuckerberg Wants a Smart Home with a 'Jarvis' AI Butler; Just How Difficult Will That Be?" *International Business Times*, January 7, 2016 (accessed June 12, 2016). http://www.ibtimes.com/mark-zuckerberg-wants-smart-home-jarvis-ai-butler-just-how-difficult-will-be-2255113

11 Andrew Bartels et al., "The Public Cloud Market Is Now in Hypergrowth: Sizing the Public Cloud Market, 2014 to 2020," *Forrester*, April 24, 2014, https://www.forrester.com/report/The+Public+Cloud+Market+Is+Now+In+Hypergrowth/-/E-RES113365 (accessed June 11, 2016).

12 Lauren F. Friedman, "IBM's Watson Supercomputer May Soon Be the Best Doctor in the World," *Business Insider*, April 22, 2014, http://www.businessinsider.com/ibms-watson-may-soon-be-the-best-doctor-in-the-world-2014-4 (accessed June 11, 2016).

13 Lia Davis and Faye Abloeser, "IBM Forms New Watson Group to Meet Growing Demand for Cognitive Innovations," news release, January 9, 2014, https://www.-03.ibm.com/press/us/en/pressrelease/42867.wss. (accessed June 11, 2016).

14 Personal Interview with Author. June 30, 2016.

15 Will Oremus, "Terrifyingly Convenient: A.I. Assistants Can Give You the News, Order You a Pizza, and Tell You a Joke. All You Have to Do Is Trust Them—Completely," *Slate*, April 3, 2016, http://www.slate.com/articles/technology/cover_story/2016/04/alexa_cortana_and_siri_aren_t_novelties_anymore_they_re_our_terrifyingly.html (accessed June 11, 2016).

Eight

1   Derek Kessler, "Model X Software Update Brings 'Umbrella Mode' to Falcon Wing Doors," TeslaCentral, April 13, 2016, http://www.teslacentral.com/model-x-software-update-brings-umbrella-mode-falcon-wing-doors (accessed June 11, 2016).

2   Michael E. Gerber, *The E-Myth: Why Most Businesses Don't Work and What to Do about It* (New York: HarperBusiness, 1986).

3   "'Gamifying' the System to Create Better Behavior," NPR.org, March 27, 2011, http://www.npr.org/2011/03/27/134866003/gamifying-the-system-to-create-better-behavior (accessed June 29, 2016).

4   Gabe Zichermann and Joselin Linder, *The Gamification Revolution: How Leaders Leverage Game Mechanics to Crush the Competition* (McGraw-Hill Education, April 16, 2013).

5   Chris Welch, "Foursquare Finally Brings Mayorships and True Competition to Swarm: Checking in Feels Like Fun Again," *The Verge*, June 22, 2015, http://www.theverge.com/2015/6/22/8825205/swarm-app-mayorships-now-available (accessed June 29, 2016).

6   Larry Mohl, e-mail to author, June 23, 2016.

INDEX

ABOUT THE AUTHOR

David Nour—CEO, The Nour Group, Inc.

Relationship Economics® Expert, Senior Leadership / Board Advisor, International Speaker and Best-Selling Author

David Nour brings a disciplined approach to the often-fuzzy subject of the value of strategic business relationships.

He originated the practice of Relationship Economics®, the concept of the quantifiable value of business relationships. Through his best-selling books, compelling speeches, and valuable consulting, Nour demonstrates how relationships are the greatest off-balance-sheet asset any organization possesses, large or small, public or private.

Nour's new book, *CO-CREATE*, illustrates how companies can use strategic relationships to create value through innovation.

He delivers over 50 keynotes a year explaining the economic value of strategic relationships and the disciplined process of investing in them. He has worked with leading global companies such as Disney, Cisco Systems, Deloitte Consulting, Hilton Worldwide, HP, IBM, and more.

His insights on driving growth through unique return on strategic relationships have been featured in top outlets like *The Wall Street Journal, The New York Times, Fast Company,* Mashable, CNBC, Knowledge@Wharton and Associations Now, as well as *Entrepreneur* and *Success* magazines. He also writes a regular column for *The Huffington Post* and *Medium.*

David is the author of ten books, including the best-selling *Relationship Economics,* as well as *ConnectAbility, The Entrepreneur's Guide to Raising Capital,* and *Return on Impact.*

Nour has guest lectured at the Goizueta Business School at Emory University and Georgia Tech's College of Management. He serves as the lead independent director on the board of introNetworks, a privately held intelligent community technology firm based in Santa Barbara, California. An Eagle Scout, Nour is involved with the Centennial Scouting movement, Junior Achievement, One Voice—aiming to create peace in the Middle East—and the High Tech Ministries. He is currently an active member of the FBI Citizens' Academy, Association for Corporate Growth (ACG), and the National Association of Corporate Directors (NACD), where he has earned the Governance Fellow accreditation.

A native of Iran, Nour came to the U.S. with just a suitcase, $100, limited family ties, and no fluency in English. He went on to earn an Executive Master's of Business Administration from the Goizueta Business School at Emory University and a bachelor's degree in management from Georgia State University. Nour resides in Atlanta, Georgia, with his family.

Other Books by David Nour

Co-Create is David Nour's fifth commercial book since 2008. A prolific writer, David has spent the past two decades becoming a student of business relationships—how individuals, teams, and organizations can deliver unprecedented growth through a unique return on their strategic relationships. Below are his other books available online or from www.NourGroup.com.

Return on Impact: Leadership Strategies for the Age of Connected Relationships (2013)

Access to information is instantaneous. Social tools put professional networks within arm's reach. What are the leadership strategies that will allow your organization to create and support differentiating value and nurture ongoing relationships with your members? In *Return on Impact: Leadership Strategies for the Age of Connected Relationships*, Nour charts the implications of a socially enabled world and the reinvention—in structure and governance, talent acquisition, listening practices, and business and revenue models—that leaders of organizations must undertake to fuel growth in the next decade.

Relationship Economics: Transform Your Most Valuable Business Contacts Into Personal and Professional Success—Revised and Updated (2011)

A revised and updated guide to bridging relationship creation with relationship capitalization. Relationship Economics isn't about taking advantage of friends or coworkers to get ahead. It's about prioritizing and maximizing a unique return on strategic relationships to fuel unprecedented growth. Based on the author's global speaking and consulting engagements, *Relationship Economics* reveals that success comes from investing in people for extraordinary returns. This version explains the three major types of relationships—personal, functional, and strategic—and how to focus each to fuel enterprise growth. It introduces new concepts in relationship management, including the exchange of Relationship Currency, the accumulation of Reputation Capital, and the building of Professional Net Worth. These are the fundamental measures of business relationships, and once you understand them, you'll be able to turn your contacts into better executions, performance, and results.

ConnectAbility: 8 Keys to Building Strong Partnerships with Your Colleagues and Your Customers (2009)

noun: 1. an agile approach to running an organization that takes into account the psychology of human interaction; 2. the only way to do business in today's economy. Drawing from the powerful lessons of emotional awareness and relationship dynamics, *ConnectAbility* promotes a sophisticated yet simple method for developing superior partnerships guaranteed to create quality results on a consistent basis. Even the best-intentioned team players too often focus more on communicating their own ideas than hearing and understanding what others have to say. *ConnectAbility* changes all this using eight steps to foster optimum communication, and is your key to getting things done in a positive manner that benefits not only you and your team—but the organization as a whole.

The Entrepreneur's Guide to Raising Capital (2009)

Ask any established business owner to identify his or her toughest challenge when just starting out, and you'll likely get this answer: raising capital. Most aspiring entrepreneurs know far too little about the sources of money that can help start a business or fuel its growth. This book answers these and many other critical questions. Even more important, entrepreneur and consultant David Nour shows how to develop long-term relationships with financial partners—the people who can help keep a business humming throughout its life.

Speaking Topics

MASTERING THE CO-CREATE EFFECT

*Driving Innovation and Growth
through Strategic Relationships*

Few companies have mastered how to drive innovation through strategic relationships. In retail, Warby Parker has. In payments, Stripe has. IBM, Toyota, and L'Oreal also excel in this regard, but the list is far shorter than it should be. This keynote shows you how to get others to invest their time and effort in your organization's success . . . and what you need to offer them in return.

The key difference between those companies that merely aspire to do this and those that have mastered the Co-Create Effect is that the best of the best employ a disciplined strategic process. Nour will take you through that process, explain how it works, and highlight where so many firms go wrong with half-hearted or poorly conceived efforts to "collaborate."

RELATIONSHIP ECONOMICS®

The Art and Science of Relationships

This is David Nour's most acclaimed keynote—based on his best-selling book of the same name—which he has delivered to over 500 corporate, association, and academic forums. This dynamic session focuses on the quantifiable value of business relationships. It describes a systematic process to build and leverage strategic relationships. This session delivers exceptional value to most audiences by sharing the battle-tested best practices for bridging relationship creation with relationship capitalization.

Additional topics . . .

Adaptive Innovation: Adaptable Business Models for Changing Market Demands
Enterprise Evangelism: The Economic Value of Exceptional Experiences, Every Time
Sharing Economy: The Disruptive Nature of Collaborative Consumption
In the Wrong Seat: Are You in the Wrong Seat on Your Own Bus?
Reverse Perspective: What If You Were a Guest in Your Customer's Journey?
Ten Critical Boxes: Using the Business Model Canvas to Tell Your Story!
Flight Risk: Why Your Most Valuable Talent Is Leaving and Strategies to Curtail

Learn More at www.NourGroup.com/speaking